THE GREAT BOOK OF COUSCOUS

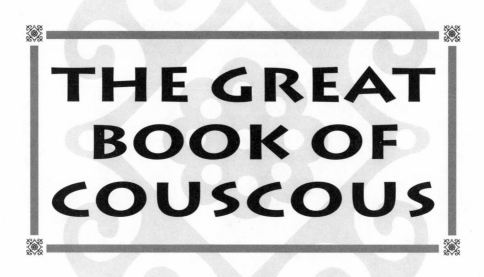

THE GREAT BOOK OF COUSCOUS

Classic Cuisines of
Morocco, Algeria and Tunisia

COPELAND MARKS

DONALD I. FINE, INC.

New York

Library of Congress Catalogue Card Number: 94-071117
ISBN: 1-55611-420-6

Manufactured in the United States of America

10 9 8 7 6 5 4 3 2 1

Designed by Irving Perkins Associates, Inc.

CONTENTS

V

ACKNOWLEDGMENTS

I am always grateful when I encounter ethnic peoples who will share their family culinary knowledge, even when some of them are secretive and hold their recipe cards close to their chests. The Moroccans gave willingly and joyously, relishing the pride in their great cooking. I list them.

Aicha Mazouz
Hamid Bernhida (in Safi)
Kamal Zokhour
Hassan Bin Lakhal (in Fez)
Hassan Chadli (in Fez)
Rachid and Amina Smina
  (in Marrakesh)

Rebecca Cohen
Anas Abouzaid
Latifa Lakhzami (in Safi)
Berji Fatna (in Safi)
Zeneb Kaffaf (in Fez)
Abdul Karim Idrissi (in Fez)

Special mention is made to Devora Avikzer Goltry, who learned her craft directly from her mother and by extension her grandmother, guardians of the Jewish cuisine of Morocco. Her attention to details and authenticity was admirable. I applaud her devotion.

Algeria was a difficult nut to crack. Everyone was not as I had expected. Travel was prohibited due to politics, which reared its ugly head. Yet, there are good people everywhere, and one has to select judiciously, which I did. My blessings to:

Zoubida Laguab
Kouider Laguab
Edmond Halimi

Samira Benaissa
Colette Schriqui

Travelling throughout Tunisia on several occasions, I was struck by the general relaxation of the people from Tunis in the north, the island of Jerba, where Ulysses found the lotus eaters, to the oasis of Nefta. Cooking, tasting and collecting recipes became a joy and an education of the psyche of the Tunisian people. I thank them all and special appreciation goes to:

Haouari Abderrazaic (in Jerba)　　Nouredinne Ben Ammar
Zorha Jeddi　　Matilda Guez
Yvette Fitoussi

GLOSSARY

Bouzelouf The roast head of a lamb, one of the popular family dishes in Algeria, especially on Ramadhan. Also, literally, to cut the head off a live lamb. And, a derogatory colloquial expression meaning "stupid."

Halal The Islamic ritual as regards the slaughtering of poultry and meat animals, with the exception of pork, which is prohibited. The animal is turned to face Mecca, the throat is cut and all the blood, which is considered unclean, drained.

   The Jewish ritual is known as making the meat kosher.

M'loukhia (Corchorus olitorius) Also known as Jews' mallow and tossa jute. The plant grows from Egypt to Japan, but I encountered it during my residence in Calcutta, India. My cook would stir-fry the fresh leaves of the plant. Jute (burlap) is derived from the stems of the mature plant. The dried leaves when crushed are used in an aromatic soup with beef in Tunisia.

Scheena The stew that Spanish Jews (those that have gone to the Maghreb) place on glowing embers on Friday evening to eat on the Sabbath. *Scheena* is the word in Arabic. *Dafina* in French; *Adafina* in Spanish; and *T'Fina* is the modified colloquial word in Tunisia. *Hameem* is the Hebrew word for this Sabbath food and is used by the Jews in India.

Jewish Holidays

Rosh Hashanah The high holy day that marks the beginning of the Jewish New Year. Observed September/October, a date determined by the lunar calendar. A day for family gatherings and holiday dining. Upon returning home from the synagogue, certain ritual foods are served and the diners offer prayers for the New Year. Eating apples dipped into honey will guarantee a sweet year, for instance, and pomegranate seeds will promise fertility.

Yom Kippur (The Day of Atonement) The holiest day in the Jewish calendar. Observed in September/October. On this day there is complete abstinence from food and drink from the afternoon of one day until the evening of the following day. A day punctuated by the recitation of prayers and repentance of sins.

Passover (Pesach) This season commemorates the Exodus of the Jews from Egypt. Celebrated for eight days. Matzoh, the unleavened cracker, is eaten and used as an ingredient in dairy, meat and sweet dishes, while bread is banished. Special foods relating to the holiday are prepared. Passover, more than any other Jewish holiday, has its own special cuisine. Observed in the spring.

Muslim Holidays

Ramadhan The most important religious holiday of the Muslim year. Ramadhan is the ninth month of the Muslim calendar when it becomes fasting time for 29 or 30 days, according to the lunar calendar, from sunrise to sunset for every adult, adolescent, girl and boy who has reached puberty. The reason for fasting is to achieve a proximity to God by the submission of the body and purification of the soul. During Ramadhan, when the fast is broken in the evening; there is an abundance of foods. Milk and dates, prunes and dry raisins are served among many others. On the 14th and 27th days of the fast, the principal dish served is chicken and lamb couscous. Other family favorites are also included.

Mosaic water fountain in Casablanca

Iд El Fitr This is the joyous end of the month of Ramadhan, at the first sighting of the moon in the month of Choual (Shawwal). It is the end of the fast and characterized by the giving of grains, dates (1/2 pound per person, including the youngest) or the equivalent in money to the poor. New clothes are worn and family members ask their relatives to forgive their sins. Pastry and coffee in abundance is served all day long. Lunch is *bourek,* meat dishes and green salads.

Iд El Aдha This holiday commemorates the event when Abraham planned to sacrifice his son, Isaac, but was prevented from doing so by the Angel Gabriel. The morning of Adha, the head of the family, reciting a formula, sacrifices a lamb. Believers must eat the liver and the meat. Douara is prepared for lunch. Evening dinner is more elaborate, with a special preparation of Bouzelouf, the lamb's head.

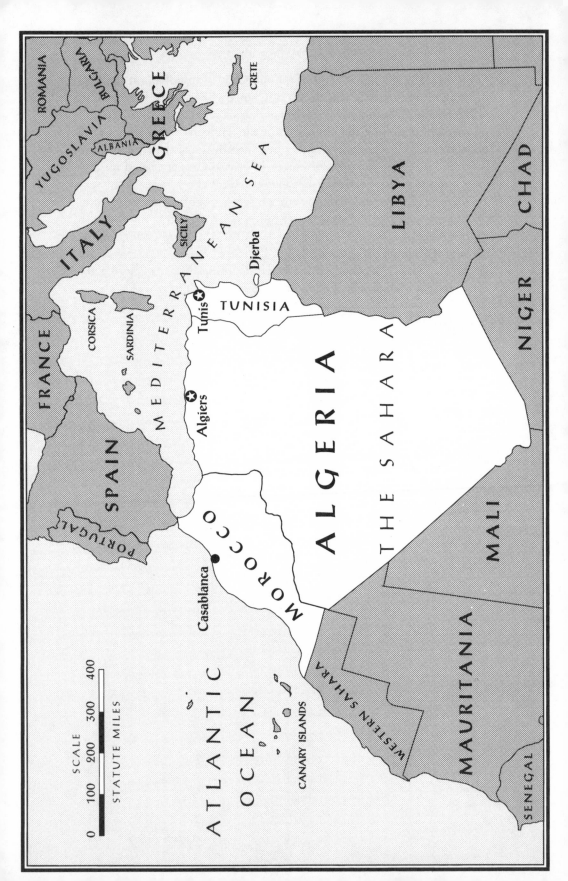

THE COOKING OF
MOROCCO

An old gate in Fez

Fez market in the medina

MOROCCO

HISTORY, agriculture and the Berbers, Morocco's earliest indigenous inhabitants, have all joined to produce one of the world's ten greatest cuisines. Perched on the northwestern edge of Africa and facing the Atlantic Ocean and the Mediterranean Sea, a stone's throw from Europe, having the best of both worlds, Morocco, that exotic and fascinating country, provided an easy route to everywhere.

The Phoenicians (Carthaginians) established a foothold in the country; followed by the Romans who turned the Maghreb into their breadbasket producing wheat for Rome.

The Ottoman Turks left their culinary mark producing sweets and perhaps the idea of the warka, that thin semolina pancake that became the lining for the famous Bestilla, Morocco's celebrated pigeon pie.

In the 6th and 7th century Islam arrived to change all that had gone before. The Muslim dynasties with their extravagant architectural genius produced mosques, palaces, walled cities and fortifications and introduced their cuisine based upon the spices and seasonings brought from the Middle East and Asia by Arab spice merchants adding to the already well established Berber dishes.

The Muslim dynasties, Berber and Arab, such as the Almoravids, Almohads, Merinids, names that emphasize the history of Morocco, were royal. It is no wonder that the techniques of cooking and lavish life styles were flamboyant in aromatic appeal for the royal tables. The cooking style afterward filtered down into the kitchens of the general population.

I have been told by a Moroccan government official that one half of the foods (recipes) in Morocco are of Jewish origin, which were introduced to the country after the expulsion of the Jews from Spain in 1492. I accept this as an idea that is arguably logical since there are similarities in the Jewish and Muslim cooking. Religious rituals and holy days of both religions, such as the Jewish Passover, have their separate ways and their own unique cuisine.

The Jewish experience in Morocco has a long pre- and post-Islamic history and is part of the patrimony of the country.

3

Although Moroccan men rarely enter the kitchen in the home they know a great deal about their traditional cuisine, how it should taste and the presentation at the table. Moroccans in general, but especially the women, have a great natural flair for cooking. It is this self-centered attitude about their cuisine that has helped to produce a great one.

The distinctive characteristic of Moroccan cooking is the ability to combine meat, mainly lamb with sweet spices such as cinnamon, coriander, cumin, paprika, saffron with toasted almonds, dry prunes and apricots. Granulated and powdered sugar may also be included in this melange of sweetness.

A variety of salads, mainly cooked, that run the gamut from carrot, eggplant, green and red sweet peppers, fennel, artichokes and countless other vegetables can adorn the table with a display of generosity.

Regional foods that are equated with a seaport town such as Safi are known for their many varieties of sardine preparations. The two greatest cooking cities are acknowledged to be Fez and Marrakesh, preparing the celebrated dishes of the country such as the Bestilla, tajines of many combinations, the Trid which uses the semolina warka (pancake), and all the other idiosyncratic features of a cuisine that knows no fear of adventurous cooking.

View of modern Casablanca

Vegetables of all kinds are an important characteristic of the diet. Meat is money and is not always available, so vegetables fill the gap replacing the meat somewhat without producing blandness since there is always a battery of spices and olive oil to provide richness.

As one Moroccan cook told me (a man) we look into the larder or refrigerator to see what we have and plan a meal on that rather than reconnoiter a market at a late hour. Flair and imagination provide the impetus with confidence to cook a traditional dish with what is immediately available. The variety of the food is considerable and a good meal is part of the spice of life. But it is the spices that provide the life of the food.

Moroccans use a greater variety of spices than any other country except India. Since I lived in India for five years and have written about the cuisine from the different regions, I often compare the cooking habits of the two countries. Basic spices such as turmeric, ginger, cumin, coriander, black pepper and saffron are common to both countries. I have the strongest intuition that spice merchants that picked up their wares in India also brought with them culinary ideas and that these have entered the mainstream.

In any event, whatever the exterior influences can have been, a great cuisine has emerged that is not elitist but can be celebrated by all.

COUSCOUS

❋ HOW TO COOK COUSCOUS ❋
THE PASTA

The pasta is steamed simultaneously in the *kesskess*, the top of the *cous-couvier*, while the meat and vegetables cook in the bottom (makfout). It is the steam emanating up from the stew in the bottom that cooks the pasta in the top container. In the event that the sheer quantity of pasta and stew are too much for the steamer, each may be made separately; one container for the stew and a separate steamer for the pasta. Here is how it is done.

Put the pasta in a large bowl and rinse it briefly in water. Drain well, toss the grains a few times and let them rest for 15 minutes to absorb the moisture. Then place the couscous in the top of the *couscousier*. Wrap a narrow piece of aluminum foil or a kitchen towel around the *couscousier* where the top and bottom of the steamer meet to prevent the steam from escaping from the sides. Steam for 1/2 hour, which constitutes the first steaming.

Turn the pasta out into a bowl and sprinkle over it 1/4 cup water. Toss well to mix, cover the bowl with a towel and let stand for 10 minutes. Add 2 teaspoons vegetable oil and toss several times to mix in the oil. Return the pasta to the steamer and steam for 10 minutes. The pasta should have expanded three times its original size and be ready to serve.

What is wanted is a light fluffy texture, not overly wet, and without lumps.

❋ COUSCOUS AVEC SEPT LÉGUMES ❋
COUSCOUS WITH SEVEN VEGETABLES

This is the classic couscous of Morocco and is prepared all over the country. The fresh vegetable assortment can vary according to personal preference and does not necessarily have seven—there may be fewer—but with seven the variety is more interesting and flavorful. My choice here is carrot, white turnip, zucchini, cabbage, butternut squash, chick-peas and fresh hot green chili to give the sauce as much spunk as you wish.

1 pound boneless lamb, cut into 6 pieces.
1/4 cup vegetable oil
1 teaspoon salt, or to taste
1 teaspoon black pepper
1/2 teaspoon turmeric
1 medium onion, cut into long slices (1 cup)
3 tomatoes (1 pound), peeled and sliced
4 cups water
1 pound carrot, quartered, inner cores discarded and scooped out
1 pound white turnip, peeled, quartered

1 pound cabbage, cut into 6 pieces
1/2 cup dried chick-peas, soaked overnight in water and drained
1 pound zucchini, cut into 2-inch cubes
1 pound butternut squash, not peeled, cut into 6 pieces
10 sprigs flat-leaf parsley, tied in a bundle
1 small fresh hot green chili, or more to taste
1 pound couscous, steamed in the traditional method

1. Put the lamb, oil, salt, pepper and turmeric in the *makfoul* of the steamer and stir-fry over moderate heat for 5 minutes. Add the onion, tomatoes and water and bring to a boil. Simmer for 1/2 hour.

2. Add vegetables in sequence, according to their degree of firmness. Begin with the carrot, turnip, cabbage and chick-peas, and cook for 15 minutes.

3. Now add the zucchini, butternut squash, parsley and chili. Check to see that there is ample sauce and add 1 more cup water. Adjust the salt and pepper. Cook until the meat and vegetables are tender, about 1/2 hour more.

4. To serve, put the cooked couscous in a large bowl and sprinkle with 1 cup of the sauce. Toss well to mix. Place the meat in the center and arrange the vegetables carefully over the meat. Put the parsley on the top of the pyramid with the chili.

Serve warm. Serves 6.

NOTE: Moroccans eat couscous with their hands, using their fingertips to grasp the pasta, vegetables and meat from the serving bowl. Other people do not care for this traditional method and serve themselves from their plate with a tablespoon.

In early times man used his cupped hand to scoop up foods. As an anthropological remembrance of things past, we scoop up soup, stews and pasta with a tablespoon or other large spoon or ladle, which is, after all, a cupped hand in the shape of a modern utensil.

VARIATION

Beef and chicken may also be used instead of the more popular lamb. Beef will require additional time to cook before the vegetables can be added. Alternately, chicken takes less time, so that one should test the meat.

✵ COUSCOUS BYTFAYA ✵

COUSCOUS WITH ONIONS, RAISINS AND CHICK-PEAS

This is a light semisweet couscous served on Fridays with tea and fruit.

1/4 cup vegetable oil
1 pound boneless lamb, cut into 6
pieces
1 teaspoon salt, or to taste
1 teaspoon black pepper
1/2 teaspoon turmeric
2 cups water

1 cup dried chick-peas, soaked
overnight in water, drained and
skins peeled off
2 or 3 large onions (2 pounds), cut
into long slices
1 cup white raisins
1 pound couscous

1. Put the oil and lamb in the *makfoul* and stir-fry over moderate heat for 5 minutes. Add the salt, pepper, turmeric and water. Bring to a boil and simmer 30 minutes. Add the chick-peas, onions and raisins and cook over low heat 15 minutes.

2. At this time, prepare the couscous according to the instructions at the beginning of this section, rinsing and steaming twice in the *kesskess* while the meat and sauce are cooking in the *makfoul* simultaneously. Total cooking time for both pasta and meat is about 1 hour.

3. To serve, put the pasta in a large bowl and level it slightly. Sprinkle about 1/2 cup of the sauce over it. Do not overdo this as it will make the pasta soggy. Toss well to mix. (Excess sauce can be served separately.)

4. Put the lamb pieces in the center of the pasta and arrange the onions, raisins and chick-peas over everything.

Serve warm. Serves 6.

❈ COUSCOUS AVEC POIS CHICHE ❈ ET RAISINS

COUSCOUS WITH CHICK-PEAS AND RAISINS

A lady in Fez produced this fine couscous for me in her home. The farm chicken was bought live, as they all are, killed, plucked and cleaned while we waited. It was then cooked in the *couscousier*, the chicken stew in the bottom (*makfoul*) and the couscous in the top (*kesskess*).

1 chicken (3 pounds), cut into 6 pieces, loose skin and fat discarded
1 cup dried chick-peas, soaked overnight in water and drained
1/2 teaspoon salt
1/2 teaspoon black pepper
2 tablespoons olive oil
2 tablespoons vegetable oil

1/2 teaspoon saffron stamens
1 sprig flat-leaf parsley, chopped
1 large onion, sliced (1 cup)
2 ripe tomatoes, sliced (1 cup)
4 cups water
1 cup dark raisins
2 pounds couscous
1 tablespoon butter, melted

1. Put all the ingredients, except the raisins, couscous and butter, in the *makfoul* of the *couscousier*. Bring to a boil, then simmer over low heat for 1/2 hour.

2. Add the raisins and simmer for 15 minutes. Set aside.

3. Mix the dry couscous with 1/2 cup water and toss well. Rub the couscous through your fingers to ensure that there are no lumps. Steam in the *kesskess* over moderate heat for 15 minutes.

4. Turn the couscous out into a large bowl or onto a tray and add the butter. Return to the *kesskess* and steam for 20 minutes. The dry couscous should expand 3 times its original size. Preparation of the

couscous takes place at the same time as the chicken and chick-peas are cooking in the *makfoul.*

5. Serve the chicken, chick-peas, raisins and sauce together in a dish or bowl. The couscous is served in another bowl.

Serves 6 with salads.

▨ COUSCOUS SEFA ▨
SAVORY COUSCOUS CASABLANCA STYLE

Sefa is a sweet couscous that is eaten as a savory after all the meat courses have been served. Butter, cinnamon, almonds, raisins and sugar are the principal flavors that dominate the steamed pasta. This is not eaten alone, but is an adjunct to a proper meal.

1 pound couscous, the small size	*1/4 pound butter, sliced*
1/2 teaspoon salt	*5 tablespoons powdered sugar*
2 tablespoons vegetable oil	*1/4 cup blanched almonds, toasted*
3 tablespoons white raisins	*2 1/2 teaspoons ground cinnamon*

1. Prepare the couscous in the traditional method: Rinse it in water, drain it well and toss with the salt. Steam in the *kesskess* for 25 minutes. Remove to a large bowl and add the oil and raisins. Toss well. Return to the *kesskess* and steam a second time for 15 minutes.

2. Place the couscous in a non-clay serving dish. Bury the butter in it with 3 tablespoons of the sugar. Toss well. Shape the couscous into a pyramid shape.

3. Grind together the almonds, 1/2 teaspoon of the cinnamon and the 2 remaining tablespoons sugar. Sprinkle this over the couscous pyramid.

4. Now decorate the pyramid with the 2 teaspoons remaining cinnamon, sprinkling it in 6 decorative stripes from the top to the bottom of the pyramid.

Serve warm, after all the meat dishes have been served. Serves 6 or more.

LAMB AND BEEF

LAMB

TAJINE D'AGNEAU AUX LÉGUMES

LAMB AND ASSORTED VEGETABLES

1/4 cup olive oil
3 pounds lamb shoulder with bone,
    cut into 3-inch serving pieces
2 onions (3/4 pound), sliced
5 sprigs flat-leaf parsley, chopped
5 cloves garlic, chopped
1 teaspoon salt, or to taste
1/2 teaspoon sweet paprika
1/2 teaspoon black pepper
1/4 teaspoon saffron stamens
1/2 teaspoon ground ginger

1 cup water
2 pounds carrot, trimmed and
    quartered
1 pound white turnip, peeled and
    cut into wedges
5 potatoes (2 pounds), peeled and
    cut lengthwise
2 large sweet green peppers
    (1 pound), cut into 1-inch
    wide strips

1. Put the oil in a pan, add the lamb, onion, parsley, garlic, salt, paprika, pepper, saffron and ginger. Stir-fry over low heat for 5 minutes.

2. Add the water, bring to a boil and cook, covered, over low heat for 1/2 hour. Add the vegetables and cook for 1/2 hour more, or until the lamb is tender and the sauce is thickened. Should the liquid evaporate too quickly, add another 1/2 cup water.

Serve warm. Serves 8 with bread and salads.

� TAJINE SFARJEL ✶

LAMB AND FRESH QUINCE RAGOUT

Quince are that hard pale-green/yellow wonderful fruit that many cooks are curious about but have never tried. When quince make their appearance in the New York markets during October, the same time as in Morocco, I immediately start making breakfast jam from Persia and this remarkable ragout from Morocco.

It is a specialty of Marrakesh. My teacher was one of the ladies of that region, a true ethnic representative of her community. The two blue tattoo marks were on her pleasant face, one in the cleft of her chin and the other between the eyebrows. The palms of her hands were red with henna. Several layers of clothing and a headband complete the costume that she wore every day.

The clay tagine was presented to the family on a low table. The lamb was piled in the center of the tagine and the large cubes of quince covered it in a high mouthwatering mound. The family ate it with their fingers, with chunks of the wonderful *khubz*, the round, flat traditional bread. Here is the recipe.

3 quince (3 pounds)	1/2 teaspoon black pepper
1/4 cup vegetable oil	1 teaspoon sweet paprika
2 pounds boneless lamb, cut into	1/2 teaspoon turmeric
2-inch cubes	1 ripe tomato, chopped (1 cup)
1 medium onion, chopped (1/2 cup)	2 cups water
5 sprigs flat-leaf parsley, chopped	2 teaspoons ground cinnamon
1 teaspoon salt, or to taste	1/4 cup sugar

1. Cut the quince into quarters; remove the seeds, core and stems. Then cut the quarters in half crosswise so that you have large cubes. Cover the cubes in water, add 1/4 teaspoon salt and cook briskly for 20 minutes, or until they are soft but with a touch of firmness. Drain and set aside.

2. Put the oil, lamb, onion, parsley, salt, pepper, paprika and turmeric in a pan large enough to hold all the ingredients and stir-fry over low heat for 5 minutes.

3. Add the tomato and water and cook for 1/2 hour or more, until the meat is soft. Now add the quince, cinnamon and sugar. Shake the

pan to mix and simmer everything together over low heat for 10 minutes. The sauce should become thick.

4. To serve, arrange the lamb and sauce on a platter and place the cubes of quince in a mound over the meat.

   If you have the classic clay tagine with the conical top, warm the round bottom dish and serve the ragout in it, bringing it directly to the table.

Serves 6 or 7 with bread, fresh salad and Harissa (Hot Chili Sauce—see page 89).

❖ TAJINE BURKOJ L'HAM ❖

Sweet Tagine of Goat and Prunes

One of my favorite tagines is this sweet one. I have a sweet tooth and cinnamon, ginger, prunes and sugar combined with the goat meat (or lamb) is foolproof. In the absence of goat, which this Berber recipe recommends, I have used shank of lamb—with no devaluation of flavor.

*1 pound large prunes, with or
   without pits
2 pounds boneless goat meat, cut
   into 2-inch cubes
2 tablespoons vegetable oil
1/2 teaspoon turmeric
1 medium onion, chopped (1/2 cup)*

*1 teaspoon ground ginger
1 teaspoon ground cinnamon
2 cups water
1/2 teaspoon salt
2–3 tablespoons sugar, to taste
1 tablespoon toasted sesame seeds*

1. Cook the prunes, covered, in water to soften them, for 15 minutes, retaining some firmness. Drain.

2. Put the goat, oil, turmeric, onion, ginger, cinnamon, water and salt in a pan and bring to a boil. Cook, covered, over low heat for 1 hour, or until the meat is tender.

3. Add the prunes and sugar and simmer for 10 minutes more.

4. To serve, arrange the meat and prunes with sauce on a platter or in the clay tray of a tagine. Sprinkle the sesame seeds on the prunes only as a decorative touch.

Serves 6 with bread and salads.

❖ TAJINE KHORCHAUF ❖

LAMB AND FRESH CARDOON RAGOUT

Occasionally I see the almost unknown stalks of cardoon in certain Italian neighborhoods in New York during their growing season, which is the same as its first cousin—the artichoke. Yet the melting texture of the cardoon, which looks like overgrown celery with large flamboyant serrated leaves, is being overlooked. During October the open-air, rather disorganized market in the Fez Medina, the old quarter, was filling with the new cardoon crop, and I capitalized on this harvest by convincing Fez friends to prepare this ragout.

1/3 cup green cracked olives
2 pounds cardoon stalks, cut into 2-inch pieces
1 teaspoon salt, or to taste
1/4 cup vegetable oil
2 pounds lamb shoulder, with or without bone, cut into 3-inch pieces
1 medium onion, chopped (1/2 cup)

6 sprigs flat-leaf parsley, chopped
1/4 teaspoon black pepper
1 teaspoon sweet paprika
1/2 teaspoon turmeric
1 ripe tomato, chopped (1 cup)
2 cups water
1/2 Preserved Lemon (see page 58), cut into 1-inch cubes

1. In a saucepan cover the olives in water and cook over low heat for 15 minutes to remove excess salt. Drain well and set aside.

2. Just cover the cardoon stalks in water, add 1/2 teaspoon of the salt and cook over low heat until soft, about 20 minutes. Drain and set aside.

3. Put the oil, lamb, onion, parsley, remaining 1/2 teaspoon salt, pepper, paprika and turmeric in a large pan and stir-fry over low heat for 5

minutes. Add the tomato and water and simmer, covered, for about 1/2 hour to soften the meat. Now add the cardoon, olives and preserved lemon. Cook for another 1/2 hour to integrate the flavors, thicken the sauce and soften the ingredients.

Serve warm. Serves 6 or 7 persons with bread and a fresh salad, the recipe for which follows.

1 ripe tomato, peeled and cut into 1/2-inch cubes (1 cup)
1/2 sweet green pepper, cut into thin 1/2-inch-long slices (1 cup)
1 tablespoon fresh lemon juice
1/2 teaspoon salt
1 tablespoon vegetable oil

Mix everything together and serve at room temperature.

❈ MECHOUI DE MOUTON ❈
Roast Lamb

A Moroccan friend told me that in his family for special occasions they usually roasted a whole or half lamb. The same method can be used for homecooking this lamb shoulder.

10 sprigs flat-leaf parsley, chopped
12 cloves garlic, chopped
1 teaspoon salt
1 teaspoon black pepper
1 teaspoon ground cumin
a 6-pound lamb shoulder or leg, trimmed of excess fat
1/4 pound butter

1. Mix together the parsley, garlic, salt, pepper and cumin.

2. Cut a number of incisions in the lamb 1 inch deep. Push 1 tablespoon of the spice mixture into each incision. Rub 2 or 3 tablespoons of the mixture over the entire lamb to use up all of the mixture.

3. Melt the butter over low heat in a flameproof roasting pan and brown the meat on all surfaces for 15 minutes. Cover the pan and roast in a 350 degree oven for 1 1/2 to 2 hours. Remove the cover

toward the end to see that the lamb is browned. Inside should be pink or well done, as desired.

Serve warm. Serves 8 with fresh salads and bread.

❖ TAJINE BIL KEFTA UL BEID ❖

TAGINE OF MEATBALLS AND EGG IN TOMATO SAUCE

Daily food can be tempting and easy to prepare. This tagine can be made in the ornate clay pot of the same name, with its pyramidal shape, or in a skillet. But if you have a tagine by all means use it.

1 pound ground lamb
1 medium onion, grated
1 teaspoon salt
1/4 teaspoon black pepper
1 teaspoon sweet paprika
2 sprigs fresh coriander, chopped fine
2 sprigs flat-leaf parsley, chopped fine

2 tablespoons olive oil
1/8 teaspoon ground ginger
1/4 teaspoon turmeric
3 tablespoons tomato paste
(tomato concentrate)
1 cup water
1/2 cup green peas, fresh or frozen
3 eggs, beaten

1. Mix together well the lamb, half of the onion, half of the salt, pepper, half of the paprika, coriander and parsley. Roll into miniature meatballs, each 3/4 inch in diameter. Set aside. Makes 35 meatballs.

2. Prepare the sauce: Add the olive oil, the remaining onion and paprika, the ginger, turmeric, tomato paste, the remaining salt and water to a tagine or skillet and simmer, covered, over low heat for 5 minutes.

3. Add the meatballs and peas, cover the pan and simmer over medium-low heat for 15 minutes. Pour in the beaten eggs in a stream over all. Cover the pan and cook for 3 minutes, or just long enough to firm up the eggs, soft or hard, whichever is desired.

Serve warm, sprinkled with black pepper or ground cumin. Serves 4 with fresh salad and bread.

❈ BOULFAF ❈

GRILLED LAMB LIVER BROCHETTE

I did most of my travelling in Morocco on the public buses, which were comfortable and allowed one to see the countryside. Every few hours the buses would have comfort stops, where there was always a restaurant serving traditional dishes, including the barbecued lamb liver on 12-inch-long metal skewers that was served on half a *khubz*, the round flat spongy and always freshly baked bread. Street food that is prepared and sold in quantity reveals the culinary ideas of a country and the Boulfaf is one of my favorites.

Usually, at bus stops the liver was grilled quickly, the 1/2-inch pieces alternated with thin slivers of white kidney fat, which melted. When ready, the cook would sprinkle the brochette with coarse salt, hot red chili powder and ground cumin to taste. The recipe that follows is done in more highly seasoned style for the home and is grilled over charcoal.

1 pound lamb or veal liver, cut into 1/2-inch cubes
six 1/2-inch-square very thin slices lamb kidney fat (optional but traditional)
10 sprigs flat-leaf parsley, chopped fine

1/2 teaspoon salt
1/2 teaspoon black pepper
1 medium onion, chopped fine (1/2 cup)
1 teaspoon sweet paprika
ground cumin to taste

Mix everything together. If you do not wish to use the kidney fat, add 1 teaspoon vegetable oil to the mixture. Put 6 cubes of liver on a skewer, alternating the cubes with the sliced kidney fat, if used.

Grill over charcoal or broil in a gas broiler for about 2 to 3 minutes. Sprinkle with ground cumin before serving for a more intense flavor.

Serve warm with bread and fresh salad. Serves 4 generously at snack time.

VARIATION
Lamb kidneys, cut into 1/2-inch cubes, can also be prepared in the same manner.

❖ TAJINE CERVELLE ❖

SPICED LAMB BRAIN

The title does not begin to explain the subtle mixture of spices and seasonings in this dish, which was served to me in the classic clay tagine that was still sizzling from the kitchen, with the aroma of olives and preserved lemon wafting around the room. Those who like brain, as I do, will embrace this preparation, and those who are not aficionados might be immediately won over.

12 lamb brains, usually 2 per person
8 cloves garlic, chopped fine
8 sprigs flat-leaf parsley, chopped fine by hand or in a processor
8 sprigs fresh coriander, chopped fine
3 tablespoons vegetable oil
1/2 teaspoon salt
1/4 teaspoon black pepper
1/2 teaspoon ground cumin

1 teaspoon sweet paprika
1/2 teaspoon ground ginger
1/4 teaspoon saffron stamens
1/4 cup green cracked olives, soaked in water for 4 hours, drained and pits removed
1/2 cup water
2 ripe tomatoes (1 pound), peeled and chopped fine (2 cups)
1/2 Preserved Lemon (see page 58), sliced thin

1. Soak the brains in cold water for 15 minutes, then pull off the fine membranes. Drain well.

2. Put the garlic, parsley and coriander in a pan and stir-fry over low heat for 2 minutes. Then add the oil, salt, pepper, cumin, paprika, ginger, saffron and olives and fry slowly for 5 minutes.

3. Now add the brains carefully, one by one, to the pan. Add the water and tomato and simmer for 20 minutes to establish the sauce. Place slices of the preserved lemon between and around the brain and simmer over low heat for 10 minutes more.

At this stage, one can transfer the brain and sauce to the clay tagine, which has been heating for 5 minutes; serve at the table. Without a tagine, serve the brains on a platter, and sprinkle with chopped parsley and coriander.

Serve with bread and salads. Serves 6 to 8.

BEEF

✱ TAJINE SALOUI BIL KIFTA ✱

MEATBALLS IN A TAGINE

This well-known dish from Sale, a seaport town just across the river from the royal city of Rabat, is described in the title as "Saloui," or from the city of Sale. Both the ground beef and the tomato sauce are well spiced in the Moroccan manner.

FOR THE MEATBALLS

1 pound ground beef, or lamb
1 teaspoon salt, or to taste
1 teaspoon paprika
1/4 teaspoon hot red chili power
1 teaspoon ground cumin
1/8 teaspoon ground cinnamon
1/4 teaspoon white pepper

1/8 teaspoon ground cardamom
1 teaspoon fresh ginger, crushed, or
1/4 teaspoon ground ginger
4 sprigs flat-leaf parsley, chopped
fine
1 small onion, chopped fine
(1/3 cup)

FOR THE SAUCE

1 tablespoon olive oil
1 large onion, chopped fine (1 cup)
2–3 cups canned or fresh ripe
tomato, peeled and chopped
4 sprigs flat-leaf parsley, chopped

1/2 teaspoon salt
1/4 teaspoon white pepper
1/4 teaspoon sweet paprika
1/8 teaspoon hot red chili powder
1/4 cup water

1. *Prepare the Meatballs:* Mix all the meatball ingredients together by hand or in a processor. Form miniature meatballs, each 3/4 inch in diameter. Set aside. Makes 40 balls.

2. *Prepare the Sauce:* Heat the oil in a tagine or in a large skillet. (I prefer the tagine since it is made for moving from the stove to the table and- can be used for serving.) Add the onion and fry over low heat until

golden, about 5 minutes. Add the tomato and all the remaining sauce ingredients. Cover the clay plate with the conical cap and simmer over low heat for 1/2 hour. Stir every now and then.

3. Drop the meatballs, one by one, into the sauce; cover and simmer over low heat for 15 minutes. The sauce will become thick and darken.

Serve warm with bread. Serves 6 to 8.

❖ M'HAMMAR ❖

BROWNED BEEF IN A CLEAR SAUCE WITH PRUNES

The system of making M'Hammar is unique in my experience since the herbs, onion and garlic are crushed in a small amount of water, enough to moisten the mixture, then the water is pressed out. But it is the liquid that is saved and the pulp that is discarded. M'Hammar also refers to a coloring or browning of the meat just before serving.

For weddings and other celebrations beef is the preferred meat here. Lamb, with or without bones, is another meat that can be used, for ordinary days. It is less expensive than beef. Substitute lamb if you wish and follow the same instructions.

8 sprigs fresh coriander, chopped
8 sprigs flat-leaf parsley, chopped
1 medium onion, sliced (1/2 cup)
4 cloves garlic, sliced
1 1/2 cups water
1 teaspoon salt
1/2 teaspoon black pepper
1 teaspoon ground ginger
1/4 teaspoon turmeric
2 cinnamon sticks, each 3 inches long

1/2 teaspoon saffron stamens
4 tablespoons vegetable oil
2 pounds boneless beef chuck, or other tender cut, cut into 2-inch cubes
1 pound large prunes
2 tablespoons sugar
1 teaspoon ground cinnamon
1 tablespoon toasted sesame seeds

1. Coarsely crush the coriander, parsley, onion, garlic and 1/4 cup of the water together in a processor. Squeeze out the liquid firmly and reserve it. There should be about 1/3 cup liquid. Discard the pulp.

2. Put the flavoring liquid in a pan, and add the salt, pepper, ginger, turmeric, cinnamon sticks, saffron and 3 tablespoons of the oil. Add the beef and mix well. Cover the pan and simmer the mixture over low heat for 1/2 hour. Add 1/2 cup of the water and cook slowly for 1 hour more. Should the liquid evaporate too quickly, add another 1/4 cup water. There should be some concentrated sauce.

3. Prepare the prunes. Soak the prunes, covered, in water for 1 hour. Drain. Mix them with the sugar, ground cinnamon, the 1 remaining tablespoon oil and 1/2 cup water. Cook over low heat for 20 minutes. Very little sauce will remain and the prunes will be soft and plump. Set aside.

4. When the meat is soft, put it in a serving dish and arrange the prunes over all with whatever sauce remains. Sprinkle only the prunes with the toasted sesame seed for garnish.

Serve warm with Safa Shaaria (see page 50) and bread. Serves 6.

NOTE: You may also remove the meat from the pan at the stage when it is tender and brown it on a charcoal grill for about 10 minutes to increase the color. Then top the meat with the prunes and sesame seeds. This is an additional flourish performed by cooks who have a great flair for their cuisine.

❈ TAJINE DE KEFTA ❈

MEATBALLS IN TOMATO SAUCE

This is one of the most ubiquitous dishes of the Moroccan countryside. Whenever I ran out of ideas for my dinner, I would fall back on this combination, knowing that it would be full of flavor and attractive to look at. There are many recipes for it and this one is a simpler version.

FOR THE KEFTA

2 1/2 pounds ground beef, or lamb　　*1 teaspoon ground cumin*
1 teaspoon salt, or to taste　　*1 tablespoon sweet paprika*
1 teaspoon black pepper, or more to　　*1 medium onion, chopped*
　taste　　　*(1/2 cup)*

2 pounds ripe tomato, peeled and   4 tablespoons olive oil
   chopped, or the same amount   1/4 cup water
   canned tomato   1 whole egg

1. *Prepare the Kefta:* Mix all the Kefta ingredients together rather well. Form miniature meatballs, *kefta,* each 3/4 inch in diameter. Set aside. Makes about 80 meatballs.

2. *Prepare the Sauce:* Put all the sauce ingredients except the egg in a pan and bring to a boil. Simmer, covered, over low heat for 15 minutes.

3. Add the miniature meatballs, one by one, and cook for 15 minutes. Make a crater in the center of the sauce and add the whole egg to the crater. Simmer for 3 minutes. The egg should be firm but still melting, which is what is wanted.

Serve hot with bread and salads. Serves 6.

❈ BROCHETTES DE VIANDE ❈

BARBECUED BEEF OR LAMB SKEWERS

Prepare the meatball mixture as for Meatballs in a Tagine (see page 17). As in that recipe lamb can also be used.

Roll the meat mixture into the shape of a cigar, 3 1/2 inches long and 1/2 inch wide, and push each roll onto a small 8-inch metal skewer. (These skewers are very much like the Seek Kebabs that I tasted many times over the years I lived in India.)

Grill the skewers over charcoal or in a gas or electric broiler for 5 to 10 minutes. Do not overcook since the kebabs become too dry.

Serve warm as a main or side dish with other Moroccan foods. It is customary to have a side dish on the table of ground cumin and salt in separate piles for those who wish to intensify the flavor of the meat.

Makes 15 skewers.

❈ HERGMA ❈

CALVES FEET IN THICK SAUCE

Here is an example of old-time homecooking in Fez, where one can see the beef, veal and lamb feet lined up in the butcher shops. During the days of my youth my mother made a similar concoction without chick-peas, which we all loved, back on the farm in Vermont. This is one of the ethnic recipes that are disappearing but it is remarkably flavorful if the effort is made to find the ingredients.

2 beef or veal feet (legs), cut into
    8 pieces
1 large onion, chopped (1 cup)
4 cloves garlic, chopped
1 teaspoon salt
1/2 teaspoon black pepper
1/2 teaspoon ground cumin
1 teaspoon sweet paprika

4 sprigs fresh coriander, chopped
2 tablespoons olive oil
2 tablespoons vegetable oil
1/2 cup dried chick-peas, soaked
    overnight in water and drained
4 cups water
2 tablespoons rice, rinsed well

Put all ingredients, except the rice, in a pan large enough to hold them and bring to a boil. Cover and simmer over low heat for 1 1/2 hours. Add the rice and simmer for 20 minutes more.

Serve warm with bread and fresh seasonal salads. Serves 6 to 8.

CHICKEN AND PIGEON

TAJINE POULET AUX PRUNEAUX

CHICKEN AND PRUNE RAGOUT

The Moroccan genius for combining meat, fruit and nuts is exemplified in this fine dish. Traditional seasonings enrich the combination in a lightly sweet sauce.

*a 4-pound chicken, cut into 8
   pieces, or chicken parts, breast,
   thigh, legs, loose skin and fat
   removed and discarded
2 tablespoons vegetable oil
1 teaspoon salt
1/4 teaspoon turmeric
1/2 teaspoon ground ginger*

*1/2 teaspoon white pepper
2 cups water
2 medium onions, grated (1 cup)
1 pound large prunes (calculate 5
   per person)
1/2 cup sugar
2 teaspoons toasted sesame seeds
1/4 cup blanched almonds, toasted*

1. Put the chicken pieces or parts in a pan with the oil, salt, turmeric, ginger and pepper and stir-fry over low heat for 10 minutes. Add 1 cup of the water and the onions and simmer over low heat for 20 minutes.

2. Put the prunes, sugar and 1 cup remaining water in a pan and cook for 20 minutes. Add the prunes and the liquid to the chicken. Simmer, uncovered, for 15 minutes to thicken the sauce and integrate the flavors.

3. Serve on a platter, sprinkling the sesame seeds on only the prunes for presentation. Scatter the almonds over all.

Serves 6 with bread and salads.

❈ DJEDJ FOUR ❈

STUFFED STEAMED CHICKEN

This is a specialty of the old city of Fez, the Medina, and I was present from the last squawk of the chicken we purchased in the market through all the steps of stuffing and steaming it. This method of preparation will appeal to those who wish to reduce their fat and oil intake. It is easily assembled and can be steamed in a Chinese-style steamer or in a large enough *couscousier,* using the *kesskess* (top) for the chicken, while the *makfoul* (bottom) is filled with boiling water.

1 tablespoon plus 1 teaspoon coarse salt
a 3-pound whole chicken, rinsed well in cold water
10 sprigs fresh coriander, chopped in a food processor
4 cloves garlic, sliced
1 tablespoon sweet paprika

2 teaspoons ground cumin
1 teaspoon black pepper
juice of 1 lemon
1 chicken liver, diced
4 potatoes (1 pound), cooked in jackets, peeled and cut into 1/2-inch cubes

1. Rub the chicken inside and out with the 1 tablespoon salt and let stand for 1 hour. Some cooks salt the chicken and let it stand overnight, planning to cook it the next day. Rinse afterward in cold water.

2. Process the coriander, garlic and 1 teaspoon salt together in a mortar and pestle (as I did in Fez) or in a food processor. Makes about 2/3 cup.

3. Mix together the garlic mélange, paprika, cumin, pepper, lemon juice and liver. Mix well.

4. Rub the chicken inside and out with 1/2 of the spice mixture (also called *chermoula*). Mix the balance of the *chermoula* with the potato cubes. Stuff the chicken tightly. Place any excess stuffing around the chicken.

5. Put the chicken and stuffing in a bowl and steam in a *couscousier* or Chinese-style steamer over moderate heat for 1 1/2 hours. Replenish the water if it evaporates too quickly. Test the chicken for doneness. If still too firm continue to steam.

Serve the chicken and stuffing warm. Serves 4.

Rice is not a popular grain in Morocco, yet this particular stuffing in the medieval city of Fez is frequently used. The same spices and seasonings are used as for the potato stuffing.

1 cup rice, well rinsed   *1 tablespoon vegetable oil*

1. Half-cook the rice in ample boiling water over moderate heat for 7 minutes. Drain and rinse in cold water.

2. Mix the rice, oil and half of the *chermoula* together. (The other half of the *chermoula* is on the chicken.) Stuff the chicken and steam over moderate heat for 1 1/2 hours. Excess stuffing can be placed in the steamer around the chicken.

❖ DJEDJ B'SLA ZAFRON ❖

Chicken with Onion and Saffron

A substantial amount of onion provides a most flavorful sauce for this chicken. The saffron adds a pale yellow tint to what is a light, fat-free preparation in the Moroccan manner. Persian cooks have told me that too much saffron in the food makes people laugh, even when the topic isn't amusing.

1 teaspoon salt
1/4 teaspoon white pepper
2 1/2 pounds chicken parts, breast,
   thighs, wings
2 tablespoons corn oil
2 large onions (1 pound), chopped
   (2 cups)
1 tablespoon peeled chopped tomato
   (optional)

1 teaspoon saffron stamens
6 sprigs flat-leaf parsley, chopped
1 cup water
1/4 Preserved Lemon (see page
   58), sliced
1/2 teaspoon olive oil

1. Mix the salt, pepper and chicken together and let stand 15 minutes while you assemble the other ingredients. Put the corn oil in a pan

over low heat, add 1 cup of the onion and the tomato and stir-fry for several minutes as the color changes. Add the chicken and saffron, mix well, cover the pan and cook for 1/2 hour as the liquid accumulates.

2. Now add 1 more cup onion, the parsley and water. Stir well, cover and cook for 15 minutes. At the end, add the preserved lemon and olive oil and simmer 15 minutes more to reduce some of the sauce. Adjust the salt and pepper to taste.

Serve warm with bread and salads. Serves 4.

❊ DJEDJ BIL ZEITOUN ❊
CHICKEN WITH GREEN CRACKED OLIVES (MOROCCO)

This is a popular and predictable combination emanating from olive country where this ancient fruit is grown for its oil and as a food. The green cracked olives, pickled in brine, are salty as well as slightly bitter. By both soaking and cooking them, they become milder without losing their character. Harissa, hot chili, is added to taste.

1 pound green cracked olives
1 tablespoon corn oil
8 whole cloves garlic, halved lengthwise
2 ripe tomatoes (1 pound), peeled and chopped
1/2 teaspoon black pepper
1/2 teaspoon turmeric

1–2 teaspoons Harissa (see page 89), or more to taste
juice of 1 lemon
1 cup water
3 pounds chicken parts, breast, thighs, legs, loose skin and fat discarded
6 sprigs flat-leaf parsley, chopped

1. Soak the olives covered in water overnight and drain. In a saucepan cover the olives again in water, bring to a boil and drain. Do this again to remove salt and excessive bitterness. Remove the pits carefully so that there are 2 intact halves if possible.

2. Heat the corn oil in a pan, add the garlic, tomato, pepper, turmeric, *harissa*, lemon juice and water. Bring to a boil and add the chicken

pieces to the sauce. Cover the pan and cook over low heat for 1/2 hour. Do not stir during this simmering process but do shake the pan several times.

3. Add the olive halves and push them to the bottom of the pan and around the chicken. Cover and continue to cook over low heat for 20 minutes more. The sauce will become thick and the chicken tender. Add the parsley 5 minutes before the completion of cooking.

Serves 6 with salads and French bread.

✸ ELRFISA ✸

SAFFRON CHICKEN AND TORN PANCAKES

This is one of the oddest names to describe this Casablanca dish known as Elrfisa. In Marrakesh this dish is known as *trid*, a regional modification, which happens frequently in Morocco. Each region produces its own dishes, but they might turn up in another locality with a different name, as happens in this case.

Moroccan cooks spend a lot of time in the kitchen as this recipe illustrates. This extremely tasty preparation is a family dish, eaten anytime rather than on special occasions. This does not detract at all from its culinary value or ingenuity.

Smen, an optional choice, is a seasoned preserved butter that has a slightly fermented taste, and one either likes it or does not. It can be stored for several years, if necessary. My teacher was adamant about the indispensable flavor of *smen* for dishes that include it.

FOR THE CHICKEN

3 tablespoons olive oil
a 3-pound whole chicken, loose skin and fat discarded
2 medium onions, sliced (1 cup)
1/4 teaspoon turmeric
1 teaspoon saffron stamens
1 teaspoon black pepper
1 teaspoon salt, or to taste

1/4 teaspoon ground ginger
1 teaspoon smen (seasoned preserved butter; optional but recommended, if available)
1/2 cup small green/brown lentil, well rinsed
3 1/2 cups water

For the Pancakes

1/2 teaspoon dry yeast
1/4 teaspoon sugar
1/4 cup water
1 cup fine semolina flour
1 cup flour

1/4 teaspoon salt
about 1/2 cup water, more or less
1/4 cup vegetable oil
1/4 cup butter, melted

1. *Prepare the Chicken:* Put everything, except the water, in a large pan and simmer over low heat for 10 minutes. Turn the chicken over several times during this period. Add the water, bring to a boil and simmer, covered, over low heat for 40 minutes. There will be a rich yellow sauce.

2. *Prepare the Dough:* Dissolve the yeast, sugar and water together and let stand 2 or 3 minutes.

3. Mix together the semolina flour and flour, equal amounts, and the salt.

4. Mix together the oil and butter.

5. Mix together the yeast, flours and enough water to form a soft dough that can be easily handled. Dust with flour, if necessary.

6. Oil your hands with the butter/oil mixture. Take 1 heaping tablespoon of the dough and roll it into a slightly flattened ball. Do this with all of the dough.

7. *Make the Pancakes:* Oil a plate, add a dough ball and press out a very thin pancake about 6 inches in diameter. Place it on a Teflon skillet lightly sprinkled with the oil. Fry for about 20 seconds, which will barely tan the pancake. Turn it over and as you fry the other side, add another pancake on top. Turn the pancake bundle over and add another pancake on top until you have 5 all browned. Set them aside and start another stack of 5 pancakes. Makes 20–22 pancakes.

8. Tear—do not cut the pancakes—in rough pieces from 1/2- to 1-inch size. Steam the pieces in the *kesskess* of a *couscousier* over moderate heat for 3 minutes.

9. To serve, place the whole chicken in the center of a large platter. Put all the torn pancakes around the chicken and pour the sauce over all. The sauce will be absorbed by the pancakes.

This dish is eaten with the fingers of the right hand (as done by the Prophet) in Morocco, with each person pulling off the chicken, as much as is wanted. Or the chicken can be disjointed with table utensils. Bread is not usually served.

Serve warm. Serves 6.

❖ DJEDJ CHIZU BATATA JILBANA ❖

CHICKEN WITH CARROTS, POTATOES AND GREEN PEAS

Chicken in a saffron-flavored sauce with an assortment of vegetables, whatever you find in the refrigerator, is quintessential Moroccan cooking. Light, emphasizing the vegetables, and without heavy oil, this dish fits our current focus on healthful foods of an ethnic origin.

2 pounds chicken parts, breast, thighs, legs, loose skin and fat discarded
1 teaspoon salt
1/4 teaspoon white pepper
1 tablespoon corn oil
1 large onion, chopped (1 cup)
4 carrots, peeled and cut little finger size
2 potatoes (1/2 pound), peeled and cut into 1/2-inch cubes

1 cup water
1 teaspoon saffron stamens or 1/2 teaspoon turmeric
8 sprigs flat-leaf parsley, chopped, 6 leaves reserved for garnish
1 cup fresh or frozen green peas
1/4 Preserved Lemon (see page 58), sliced
1 teaspoon olive oil

1. Mix the chicken pieces with the salt and pepper. Let stand for 15 minutes.

2. Heat the corn oil in a pan, add the onion and stir-fry over low heat for 3 minutes. Add the chicken and mix. Cover the pan and simmer for 20 minutes, or until the chicken is tender. Now add the carrots, potatoes, water, saffron or turmeric and cook for 15 minutes.

3. Add the parsley, green peas, preserved lemon and olive oil and simmer 10 minutes more. There is substantial sauce, but the vegetables will absorb it and the flavors.

Serve warm with salad side dishes. Serves 4.

❈ TRID ❈

CHICKEN WITH SAFFRON AND PASTRY LEAVES

Trid was called a "poor man's bestilla" by a Moroccan homecook who prepares it frequently for her family. It also involves using *warka* (pastry leaves) in layers with chicken stew seasoned with saffron, among other things. The difference is that the entire concoction is baked lightly in the oven but is not sealed as a bestilla pie. This combination is from Casablanca. Other regions have their own modifications on the same theme.

a 3 to 3 1/2-pound chicken, cut
    into 8 pieces, loose skin and fat
    discarded
3 tablespoons vegetable oil
1/2 teaspoon salt, or to taste
1 teaspoon black pepper
1/4 teaspoon turmeric
1 teaspoon saffron stamens
1/4 teaspoon ground ginger
2 cinnamon sticks, each about 3
    inches

1 cup water
2 large onions (1 pound), cut into
    long slices
1/2 cup white raisins
1 tablespoon butter
6–8 warka (substitute Shanghai-
    style round spring roll wrap-
    pers)

1. Put the chicken in a pan large enough to hold it, add the oil, salt, pepper, turmeric, saffron, ginger and cinnamon sticks and sauté over low heat for 10 minutes. Add the water, onions and raisins and bring to a boil. Simmer, covered, over low heat until the chicken is tender, about 35 minutes.

2. Butter a round baking dish. Place 2 *warka* on the bottom of the dish. Then place 1/4 of the chicken mixture on the *warka* and cover with 1 *warka*. Prepare 3 more layers, each separated by a *warka* until the chicken and sauce are finished. Cover the last layer with 1 *warka*.

3. Bake in a preheated 350 degree oven for 10–15 minutes, which is time enough to heat through all the ingredients.

Serve hot. Serves 6.

NOTE: Old-time cooks serve this to guests or family with a glass of milk lightly perfumed with a drop of rose water. Surprisingly tasty!

Another method is to use 2 1/2 to 3 pounds of boneless and skinless chicken parts, breast and thighs. The flat boneless pieces allow for a more professional presentation and convenience. All the steps above and the amounts of ingredients are the same.

❈ POULET AU CITRON ❈

WHOLE CHICKEN IN PRESERVED LEMON SAUCE

Cooking a whole chicken has more presentation possibilities than cooking cut-up pieces does. Saffron, parsley and fresh coriander add one set of seasonings here, while green olives and preserved lemon add another, plus all the culinary influences that abound in this combination.

1 whole 3 1/2 to 4-pound chicken,
*   loose skin and fat discarded*
1/2 teaspoon saffron stamens
6 sprigs flat-leaf parsley, chopped
6 sprigs fresh coriander, chopped
1 large onion, grated (1 cup)
1 teaspoon black pepper
1 teaspoon salt
5 cloves garlic, chopped fine

3 tablespoons olive oil
1 tablespoon vegetable oil
1 teaspoon tomato paste
2 tablespoons sliced Preserved
*   Lemon (see page 58)*
1 pound green cracked olives
*   soaked in water to cover*
*   overnight and drained*
2 cups water

1. Rub the chicken on the outside with the saffron.

2. Mix the parsley, coriander, onion, pepper, salt and garlic together into a paste. Rub the chicken with 1 heaping tablespoon of the paste.

3. Put both oils in a pan over low heat, add the chicken, tomato paste, the balance of the spice paste, the preserved lemon, olives and water. Bring to a boil and cook, covered, for 10 minutes. Reduce the heat to low and simmer for 1/2 hour, basting now and then as it cooks. Should too much liquid accumulate simmer until the sauce has been reduced to a thick consistency.

Serve warm. Serves 6 with bread and salads.

M'HAMMAR DJEDJ

TWICE-COOKED CHICKEN

This is a fascinating chicken dish for several technical reasons, resulting in an extremely tasty preparation with considerable dimension of flavor. The chicken is simmered in an essence of herbs, onion and garlic, with the pulp of these flavorings discarded. Secondly, after the chicken has been cooked, it is browned in a hot oven to intensify its color and slightly reduce the sauce. All this with preserved lemon and green olives. Who could ask for anything more?

The M'Hammar Djedj is a popular wedding dish, but then the chicken is prepared whole, well rinsed in lemon juice and salt and cooked in the same way as for the cut-up pieces. The French fried potatoes are omitted at weddings. When served, guests pull at the chicken with their fingers, making table utensils unnecessary. Bread is always served with the M'Hammar.

a 3 1/2-pound chicken, cut into 8
pieces, or an equal amount of
chicken parts, loose skin and fat
discarded
juice of 1 lemon
1 1/2 teaspoons salt
10 sprigs fresh coriander, chopped
10 sprigs flat-leaf parsley, chopped
4 large cloves garlic, sliced
1 large onion, sliced (1 cup)
2 cups water
3 tablespoons vegetable oil

1/2 teaspoon saffron stamens
1/2 teaspoon black pepper
1/4 teaspoon ground ginger
1 teaspoon smen (seasoned
preserved butter; optional)
a 3-inch stick cinnamon
1/2 pound green cracked olives
1-inch square piece Preserved
Lemon (see page 58)
1 pound potato, sliced and fried as
for French fries (optional)

1. Rinse the chicken well with cold water, then rub with the lemon juice and 1 teaspoon salt. Let stand for 15 minutes, then rinse and drain. This procedure is done to remove the sometimes strong aroma of chicken.

2. In a mortar or food processor crush together the coriander, parsley, garlic and onion with 1/4 cup water to moisten the combination. Firmly squeeze out all of the liquid and add it to the chicken in a pan. Discard the pulp.

3. Now add the oil, 1/2 teaspoon remaining salt, saffron, pepper, ginger, *smen*, if used, and cinnamon and mix everything together. Cover the

pan and simmer over low heat for 10 minutes. Add the balance of the water, about 1 1/2 cups or more and simmer, covered, for 20 minutes.

4. Cover the olives with water, bring to a boil for 1 minute and drain. Add them to the chicken with the preserved lemon. Continue to simmer for 1/2 hour.

5. Remove the chicken, sauce and olives and transfer them to a roasting pan. Brown lightly in a 350 degree oven for 15 minutes, turning the chicken pieces over once. If the sauce evaporates too rapidly, add another 1/4 cup water. There should be enough sauce to keep the chicken moist.

Serve warm, garnished with the French fries, which are optional but a popular choice in Morocco. Serves 6.

NOTE: To prepare French fries the Moroccan way, slice the potatoes as you like, cover them with 1 cup water and 1 teaspoon salt for 10 minutes. Drain well and dry on a kitchen towel. Crisp brown in hot vegetable oil, then drain briefly on paper towels.

❈ BASTILLA ❈

CLASSIC PIGEON PIE

When the cuisine of Morocco is mentioned by those who are not really acquainted with its culinary treasures, they do know, have tasted or at least heard about pigeon pie. Complex and somewhat arduous to assemble, the pie is the great preparation of North Africa and a world-class taste—when properly baked. The recipe given here is eminently fragrant and when baked in my own home was superior to the commercial ones served to me in Morocco.

It is the *warka*, the very thin and translucent round leaves, that are vital for the assembly of the pie. Nowadays, Greek-style fillo sheets are used, but the chewy texture of the *warka* is not the same as the crisp and ultimately dry texture of the fillo. No matter, fillo is available—and any port in a storm.

In the recipe that follows I recommend using the round egg roll wrappers sold in New York and elsewhere by the Chinese community. Each is about 8 inches in diameter and is a legitimate substitute for Moroccan *warka*. Also, but not so convenient is the Shanghai-style egg roll skin, which is made the same way but is only about 7 inches in diameter. (One would have to work harder to lay down and fit more skins.) The original *warka* in Morocco is the most convenient, since the leaves can be made in the size needed or large enough so that one *warka* can cover the baking pan with extra inches to hang over the sides and to fold under the pie.

The following recipe is the old-time, traditional way of preparing the dish.

FOR THE CHICKEN

> *a 3-pound chicken, cut into 8*
> *pieces, well rinsed in cold water,*
> *loose skin and fat discarded*
> *1 teaspoon ground ginger or 2*
> *teaspoons grated fresh ginger*
> *1 teaspoon black pepper*
> *2 teaspoons salt*
> *2 cinnamon sticks, each 3 inches*
> *long*
>
> *2 medium onions, grated (1 cup)*
> *1 bunch, about 20 sprigs, flat-leaf*
> *parsley, ends trimmed and*
> *chopped*
> *1/2 teaspoon turmeric*
> *8 tablespoons butter, sliced*
> *1 cup water*
> *2 tablespoons sugar*

1. *Prepare the Chicken:* Put the chicken pieces in a pan, add the ginger, pepper, salt, cinnamon sticks, onions, parsley, turmeric and butter and sauté together over low heat for 15 minutes. Turn the chicken over so that the turmeric colors the meat. Add the water, bring to a boil and simmer over low heat for 1 hour.

2. Remove and discard the cinnamon sticks, bones or other foreign objects. There should be 1 cup of thick seasoned sauce. Set aside.

3. Remove the chicken, pull off and discard the skin and bones. Shred the meat into thin pieces about 2 inches long. Mix in the sugar. Set aside.

FOR THE ALMONDS

> *1 cup vegetable oil*
> *1 cup blanched almonds*
>
> *4 tablespoons sugar*
> *1 tablespoon ground cinnamon*

1. *Prepare the Almonds:* Heat the oil in a large skillet and brown the almonds over low heat for about 3 minutes, stirring constantly. A

light tan should evenly color each almond. Drain on paper towels. Cool and reserve the oil for another purpose.

2. Put the almonds, sugar and cinnamon in a processor and grind coarse.

FOR THE EGGS

1 cup of the reserved chicken sauce   *8 large eggs, beaten*
juice of 1 lemon

1. *Prepare the Eggs:* Warm the sauce from the chicken over low heat in the original pan, add the lemon juice and bring to a slow boil. (The lemon juice is added to remove a "too strong egg smell," according to my teacher.) Add the eggs in a steady stream. Stir slowly and continuously until the mixture achieves a dry scrambled texture combined with the seasoned sauce.

2. Since some liquid will accumulate, drain it off in a colander. Set the eggs aside to cool.

FOR THE PIE

about 30 warka, Shanghai-style   *8 tablespoons butter, melted*
  egg roll wrappers, 8 inches in   *1 egg yolk, beaten*
  diameter   *1/2 cup powdered sugar*
1 round metal pan, 14 inches in   *1 tablespoon ground cinnamon*
  diameter and 1 1/2 inches high

1. *Assemble the Pie:* Brush the pan generously with the melted butter.

2. Arrange 6 *warka* around the perimeter of the pan, leaving about 2 inches draped over the edge. Butter the *warka*. Add 1 more *warka* to the center of the pan and butter it. This will support the pie contents.

3. Add 1/3 of the chicken as part of the first layer of the pie and distribute it over the *warka.* Add 3 *warka,* placing them up to the inner edge of the pan and overlapping each other. Butter them well.

4. Add 1/3 of the ground almond mixture. Cover with 3 *warka* and butter them.

5. Cover with 1/3 of the egg mixture. Cover with 3 *warka* to the inner edge of the pan and butter them.

6. Start second complete layer, using 1/3 of the chicken, the almonds and eggs, separating the layers as directed above. Make a third layer, using the balance of the fillings, covering the top with *warka*. Now fold the *warka* draped over the edge of the pan toward the center of the pie. Brush these *warka* with the beaten egg yolk so that they stick together. Cover the center of the pie with 1 *warka* and butter it well.

7. Add 4 more *warka*, which should overlap each other, and butter them. Tuck each one into the sides of the pan. This will close or seal in the pie contents. Brush the top with the balance of the egg yolk.

8. Bake in a 425 degree oven for 15 minutes, or until just a golden color. Do not overbake. I was cautioned to turn on the oven to 425 degrees and put the pie in immediately, without preheating. The gradual increase in the oven heat was sufficient to bake the pie without drying out the *warka*. This makes sense since all the ingredients are cooked.

10. Remove the pie from the oven and turn it over onto a serving platter. Cover the still-warm pie with a generous amount of the powdered sugar. Sprinkle the cinnamon over the sugar with your fingertips to shape a 2-inch grid pattern. Some Moroccan cooks with a more artistic bent use the brown cinnamon to sprinkle on the design of a tree or other botanical design. The grid, however, is the easiest and most common.

11. Bastilla should be served warm. It is not daily fare, but reserved for special occasions, such as weddings or other ceremonies.

    The pie is not usually cut into slices, but it can be for western dining. In Morocco, the pie is placed in front of the guests, who pull at it with their forefingers delicately eating one morsel after another.

Serves 8.

VARIATION

A modern way of filling the pie wrapper is to mix together the 3 principal fillings of chicken, egg and sauce, plus the almonds. Pour this into the already assembled pie casing and cover it with *warka*, as indicated in the above recipe, then bake. All the steps and the baking are exactly the same, except that no layers of *warka* are laid down. The complete filling is added at one time in the European pie fashion.

✸ H'MEM ✸

PIGEON IN ALMOND SAUCE

Pigeons are a popular food in Morocco and are seen for sale in round covered baskets in the public markets. Those that are not in baskets are flying around the city, just like in New York City.

2 tablespoons vegetable oil
2 tablespoons olive oil
4 whole pigeons (about 3 pounds), cleaned
3/4 cup blanched almonds
1 teaspoon black pepper
1/4 teaspoon saffron stamens

1/2 teaspoon salt
2 cloves garlic, chopped
6 sprigs flat-leaf parsley, chopped
3 medium onions, sliced (1 1/2 cups)
2 cups water

Mix everything together in a pan and simmer, covered, over low heat for 1 hour. Should too much liquid accumulate in the pan, toward the end of the cooking time, uncover the pan and reduce the sauce by evaporating it somewhat.

Serve with bread and salads. Serves 4.

NOTE: If pigeon is not available, try small Cornish game hens.

✸ EL H'MEM FARCIE ✸

PIGEONS STUFFED WITH ALMONDS

Within the walls of the old Medina of Fez are a small number of beautiful restaurants built in the old style with high domed ceilings and ornate fixtures, carved walls, colored glass and painted doors. These were once private homes but are now restaurants catering to tourists. It was in one of these that I sampled stuffed pigeons. Pigeons are a common food in the old cities. There are two types—the domesticated house pigeon and the forest variety, which is reputed to be tastier and not so readily available.

2 whole pigeons (about 2 pounds), cleaned
2 tablespoons white vinegar combined with 2 tablespoons water and 1 teaspoon salt
1/2 pound blanched almonds, chopped fine

1 tablespoon olive oil
1 tablespoon butter
salt and pepper to taste
fresh mint leaves

1. Rinse the pigeons in the vinegar mixture. This is done, according to the cook, to remove the strong aroma of pigeon.

2. Stuff the pigeons with the chopped almonds and sew up the cavities. Put them in the *kesskess* of a *couscousier* and steam over moderate heat for 1/2 hour.

3. Now put the pigeons in a pan with the oil and butter, rolling them in it, and sprinkle with salt and pepper. Bake in a 350 degree oven for 1/2 hour to brown.

Serve warm on a bed of fresh mint leaves. Serves 2.

VARIATION
The same can be done with Cornish game hens; double the recipe and steam the birds for 1 hour before baking.

FISH

❧ SHORBA DE POISSON ❧

FISH SOUP FROM SAFI

With an unlimited supply of fresh fish brought to Safi's harbor by trawlers, my teacher only had to make an instant decision on the quantity, then start the proceedings. Some cooks prefer fish heads and bones to prepare the soup, and others use the whole fish, which is steamed and served separately from the bouillon. This is the case here. Neither garlic nor onion is included in the broth as it would erase the pure flavor of the fresh fish.

2 pounds of any ocean fish such as mérou, red snapper or porgy
8 cups water
1 pound carrot, cut into 1/4-inch dice
1 pound white turnip, peeled and cut into 1/4-inch dice
1 pound potato, peeled and cut into 1/4-inch dice

1 pound leek, white and green part, sliced thin, well rinsed in cold water
1 rib celery, diced
4 sprigs fresh coriander, chopped
1 teaspoon black pepper
1/2 teaspoon salt

1. Prepare the soup in a *couscousier* if you wish or in a standard Chinese steamer (you will need two to stack one on top of the other): Place the whole fish (or fish slices) in the top of a steamer on the perforated platform. Place the water, vegetables and seasonings in the bottom of the steamer. Bring the water to a boil, arrange the top of the steamer containing the fish over the bottom steamer and cover the top. Steam over low heat for 30 minutes, which is sufficient to cook the fish and allow the juices to drop into the broth and enrich it. Serve the fish separately and the soup with the vegetables in bowls.

    Another method of preparing this soup is to use a standard pot, put the water and vegetables in, bring to a boil and cook over low heat for 10 minutes. Then add the fish and cook for 1/2 hour. Serve as directed above.

Still another method is to remove the meat from the steamed fish and add it to the soup. The choice is according to one's personal preference.

A garnish for the soup: Mix together 1 cup of toasted bread crumbs with 1 clove garlic, crushed. Serve separately, for those who care to add it.

Serves 6 to 8 with plain cooked rice.

❈ SARDINE M'CHERMOULA ❈

STUFFED SARDINES (MOROCCO)

When the seaport of Safi is mentioned, the immediate response is that it is the home of sardines. They are caught seemingly by the millions and prepared in many ways. I went there and tasted sardines in one form or another every day. Stuffed sardines are street food, prepared for passing shoppers in the port area.

2 pounds fresh sardines
1 tablespoon sweet paprika
1 tablespoon ground cumin
1 clove garlic, chopped fine
2 tablespoons chopped parsley
1/2 teaspoon salt

juice of 1 lemon, plus lemon wedges
for serving
1/2 teaspoon black pepper
flour
1/2 cup vegetable oil

1. Remove the head and tail of each sardine, open up the stomach and clean everything out. Pull out the soft and easily removed spine and small bones. Flatten out the boneless fillet. Repeat with the remaining sardines. Rinse the fillets well in cold water and dry them.

2. Mix together the paprika, cumin, garlic, parsley, salt, lemon juice and pepper. This can be done in a processor. Take 1 heaping teaspoon of the seasoning mixture and smear it over 1 fillet on the stomach side. Press another fillet over this; roll the sandwich in flour. Heat several tablespoons of the oil in a skillet and pan-fry the stuffed

sardine on both sides for about 3 minutes. Drain on paper towels. Stuff, flour and pan-fry the remaining fillets in the same manner, adding more oil to the skillet as needed.

Serve warm with wedges of lemon and bread. Serves 6.

❋ SEMK FILFARAN ❋

BAKED FISH WITH VEGETABLES

The fish from Moroccan waters is of the highest quality and freshness is much prized. In fact, freshness is *de rigueur* with homecooks who search out their favorite fishmonger.

The title of this Casablanca recipe is in Arabic but it would have been just as accurate to call it *poisson au four*. Although Arabic is the national language, Moroccans throw French words into their daily conversation, not as much, though, as the Algerians, who have developed their own *patois* that combines both languages.

a 1 1/2- to 2-pound whole red
   snapper, porgy or similar fish
1 lemon, sliced
6 sprigs flat-leaf parsley, chopped
6 sprigs fresh coriander, chopped
2 cloves garlic, crushed in a garlic
   press
1/2 teaspoon salt, or to taste
1 teaspoon black pepper
1/4 teaspoon ground ginger
1/4 teaspoon turmeric
1/4 teaspoon saffron stamens
1 teaspoon sweet paprika

1/4 cup olive oil
1/2 cup water
2 large potatoes (1 pound), peeled
   and sliced into rounds 1/4 inch
   thick
3 sweet green or red peppers
   (1 pound), sliced into rounds
   1/4 inch thick
1 large tomato (1/2 pound), sliced
   into rounds
1 semi-hot fresh chili pepper, whole
1/4 cup green cracked olives

1. Clean the whole fish, including the head and tail. Score the fish 3 times diagonally on each side. Rub with a slice of lemon inside and out, including the scored cuts. Let stand 10 minutes, then rinse and drain.

2. Mix together in a bowl the parsley, coriander, garlic, salt, pepper, ginger, turmeric, saffron, paprika and oil. Rub 1 tablespoon of the spice mix (*chermoula*) into the fish. Add the water to the balance of the *chermoula* and mix well. Adjust the salt and pepper for the sauce at this time.

3. Put the fish into an oiled baking dish. Place over and around it in layers the potato slices, sweet pepper, tomato slices, and add the hot chili; scatter the olives over all. Pour the sauce over everything. Cover the dish with aluminum foil.

4. Place in a preheated 350 degree oven and bake for 20 minutes. Remove the foil and reduce the heat to 300 degrees. Bake for 15 minutes more, which is enough to soften the vegetables and fish. Baste once or twice.

5. Serve the whole fish on a platter and surround with the vegetables. Pour the sauce, somewhat reduced, over all.

Serve warm. Serves 6.

✵ KEFTA DE SARDINE ✵

SARDINE BALLS IN OLIVE SAUCE

These miniature chopped sardine balls are served in a sauce seasoned in the Moroccan manner with tomato, preserved lemon and olives. It is outstanding. Note that the traditional manner of preparing the Kefta is to include in the mixture some of the white kidney fat of lamb. This is optional, and 1 tablespoon vegetable oil is an effective substitute.

FOR THE KEFTA

2 pounds fresh sardine fillets, skins removed

3 tablespoons finely chopped lamb kidney fat or 1 tablespoon vegetable oil

4 cloves garlic, chopped

1 tablespoon ground cumin

1 tablespoon sweet paprika

1 tablespoon chopped flat-leaf parsley

1 tablespoon chopped fresh coriander

1/2 teaspoon black pepper

1/2 teaspoon salt

1/2 cup uncooked rice, well rinsed in cold water

3 ripe tomatoes (1 pound), peeled,
  seeds removed and chopped
1/4 cup vegetable oil
2 teaspoons chopped flat-leaf
  parsley
1 clove garlic, chopped
1 teaspoon ground cumin

2 teaspoons chopped celery
1 tablespoon tomato paste
25 green cracked olives, halved and
  pitted
1/2 small Preserved Lemon (see
  page 58), sliced thin into 2-inch
  slivers

1. *Prepare the Kefta:* Mix everything together. Form miniature balls, each 1 inch in diameter. Set aside.

2. *Prepare the Sauce:* Mix everything together and simmer over low heat for 15 minutes.

3. Add the sardine balls, one by one, to the sauce and cook, covered, for 15 minutes. This can be done in a traditional clay tagine or in a modern skillet.

Serve warm with bread and salads. Serves 6.

❈ KABOB DE SARDINE ❈

SARDINE PATTIES (MOROCCO)

Using the Kefta preparation in Kefta de Sardine, one can play with this spiced mixture and prepare patties 2 inches in diameter and 1/4 inch thick that are then dusted in flour and pan-fried in vegetable oil. I have also had served to me a finger- or cigar-shaped kebab that was 2 inches long and 1/2 inch thick, which was also dusted in flour and fried.

Then there were the variations—3-inch-diameter pattie, not quite 1/2 inch thick, which can be pan-fried as well or barbecued over charcoal.

I was involved in researching all this when I was down in the bazaar area of the Port of Safi, writing recipes and tasting the fried or barbecued patties as they were cooked in the very simplest of street-food charcoal-stove eateries. While this was happening, the real drama was occurring in a small shop directly behind the sardine action. A water diviner was in the shop, investigating the underground water sources. There was standing room only in this display of witchcraft as the diviner with his long *djellaba* and small pointed beard exuded an air of mystery and magic. Two metal branches quivered in his hands, then pointed downward, indicating the directions of pipes or an underground stream. The public were impressed.

I had my pattie sandwich with a *khubz*, the round, flat loaf of bread that is found all over Morocco and sells for about 15 cents.

❖ SALADE DE SARDINE ❖

ROASTED SARDINE SALAD

These sardines are not opened and cleaned out after a light baking as the intestines have their own flavor. When one buys sardines in a can, they are preserved with everything except the head and tail, so the preparation of this salad should not seem so outrageous.

2 pounds fresh sardines
1 medium onion, chopped
   (1/2 cup)
1 tablespoon chopped fresh
   coriander
1/2 teaspoon black pepper
1/2 teaspoon salt

1/4 cup vegetable oil
1/4 cup black olives, pitted and
   coarsely chopped
1/4 cup white vinegar or lemon
   juice
2 ripe tomatoes (1 pound), peeled
   and chopped

1. Salt the sardines lightly and bake them in a 350 degree oven on a baking pan for 15 to 20 minutes. Remove the heads, tails and skin. Do not open the stomachs.

2. Mix together into a seasoned sauce all the remaining ingredients.

3. Arrange the sardines on a serving platter and pour the sauce over them.

Serve cold. Serves 6 with salads and bread.

SALADS, VEGETABLE DISHES AND CONDIMENTS

❈ SALADA DEL CHUS ❈

SIMPLE TABLE SALAD

1/2 head Romaine or green leaf
   lettuce
1 small onion, coarsely sliced
   (1/4 cup)

2 tablespoons corn oil
2 tablespoons white vinegar
3/4 teaspoon sugar
1/2 teaspoon white pepper

Tear the lettuce leaves into 2-inch pieces, more or less the same size.
Then toss with the remaining ingredients, mixing well.

Serve at room temperature. Serves 6.

❈ SALADA DEL FOUL KHADAR ❈

FRESH FAVA BEAN SALAD

Fava beans are an ancient vegetable of the Mediterranean area.
When the green beans are young and tender the entire pod can be eaten,
as it is in this case. The concept of this preparation is that of a sharply

flavored condiment and not that of a western-style salad. This is served in small plates with a variety of other condiments, with diners helping themselves to small amounts as an adjunct to the entrées.

*1 pound fresh green fava beans
(broad beans)
1/2 teaspoon salt, or to taste
1/2 teaspoon black pepper
1/4 cup chopped fresh coriander
1 teaspoon ground cumin*

*3 large cloves garlic, crushed
in a garlic press
juice of 1 large lemon or 3
tablespoons white vinegar
2 tablespoons olive oil*

1. Remove the tough strings from the bean pods. Then cut the pods into 2-inch pieces. Cook to soften in lightly salted water over moderate heat for 10 to 15 minutes. Drain well.

2. Prepare the dressing by mixing together briskly the salt, pepper, coriander, cumin, garlic, lemon juice or vinegar and oil. Add it to the well-drained fava beans and toss to mix. Refrigerate to chill before serving. Can be refrigerated for 1 week during which time the flavor becomes more vivid.

Serves 6.

❊ SALADA DEL CHIAR ❊

CUCUMBER SALAD

*2 Kirby cucumbers, not peeled,
sliced (2 cups)
1 tablespoon fresh lemon juice or
1 tablespoon white vinegar
2 teaspoons olive oil
1/2 teaspoon salt*

*1/4 teaspoon white pepper
1 small clove garlic, crushed in a
garlic press
4 fresh mint leaves, or more to
taste, sliced thin*

Mix everything together and toss well. Refrigerate for 1 hour.

Serve cool. Serves 4 to 6.

✺ SALADA LIM B'ZEITOUN ✺

Orange and Olive Salad

An odd combination as a condiment, with contrasting textures and flavors, and especially good with meat and poultry dishes.

*1 large orange, peeled and divided
  into segments
10 black Moroccan oil-cured olives
1 tablespoon strong-flavored olive
  oil
1 teaspoon Harissa (see page 89),
  or more to taste*

*juice of 1/2 lemon
1 teaspoon sweet paprika
1/4 teaspoon salt
1/4 teaspoon ground cumin
1 clove garlic, crushed in a garlic
  press*

1. Trim the orange segments and pull off skin. Cut into 1/2-inch pieces.

2. Pit the olives and cut into 1/2-inch pieces.

3. Toss all the ingredients together and refrigerate.

Serve with meat and poultry dishes. Double the recipe for larger groups. Serves 4.

✺ LE ZALUK ✺

Strips of Green or Red Pepper Salad

I tasted this salad at a Friday evening dinner in a Jewish home. There were six other salads—really appetizers—on the table as a first course.

*3 sweet red or green peppers
  (1 pound)
1/2 teaspoon salt
3 tablespoons vegetable oil*

*juice of 1 lemon, or more to taste
2 cloves garlic, crushed in a garlic
  press*

1. Char the peppers over charcoal or under a gas or electric broiler until the skins are black. Put the peppers in a paper bag to cool for

10 minutes, which will make it much easier to pull off the charred skins. Peel each pepper, cut open and discard the seeds and stem. Slice the flesh into 1-inch-long pieces 1/2 inch wide. These are the "fillets."

2. Combine the peppers with all the remaining ingredients, toss well and refrigerate.

Serve cool or at room temperature. Serves 6 with other salads as an appetizer.

❈ ZALOOK ❈

COOKED EGGPLANT SALAD

Zalook is a summer salad that is prepared all over Morocco. This is a Casablanca version, which can be peppery hot if you allow it to be. The salad can be eaten warm, at room temperature or cold. In my opinion, cold is better. This is often served with M'Hammar Djedj (Twice-Cooked Chicken, see page 33) with which it is compatible.

4 small eggplant (1 pound), peeled
2 cloves garlic, chopped fine
4 sprigs flat-leaf parsley, chopped
* fine*
1 teaspoon sweet paprika
1/2 teaspoon salt

1/4 teaspoon black pepper
1/4 teaspoon ground cumin
1/8 teaspoon turmeric
3 tablespoons olive oil
2 tablespoons tomato paste
1 cup water

1. Rinse the whole peeled eggplant in cold water and drain. Put them in a pan, cover with water and simmer, covered, over low heat for 15 minutes. Drain and cool.

2. In a saucepan, mix together the garlic parsley, paprika, salt, pepper, cumin, turmeric, olive oil, tomato paste and water. Simmer over low heat for 5 minutes. Add the eggplant, cover the pan and cook for 20 minutes. The eggplant should melt down, helped along by some coarse mashing with a spoon.

Serve warm, room temperature or cold. Serves 6.

✸ SAFA SHAARIA ✸

VERMICELLI WITH SWEET GARNISHES

Steamed, not boiled in water, vermicelli is glorified in the Moroccan manner—with butter, almonds, cinnamon, raisins and powdered sugar. Aromatic and sweet are the hallmarks of this fine noodle dish, a rarity in couscous land. Safa Shaaria is traditionally served with M'Hammar (see page 20), but need not be confined to that beef dish.

*2 pounds vermicelli, broken into
  2-inch pieces
5 teaspoons plus 3 tablespoons
  vegetable oil
4 tablespoons white raisins
1/3 cup blanched almonds*

*1 teaspoon ground cinnamon
1 cup powdered sugar
8 tablespoons butter, sliced
1/2 teaspoon salt*
a couscousier *or Chinese-style
  steamer*

1. Boil water in the bottom section of your steamer. Mix the noodles with 1 teaspoon oil in a dish large enough to hold them and add the noodles to the top (*kesskess*) of the steamer. Cover and steam over moderate heat for 1/2 hour.

2. Remove the noodles to the dish and mix with 1 teaspoon of the oil and 3 tablespoons water. Do this a total of 4 times to soften the noodles. The last 3 times steam for only 15 minutes as the noodles change color and become white, which indicates that they are tender. For the fourth or last steaming, add the raisins, which will soften and expand.

3. Brown the almonds in the 3 tablespoons oil over low heat and drain on paper towels. Cool and grind them in a food processor—not too fine, retain some texture—with the cinnamon and 2 tablespoons sugar.

4. Place the noodles in a serving dish, add the butter, 3 tablespoons sugar and salt. Toss well to mix and shape the noodles in a peaked pyramid form with the raisins hidden within. Decorate the top of the pyramid with 3 tablespoons sugar, like snow on a mountain. Cover the pyramid with the ground almonds.

5. Sprinkle 5 thin lines of cinnamon, equidistant, from the top to bottom of the pyramid.

6. Serve the balance of the powdered sugar as a side dish for those who wish a sweeter concoction.

Serve warm with M'Hammar. Serves 6.

VARIATION

For those who prefer rice the following recipe, Safa Roz, offers the same aromatic and sweet flavor, with rice in place of the vermicelli.

❊ SAFA ROZ ❊

AROMATIC RICE WITH GARNISHES

The same ingredients and decorative devices found in the Safa Shaaria are followed in the Safa Roz, except 2 cups of rice are used in place of the vermicelli.

2 cups rice

1. Half-cook the rice in boiling water with 1/2 teaspoon salt for 5 minutes. Drain and rinse under cold water.

2. Steam the rice over hot water twice, 15 minutes each time, mixing the rice with 1 teaspoon oil. Do not add water as in the noodles.

3. Test the rice for doneness the second steaming. It should be soft, with individual kernels. The raisins are steamed at this time. Then garnish and decorate the rice in the same manner as the noodles.

Serve warm with M'Hammar. Serves 6.

❊ TAJINE KHOUDRA ❊

VEGETABLE RAGOUT

Not all *tajines* contain meat or poultry. The Moroccan love of vegetables, always fresh in the public markets, is evident in this vegetarian side dish, which could also be considered as an entrée for the dedicated vegetarian.

1/4 cup vegetable oil
1 medium onion, chopped (1/2 cup)
5 sprigs flat-leaf parsley, chopped
1 teaspoon salt
1 teaspoon black pepper
1 teaspoon sweet paprika
1/2 teaspoon turmeric
1 large ripe tomato, chopped
    (1 cup)

1/2 pound carrot, cut into 1/2-inch
    dice
1/2 pound potato, peeled and cut
    into 1/2-inch dice
1/2 pound zucchini, cut into
    1/2-inch dice
1/2 pound white turnip, peeled and
    cut into 1/2-inch dice
2 cups water

Heat the oil in a large pan, add the onion and stir-fry over low heat for 1 minute. Then add all the remaining ingredients except the water and stir-fry for 10 minutes. Add the water, bring to a boil and cook, uncovered, for 1/2 hour to soften the vegetables. Some sauce should remain at the end of this cooking time. Adjust salt if necessary.

Serve warm with bread. Serves 6.

❈ LOOBIA BLANC ❈

WHITE BEAN STEW

Here is a Berber recipe, although it could be prepared by any community. Vegetarian, with a gamut of spices and seasonings, it transforms white beans into a production. This is a side dish, eaten with fish, meat or chicken.

1 pound dried white beans
    (haricots), soaked overnight
    in water to cover and
    drained.
3 tablespoons olive or vegetable oil
1/2 teaspoon turmeric
1/2 teaspoon black pepper
1/2 teaspoon ground ginger
1/2 teaspoon sweet paprika

1/2 teaspoon salt
2 ripe tomatoes, peeled and chopped
    (1 cup)
5 sprigs flat-leaf parsley, chopped
2 medium onion, chopped (1 cup)
3 cloves garlic, chopped
2 fresh red or green hot chili
    peppers, whole
8 cups water

Put everything into a pan large enough to hold all the ingredients, bring to a boil, then simmer over low heat for 1 hour, which should be enough time to soften the beans and integrate the seasonings. Some of the liquid does evaporate but there should still be ample sauce.

Serves 6 to 8 with salads and bread.

MACARONIA

MACARONI WITH SIMPLE SAUCE

This is not Italian but possibly was influenced by them. Various sizes and shapes of dry pasta are used by Moroccans, with elbow macaroni being popular. Macaronia cannot be considered one of the old-time traditional foods, although it is most often served with dishes such as the Semk Filfaran (Baked Fish with Vegetables, see page 42).

1 pound elbow macaroni or other pasta of choice
1 1/2 teaspoons salt
1 tablespoon vegetable oil
2 tablespoons butter
3 tablespoons olive oil
1 small onion, sliced, then crushed (1/3 cup)
1/4 teaspoon turmeric
1 clove garlic, crushed in a garlic press
1/2 teaspoon black pepper
1/4 teaspoon ground ginger
1 cup water
4 tablespoons tomato paste

1. *Prepare the Macaroni:* Cover with water, add 1 teaspoon of the salt and the vegetable oil and bring to a boil. Cook over moderate heat until al dente, about 10 minutes, or more depending upon the size of the pasta. Drain, return to the pan and add the butter. Keep warm, covered.

2. *Prepare the Sauce:* Put the olive oil, onion, turmeric and remaining 1/2 teaspoon salt in a saucepan and simmer, covered, over low heat for 10 minutes. Add the garlic, pepper, ginger and water and continue to cook for 10 minutes. Add the tomato paste and simmer for 10 minutes more to thicken the sauce.

3. To serve, place the warm macaroni in a bowl and add the sauce, mixing everything together.

Serve warm. Serves 6 with fish dishes.

❈ BATATA M'CHERMLA ❈

Spiced Potato Side Dish

Here is a well-seasoned side dish that could provide the basis for a completely vegetarian meal. The spicing is vivid, but does not sting the palate and is compatible with the melting texture of the potatoes.

*1 pound potato, peeled and cut into
   2-inch cubes
2 tablespoons corn oil
1 large onion, chopped (1 cup)
1 tablespoon tomato paste
2 cups water
1/2 teaspoon salt*

*1/4 teaspoon white pepper
1/4 teaspoon sweet paprika
1/4 teaspoon hot red chili powder
6 sprigs fresh coriander, chopped
1 bay leaf
1/2 teaspoon olive oil
1/2 teaspoon ground cumin*

1. Cover the potato cubes in lightly salted cold water for 15 minutes. Drain.

2. Heat the corn oil in a pan, add the onion and stir-fry over low heat for 3 minutes. Add the potato cubes, tomato paste and water and bring to a boil. Add the salt, pepper, paprika and chili powder, stir the mixture, cover the pan and simmer for 20 minutes.

3. As the potatoes soften (test with a fork), add the coriander, bay leaf, olive oil and cumin. Stir and cook for another 10 minutes to reduce the sauce slightly.

Serve warm. Serves 4.

❈ SALADA MITBOCHA BIL BEYD ❈

Cooked Tomato Salad with Poached Eggs

In spite of its title, this is not a salad. Like so many of the Moroccan concoctions that are really side dishes, it, too, is light and vegetarian for hot summer days.

3 tablespoons corn oil	1/2 teaspoon sugar
2 pounds ripe tomato, peeled and cut up coarsely	1/4 teaspoon ground cumin
3 large cloves garlic, quartered	1–2 teaspoons Harissa (see page 89), to taste
1 tablespoon sweet paprika	6 sprigs flat-leaf parsley, chopped
1/2 teaspoon salt	1/2 cup water
1/2 teaspoon black pepper	6 whole eggs

1. Heat the corn oil in a large skillet, add the tomato and stir-fry over low heat to evaporate the excess liquid. Add the garlic, paprika, salt, pepper, sugar, cumin, harissa, 3 sprigs of the parsley and water. Simmer 30 minutes to integrate the flavors and thicken the sauce.

2. Now make 6 depressions in the thick sauce. Break one whole egg into each depression. Scatter the 3 remaining sprigs parsley over the eggs. Cover the pan and simmer over low heat for 5 minutes for soft eggs and 10 minutes for firm ones.

Serve each person an egg and sauce with bread and condiments on the side. Serves 4 to 6.

❈ SALADA DI CHIZU ❈

SPICED CARROT CONDIMENT

This is not really a salad and leans more toward a condiment that is served Moroccan style, in a small platter with an assortment of other condiments. These can be considered as appetizers to be tasted prior to the main dining events. Spicy and intense, Chizu is used sparingly and can be refrigerated for up to one week.

1/2 pound whole carrots, cooked briefly until soft but firm	1/4 teaspoon white pepper
1 teaspoon ground cumin	4 sprigs fresh coriander, chopped
1 teaspoon sweet paprika	1 clove garlic, crushed in a garlic press
1/2 teaspoon hot chili powder	2 tablespoons white vinegar
1/2 teaspoon salt	2 tablespoons corn oil

Slice the carrots into rounds 1/4 inch thick. Put into a serving bowl, add all the remaining ingredients and toss well to mix.

Serve as a condiment. Serves 6.

❖ ZEITOUN BIL BEYD ❖

OLIVES AND EGGS

A delicious concoction that fulfills all the yearnings for a summer dish, this can be thought of as a main course or as an appetizer to introduce the main events. In addition, it illustrates the important and exotic use of olives as food.

1 pound green cracked olives
2 tablespoons corn oil
6 cloves garlic, crushed in a garlic press
1 1/2 pounds ripe tomato, peeled and chopped
1 tablespoon tomato paste
1 tablespoon Harissa (see page 89), or more or less to taste

1/2 teaspoon turmeric
1/4 teaspoon black pepper
1/4 teaspoon salt
1 cup water
juice of 1 lemon
6 whole eggs
1/2 cup coarsely chopped parsley

1. *Prepare the Olives:* Carefully remove the pits from the olives so that each olive has 2 intact halves if possible. Soak covered in water overnight. Drain. In a saucepan cover the olives again in water, bring to a boil and drain. Do this once more to remove salt and excessive bitterness. Set aside.

2. Heat the oil in a large flat skillet, add the garlic, tomato, tomato paste and harissa and stir-fry over moderate heat for 10 minutes.

3. Now add the turmeric, pepper, salt, olives and water and bring to a boil. Simmer over low heat for 45 minutes and add the lemon juice. When the sauce becomes thick, at about this time, turn the heat down to the lowest setting. Make 6 depressions in the sauce mixture. Break a whole egg into each depression. Scatter the parsley over all.

Cover the pan and cook over low heat for 10 minutes. The eggs will become firm, the sauce thick and the olives soft.

Serve warm with French bread as an appetizer or main course. Serves 6.

✷ SALADA FELFLA MECHOUIA ✷
ROASTED PEPPER CONDIMENT

This is a condiment to be served in small quantities with a variety of others, depending upon the occasion and the personal preference of the diners.

2 large sweet green or red peppers, whole
1 clove garlic, sliced very thin lengthwise
1/2 teaspoon salt, or to taste

4 tablespoons olive oil
2 tablespoons white vinegar (optional)
1/4 teaspoon white pepper

1. Char the peppers over charcoal or an open gas burner. Put the peppers in a paper bag for 15 minutes, which steams and loosens the blackened skins. Pull off as much of the skin as possible. Cut the peppers open and remove and discard the stems and seeds. Do not rinse off the peppers since the flesh will absorb the water.

2. Cut the peppers into 1/2-inch-wide strips and toss them well with the garlic, salt, oil, vinegar, if used, and the white pepper. Chill in the refrigerator before serving. The condiment can be refrigerated for 2 weeks.

Serves 6.

VARIATION
Do the same thing with 1/2 pound (6) semi-hot green chili peppers, the long twisted variety sometimes known as elephant trunk chili. Open the roasted chilies; remove and discard the stems and seeds. Do not cut the chili peppers up, but toss with the seasonings. Serve whole.

SALADA DEL B'DILGAN

SMOKED EGGPLANT AND PEPPER CONDIMENT

The combination of sweet green and semi-hot peppers gives this salad its character, which otherwise might be considered banal. Garlic is admired for its health-giving properties in addition to its flavor.

2 eggplant (2 pounds)
2 sweet green peppers
2 semi-hot green chili peppers
1 firm ripe tomato (1/2 pound),
*   coarsely cut up*
1 small onion, sliced thin (1/3 cup)
1 clove garlic, crushed in a garlic
*   press*

1 teaspoon salt
1/2 teaspoon white pepper
2 tablespoons olive oil
1 tablespoon white vinegar or
*   lemon juice*
1 tablespoon chopped flat-leaf
*   parsley*

1. Char the eggplant, sweet peppers and hot chili peppers separately over charcoal or an open gas flame. Let cool, then pull off the eggplant skins and stems; remove and discard most of the seeds inside. Cool and drain. Peel, stem and seed the sweet and hot peppers.

2. Cut the sweet peppers into 2-inch-long strips and the hot chilies into 1/2-inch pieces. Coarsely cut up the eggplant pulp. Then mix everything together in a bowl and refrigerate.

Serve cool as a starter with French bread and also as a condiment along with others. Serves 8.

HAMAD MRAKAD

PRESERVED (OR PICKLED) LEMON

Preserving the small, squat lemon as the Moroccans do ensures that they will have it during the season when it is not available in the market. In addition and perhaps more important is that the lemons are included in so many Moroccan dishes as a vivid seasoning. During my residence there I used to occasionally preserve the small, round lemons of India, but they were used as table chutney.

Some Moroccans use only the preserved peel of the lemon and discard the pulp. Others use the whole lemon, which is what I do, and employ the liquid for seasoning some salads. It may not be traditional, but it is effective as the liquid includes salt as well as lemon flavor.

6 lemons
1/4 cup coarse salt
water

2 tablespoons olive or vegetable oil
(olive is better)

1. Make cross cuts into the bud end of a lemon in each direction, cutting to within 3/4 inch of the stem end to hold the lemon together. Open the lemon up like the petals of a flower and rub about 1 heaping teaspoon salt into the openings. Do this for all the lemons.

2. Fit the lemons into a glass jar, cover with water and dribble the oil on top, sealing in the contents. Cover and refrigerate.

3. Let the lemons pickle for 2 to 3 weeks before using. As the fermentation process proceeds, the liquid in the jar will thicken and assume the rich, characteristic lemon aroma of the preservation.

VARIATION

Some cooks use lemon juice instead of water to cover the lemons. My man in his public market stall in Casablanca is adamant about the virtues of lemon juice over water. This is, however, a modern modification, resulting in a more intense lemon flavor.

❈ SPICED OLIVES ❈

Public markets in Morocco are a great place to check out the varieties of olives and taste them as well. I was given a lesson preparing this olive pickle at a fine market in Casablanca, where the merchant and the observing public had much to say and instruct as I was taking notes.

These spicy morsels can be served as one of the group of salads as a first course of appetizers at dinner. Or serve as is with drinks.

1 pound green cracked olives
1–2 teaspoons hot red dried chili flakes, crushed slightly

4 cloves garlic, crushed in a mortar or in a garlic press

1. Rinse the olives well in cold water to remove excess salt. Some cooks prefer to soak them all day as a more effective way to reduce salt. Drain and dry the olives.

2. Then mix together with remaining ingredients.

Serve as an appetizer with drinks or as a condiment with meals.

❖ QUATRE ÉPICES ❖
FOUR SPICES

This Moroccan version of combined spices is used in some dishes according to the personal preference of the cook. The Tunisians also dote on four-spice mix, as do the Indians with the *garam masala* — a mélange of many spices. It is indispensable in the kitchen. In order to have a continuous supply of fresh spices, it is better to combine small amounts.

1 tablespoon ground cumin   *1 teaspoon ground ginger*
1 teaspoon ground cinnamon   *1/4 teaspoon ground nutmeg*

Mix everything together and store in a jar with a tight cover.

Makes almost 2 tablespoons.

❖ A NOTE ABOUT SWEET PAPRIKA ❖

The red sweet peppers that are transformed to paprika were dried whole, in this case, family style on the roof of my friend's house. Then the well-dried peppers, which were flat due to the loss of moisture, were opened and the stems and seeds were removed and discarded.

The dried peppers were then ground into bright red sweet paprika, fresh and aromatic. Both the color and flavor were infinitely superior to the commercial supermarket variety.

BAKED GOODS, SWEETS AND A BEVERAGE

L'HARSHA

BERBER SEMOLINA FLAT BREAD

Semolina is the heart of a grain of wheat that ultimately is turned into couscous. Semolina fine-ground into a flour is used to prepare L'Harsha. Wandering around the public markets in the early morning hours, hungry commuters en route on foot to work buy pieces of this golden brown fried bread, which are sold by weight. They point out the amount wanted and the street-food shop man cuts off a chunk. The flat, firm, dense bread, as I saw it, is traditionally about 14 inches in diameter and perfectly round.

4 tablespoons butter
1 cup olive oil
2 pounds fine-ground semolina
    flour

1 teaspoon salt
4 eggs, beaten
1/2 cup water

1. Warm the butter and oil together. Add all the remaining ingredients and mix together, stirring vigorously. Knead the dough for 10 minutes.

2. Oil an 8- or 10-inch skillet lightly. Take a ball of the semolina dough and press it into the skillet with your fingers to shape a round flat disc not quite 1/2 inch thick. Fry over low heat for 10 minutes on each side, until light brown.

The disc is served at room temperature with coffee or soups. Makes 3 round loaves.

❈ MALAWI ❈

BERBER SOFT BREAD

In the early morning this soft, round flat bread, which is really a fourteen-inch-in-diameter rather floppy circle is sold by weight in the old city of Fez. The street shop owner pulls off and weighs a piece large or small for the buyer's breakfast with a bowl of *herissa*, the national soup (see pages 109 and 110 for the same soup that is made in Algeria). Malawi is reminiscent of the *roti* made by the Indians in Trinidad and Guyana who, in turn, brought it with them from India.

> *2 pounds flour (7 cups)*   *1 1/2 cups hot water*
> *1 teaspoon salt*   *1/2 cup olive or vegetable oil*

1. Put all the ingredients in a food processor and mix until the dough forms a ball. (The longer the processing the softer the dough. The same is true if the dough is prepared by hand, as it is in Moroccan homes.)

2. Oil your hands and divide the dough into 5 balls. Oil an 8- or 10-inch skillet lightly and press 1 ball out quite thin into the skillet, almost to the edge. Fry over low heat for 5 minutes on each side. When done the color should be light brown and the texture soft-flaky.

Serve with generous amounts of honey for breakfast. Makes 5 flat breads.

❈ SFENJ ❈

STREET DOUGHNUT

Sfenj, the Moroccan breakfast doughnut, is the morning street food *par excellence*. I would watch the *sfenj* maker in a small cubbyhole on a street corner in Fez servicing hungry diners. One of his vats contained hot vegetable oil and very close to it was an equally large container holding sticky white dough batter. Taking a big fistful of this viscous dough, he would dexterously squeeze a ball the size of a large lemon through his fist, pull it open in a rough and ready doughnut shape, then lay it down carefully into the oil. All orders were *à la carte*, freshly made for patient customers.

It was a common sight to see buyers walk off with any number of the doughnuts tied together on a thin bamboo string. Pedestrians on their way to work stopped by for their Sfenj fix for the day. Sometimes there was a plate of sugar to sprinkle on the hot, oily doughnut.

Occasionally a customer would ask that an egg be added to the frying *sfenj*. In which case, at an appropriate time, a corner of the *sfenj* was torn open, an egg dropped in, the whole was fried to completion, brown and firm—a meal on the street when time is short. These are served as a snack, especially on Ramadhan.

1 1/2 teaspoons dry yeast	*3 1/2 cups flour*
1 cup warm water, or more	*1/2 teaspoon salt*
1/2 teaspoon sugar	*4 cups vegetable oil*

1. Mix the yeast, 1/4 cup of the water and sugar together and let proof about 15 minutes.

2. Put the flour and salt in a bowl, add the yeast mixture and sufficient water (about 1 cup) to form a loose, sticky dough. Cover the bowl and let the dough rise for 1 hour.

3. Heat the oil in a wok or deep skillet to 375 degrees for deep frying. Moisten your hand with water to handle the sticky dough. Grasp a ball of dough (1/2 cup) and pull it open to make a hole like a doughnut. Place it carefully into the oil and brown on one side. Flip it over (the *sfenj* maker in Fez used a long metal hook) and brown the other side. Fry 2 doughnuts at a time.

4. Remove and drain briefly on paper towels. The Sfenj will be slightly oily, which is desired.

Serve warm with tea or coffee. Makes about 10 Sfejn.

❀ BEGHRIR ❀

MOROCCAN PANCAKES

These pancakes, with a simple yeast batter, are pan-fried on one side only. As the frying progresses, bubbles appear to pop into what could be described as very miniature volcanic mouths. The pancake is then ready to be glorified by melted butter and honey. Have for breakfast or morning snack with coffee or Fresh Mint Tea (see page 71). The first time I tasted one of these was on a street corner in the Safi bazaar. A tiny elderly lady covered to her eyes was selling them. The open bubbles seemed to be perfectly equidistant—precision cooking; she selected one, tore it in half and gave it to me to try.

4 cups flour
1/2 teaspoon salt
1 tablespoon dry yeast
1/2 cup warm plus 1 1/2 cups water

1/2 teaspoon sugar
melted butter and warmed honey
for serving

1. Put the flour and salt in a large mixing bowl. Proof the yeast and sugar in 1/2 cup warm water for 15 minutes. When proofed, mix all the ingredients together, including the 1 1/2 cups water, to form a thin batter. Let stand for 1 hour in a warm spot.

2. Using a Teflon skillet, brush the pan with a piece of wax paper and a few drops of oil. Pour in about 1/3 cup of the batter and fry slowly over low heat. The pancake will soon be covered with open bubbles; the texture will be soft. Full flavor is produced by butter and honey. Make pancakes with the remaining batter. Makes 20 to 25.

Serve with melted butter and warm honey—as much as desired. Serves 6 to 8.

NOTE: There are cooks who prepare this batter with milk and egg, but the traditional method uses water and no egg.

❊ BRIOUATS ❊

Pastry Triangles

Briouats (pronounced *bree-wats*) are filled pastry triangles traditionally prepared with *warka*, but which can be effectively made with commercial fillo dough sheets. I have used both methods, and now prefer the fillo since it is so easily available to me.

Almond Filling

1 pound blanched almonds
1 teaspoon ground cinnamon
1 cup sugar
2 tablespoons orange blossom water (available in Middle Eastern groceries)
2 tablespoons melted butter

1 pound fillo sheets, each 12 × 17 inches

1 cup vegetable oil
1 cup honey, warmed
2 tablespoons sesame seeds, toasted

1. *Prepare the Almond Filling:* In a food processor, chop the almonds to a coarse consistency, then add the cinnamon, sugar, orange blossom water and melted butter and process to combine the filling.

2. *To Shape Triangles:* Take several fillo sheets and divide them in half lengthwise and crosswise so that you have sheets that are 6 inches wide by 8 1/2 inches long. Fold them lengthwise so that you have fillo strips 3 inches wide. This is the size that will be filled and folded into triangles.

3. Take 1 heaping teaspoon of the filling and put it on the lower left-hand side of the fillo. Fold it over to the right to make a triangle. Then fold it over to the left and to the right again until you have folded the entire sheet into a triangle. Seal the package with beaten egg or a light mixture of flour and water.

4. Heat the vegetable oil in a skillet over moderate/low heat and brown the pastries for about 2 minutes.

5. Plunge them into the honey and leave them for 10 minutes, turning them over. Remove and sprinkle with sesame seeds. Set aside to cool and dry.

Serve as a sweet. Serve at room temperature with Fresh Mint Tea (see page 71) or coffee. Makes 20.

DATE AND ALMOND FILLING

This is a sweet filling, a predictable one since Morocco is date country. I purchased large, ripe, soft, melting dates that were almost the size of an egg from a street hawker in Casablanca.

1 cup chopped pitted dates
1/2 cup blanched almonds, chopped

1/8 teaspoon ground cinnamon

Mix everything together and use to fill for fillo triangles. Fry, then soak in honey as described above.

Serve as a sweet.

GROUND BEEF FILLING

1 pound lean ground beef
1 medium onion, grated
  (1/2 cup)
1/2 teaspoon ground cinnamon
1/2 teaspoon salt
1/4 teaspoon black pepper
1/4 teaspoon Harissa (see page 89)

1/4 teaspoon turmeric
3 sprigs fresh coriander, chopped fine
juice of 1 lemon
2 tablespoons vegetable oil
1 egg, beaten

1. Put all the ingredients, except the egg, in a skillet and stir-fry over low heat for 10 minutes to evaporate the moisture. The mixture should be dry. Cool well. Add the egg and mix.

2. Prepare triangles as instructed above. They may be pan-fried or baked on an oiled baking sheet in a 350 degree oven for 20 minutes, or until brown all around.

Serve as an appetizer. Makes 20 triangles.

❈ CIGAR BRIOUATS ❈

These popular *briouats* are made in the shape of cigars, 3 inches long and 1 inch thick.

1. *To Shape Cigars:* Take 1 fillo sheet, cut 6 inches wide by 8 1/2 inches long, and on the short end nearest you put 1 heaping tablespoon of the ground beef filling (above). Fold the long left and right sides of the fillo over to meet in the center into a cigar shape 3 inches wide, covering the filling. Fold the short end near you over once firmly. Then fold it two times more to shape the cigar. Seal the final fold by smearing the fillo end with either beaten egg or flour paste.

2. Deep-fry cigars in vegetable oil over moderate heat for 3 minutes. Drain on paper towels.

Serve as an appetizer. Makes 20 cigars.

❈ BRIOUATS DE RIZ ❈

RICE-FILLED PASTRY TRIANGLES OR CIGARS

An unexpected pleasure that uses a seasoned rice filling.

1 cup cooked rice   *1/4 teaspoon ground cinnamon*
1 teaspoon sugar

1. Mix the rice, sugar and cinnamon together for the filling.

2. Make *briouats* or cigars, whichever you prefer. However, I point out that rice filling is usually used for cigars. Follow the same instructions for frying and soaking in honey for 10 minutes as for the briouats with almond filling. Do not sprinkle with the sesame seeds.

   In Fez I have also tasted cigars that have been crisp-fried without any other embellishment, no honey or sesame seeds.

Serve as an appetizer. Makes 20 cigars.

❈ BRIOUATS DE CREVETTE ❈

SHRIMP-FILLED PASTRY TRIANGLES

1 pound small shrimp, cooked in
plain water and peeled
1/2 teaspoon black pepper
1/4 teaspoon salt

1 tablespoon chopped flat-leaf
parsley
3 cloves garlic, chopped fine or
crushed in a mortar

Mix everything together for the shrimp filling. Fill and fold triangles as directed above in almond-filled triangles.

NOTE: One pound of fillet of flounder or other white fish can also be used as a filling. Cook, cool and chop into 1/2-inch pieces. Add the seasonings and fill, fold and fry the fillo triangles as above.

❈ HALWA SHEBAKIA ❈

RAMADHAN SPECIAL SESAME COOKIES

This recipe is frankly for historical purposes as its yield indicates suitability for commercial or restaurant production rather than home baking. With unusual proportions of butter, oil and honey in the batter, yeast for rising and more oil for frying, making the cookies would be rather daunting were it not for the fact that they help glorify a particularly holy celebration.

4 pounds flour
3 pounds butter
2 pounds sesame seeds, plus
additional toasted seeds for
sprinkling
1 tablespoon dry yeast dissolved
in 1/2 cup water
20 grams gum arabic (optional)

1 tablespoon saffron stamens
1/2 pound smen (seasoned
preserved butter, similar
to the Indian ghee)
1 tablespoon ground cinnamon
1 quart vegetable oil, plus 1 quart
for deep-frying
10 pounds honey

1. In a food processor process all the ingredients, except the honey, into a paste.

2. Take a walnut-sized piece of paste and roll it out very thin. Using a metal cut-out typically found in Morocco, with different designs, cut out cookies and let them rise for 15 minutes. Deep-fry the cookies in the remaining quart of oil in batches over low heat just to brown.

   Soak the cookies in the honey for 15 minutes. Remove and sprinkle with toasted sesame seeds.

Makes several hundred cookies.

❈ GREBA BIL KUK ❈

COCONUT COOKIES

You may prefer to make half a recipe of these.

1 pound fine-ground semolina flour	*1 pound powdered sugar, plus 1/4 cup for sprinkling*
1/2 pound unsweetened grated coconut	*1/2 cup vegetable oil*
4 eggs, beaten	*1 tablespoon baking powder (7 grams)*
1/8 teaspoon salt	*1/2 teaspoon vanilla*

1. Mix the flour and coconut together in a large bowl. Add all the remaining ingredients, reserving 1/4 cup sugar, and mix well by hand.

2. Oil a baking sheet lightly. To shape cookies, pull off a tablespoon of the batter and roll it into a ball. Then flatten it slightly to a round cookie shape. Sprinkle 1/4 teaspoon sugar on top.

   Bake in a 350 degree oven until a light tan color, about 20 minutes. Cool.

Serve with Fresh Mint Tea (see page 71) or coffee. Makes 40 cookies.

❧ HALWA CIZAME ❧

SESAME SEED CARAMEL

Another street sweet found in one of the narrow lanes of the Fez Medina.

2 pounds sesame seeds, toasted   *1 pound sugar, caramelized to a*
                                          liquid

Put the sesame seeds in a container such as a small loaf pan. Pour the caramelized sugar slowly over the seeds.
   Cool and cut into slices or chunks.

Makes about 1/2 pound caramel.

❧ JABAN ❧

PEANUT NOUGAT

This firm, white, chewy nougat—a typical sweet—is found in the old Medina in Fez. Buy this candy at small shops or at the occasional sweets seller who sets up his business on a narrow, busy intersection. This nougat is not so hard that it pulls the fillings out of your teeth, but is a most delicious chew.

2 pounds sugar (4 cups)   *4 egg whites, beaten by hand or in*
1 teaspoon white vinegar   *an electric mixer until stiff*
                                   1 cup shelled roasted peanuts

1. Caramelize the sugar slowly over low heat in a heavy skillet until it is melted down into an amber liquid. Add the vinegar and mix.

2. Pour the caramel in a steady stream into the beaten egg whites, mixing constantly, preferably with an electric beater. Stir in the peanuts.

3. Cool the mixture for 5 minutes, then scoop it quickly into a loaf pan or other container.

   Cool well. Cut the nougat with a knife into chunks.

Makes about 2 pounds nougat.

❊ THÉ À LA MENTHE ❊

Fresh Mint Tea

The ritual of mint tea—and it is one that takes place everyday, all day long, all over Morocco. How to explain this national passion that visiting foreigners quickly assume? The tea is refreshing, traditional, and is reputed to be an effective digestive: Its health-promoting qualities cannot be ignored.

1 teaspoon green tea leaves　　　*4 sprigs fresh mint*
3 cups boiling water　　　*4–6 teaspoons sugar, to taste*

1. Put the green tea leaves in a teapot, and add 1/4 cup of the boiling water to warm the pot and also lightly color the tea. Let steep over very low heat for 2 minutes until the tea comes to a boil.

2. Add the balance of the water (2 3/4 cups) and push the mint sprigs into the pot. Pour the sugar on top, but do not stir. Rather let the tea steep again over low heat for 2 minutes.

Serve the tea without the mint leaves in the small traditional glasses. Serves 4.

Jewish quarter in the walled city of Fez

THE JEWISH CUISINE OF MOROCCO

❈ HAROSETH POR PESACH ❈

Haroseth for Passover

Every Jewish community has its own traditional way of preparing haroseth, that ritual part of the Passover seder table. The Moroccan version uses the fruit and nuts of the countryside, ground into a delectable paste, then rolled into balls.

1 cup blanched almonds
1/2 cup lightly toasted walnuts
1 cup pitted dates

1/2 cup white or dark raisins
1/8 teaspoon ground nutmeg

1. In a food processor process first the almonds, then the walnuts, into a smooth paste. Add the dates, raisins and nutmeg and combine.

2. Roll heaping teaspoons of the paste into balls about 3/4 inches in diameter.

Serve at Passover or any other time as a sweet snack. Makes about 50 balls.

❈ MARAG L'HAMED ❈

Sour Soup

It is the lemon juice that gives this soup its name. The classic method of making it is to use both boneless beef chunks and beef bones to enrich the broth. Lamb, a most popular meat in Morocco, and chicken may also be used, but it is the beef that is preferred by the Jewish community. This is prepared in the winter.

1 pound boneless beef chuck, cut into 1-inch cubes

2 pounds beef marrow bones, divided into sections

1 1/2 pounds potato, peeled and cut into 1-inch cubes

1 pound leek, green and white parts, well rinsed in cold water and cut into 1-inch pieces

1 1/2 pounds Swiss chard, cut into 1-inch pieces

6 cloves garlic, crushed in a garlic press

1 cup coarsely chopped fresh coriander

1 tablespoon corn oil

12 cups water

1/4 teaspoon turmeric

1 teaspoon salt, or to taste

1/2 teaspoon black pepper

juice of 2 large lemons, or more to taste

1. Put the beef, beef bones, potato, leek, chard, garlic, half of the coriander and the oil in a large pan. Brown over moderate heat for 10 minutes, reducing the bulk.

2. Add the water, bring to a boil and add the turmeric, salt and pepper. Cover the pan and simmer over low heat for 2 hours, or until the meat is tender.

3. About 15 minutes before the end of the cooking time, add the lemon juice and remaining fresh coriander. Adjust the salt if necessary.

Serve as a main dish with French bread. Serves 8.

❀ TAJINE DE MOUTON ❀

JEWISH LAMB STEW

This rich lamb dish is flavored, seasoned and colored with real saffron used by the well-to-do families. Those who cannot afford this mega-expensive seasoning use turmeric, which is cheap and is referred to as French saffron.

1/2 teaspoon saffron stamens
1 cup boiling water
5 pounds lean lamb shoulder, cut
   into 2-inch cubes
1/4 cup water
3 pounds whole small white
   pickling onions, peeled

2 large cans (1 1/2 pounds each)
   whole tomatoes
1 teaspoon salt, or to taste
2 teaspoons ground cinnamon
3–4 tablespoons sugar, to taste

1. *Prepare the Saffron Water:* Combine the saffron with the boiling water. Let stand for 15 minutes to cool. Put into a bottle and refrigerate.

2. Rinse the lamb well and dry. Put into a pan and cook, stirring over low heat until the color changes. Add 1 tablespoon of the saffron water at a time plus the 1/4 cup water. Cover the pan and simmer for 45 minutes. Add the balance of the saffron water and combine with the lamb.

3. In a saucepan cover the onions with water, bring to a boil, then drain immediately. Pour the tomatoes over the lamb and scatter the onions over that. Sprinkle the salt, cinnamon and sugar over all. Simmer, covered, for 20 minutes.

4. Uncover the pan and place it into a 300 degree oven for about 2 hours, or until all the liquid has evaporated. The tagine will be reduced to a thick jam-like consistency and the lamb will be tender and full of flavor.

Serve warm with bread as a main dish for Sabbath evening or any other time. Serves 8.

❖ SCHEENA L'HOUMOUS UL LOOBIA ❖

SABBATH BAKE OF CHICK-PEAS, WHITE BEANS AND BEEF

Depending upon the country, there is a connecting link between most of the Sephardic communities that prepare, in one form or another, for the Sabbath a baked one-dish combination of beans, peas, rice, meat and chicken. Included here are the famous eggs baked in their shells. This is the *scheena* of Morocco, the *tafina* of Algeria, *t'fina* of Tunisia and the *hameen* of Calcutta, India. The baked eggs are first tinted by onion skins and tea, hard-cooked, then added to the *scheena* that is baked overnight with the other ingredients. The ritual purpose is to celebrate the Sabbath by not working or lighting fires in the kitchen or in any way disturbing a day of rest.

8 eggs in the shell
several onion skins
1 tablespoon tea leaves
3/4 cup dried white beans, covered
 in water, soaked overnight and
 drained
3/4 cup dried chick-peas, covered in
 water, soaked overnight and
 drained
2 pounds beef bones, preferably
 from the knee, well rinsed
2 pounds boneless beef chuck, cut
 into 8 pieces

8 small potatoes, peeled
 (2 1/2 pounds)
10 whole small onions, peeled
 (2 pounds)
1 whole head garlic, not peeled
 (optional, personal preference)
1 teaspoon salt, or more to taste
1 teaspoon black pepper
1/4 teaspoon turmeric
1 cup rice, well rinsed
12 cups water

1. Put the eggs, a half dozen onion skins and the tea in a pan, just cover with water and bring to a boil. Cook over moderate heat for 20 minutes to hard-cook the eggs. The onion skins and tea will color the shells. Drain and set the eggs aside.

2. Select a very large pan that will hold all the ingredients. Put the beans and chick-peas in the bottom of the pan. In layers, add the beef bones and beef, the potatoes over them, then the onions, garlic, salt, pepper and turmeric.

3. Combine the rice with a dash of salt, pepper and turmeric. Wrap the rice in aluminum foil to form a package. (Old-time cooks used beef skin as the wrapper.) Poke several holes in the foil with the tines of a fork so that liquid will seep into the package and cook the rice. Make a well in the center of the ingredients in the pan and fit the rice package into it; surround with the meat, potatoes and onions.

4. Add the water, which should almost cover everything, place the eggs over the surface of the ingredients and bring to a boil. Simmer, covered, over low heat for 1 hour. Then bake in a 250 degree oven

overnight; do not disturb the *scheena*. Most of the liquid will evaporate and it may be necessary during the long baking process to add another 1/2 cup water.

Serve warm after the synagogue service on the Sabbath. Serves 8.

NOTE: The garlic and the eggs are both peeled and eaten with the *scheena*.

❧ TAJINE DE HARICOTS VERTS ❧
GREEN BEAN AND BEEF STEW

I refer to green beans as string beans. This Jewish ragout, which combines beef, the preferred Jewish meat, with traditional seasonings, is for all seasons.

2 pounds string beans
3 tablespoons vegetable oil
2 pounds boneless beef chuck, cut
  into 8 pieces
1 large onion, sliced (1 cup)
2 ripe tomatoes, diced (2 cups)

1 clove garlic, chopped
1 teaspoon salt, or to taste
1/2 teaspoon turmeric
1/2 teaspoon black pepper
4 cups water

1. String the beans and cut in half crosswise. Just cover them in water and cook over moderate heat for 10 minutes. Drain and set aside.

2. Heat the oil in a pan, add the beef, onion, tomatoes, garlic, salt, turmeric and pepper and stir-fry over low heat for 10 minutes.

3. Add the water, bring to a boil, cover the pan and simmer over low heat for 45 minutes, or until the meat is soft. Add the beans and cook for 20 minutes more, which is enough time to tenderize everything and thicken the sauce. Adjust the salt if necessary.

Serves 8 with bread and salads.

CERVELLE AVEC PIMENT ROUGE

BEEF BRAINS WITH RED PEPPERS

Red is the color here, with the sauce tinted by both paprika and red peppers. The melting flavor of brain in this Jewish recipe is one of my favorites.

2 beef brains
1 teaspoon salt
3 red sweet peppers (1 pound), cut into 4 strips each, seeds and stems discarded
4 whole cloves garlic, peeled
1/4 teaspoon turmeric
1 teaspoon sweet paprika
2 tablespoons vegetable oil
1 1/2 cups water

1. Cover the brains in water, add 1/2 teaspoon of the salt and cook, covered, over moderate heat for 10 minutes. Drain, cool and peel off the membranes. Cut each brain into 3 pieces.
2. Put the red peppers, garlic, turmeric, paprika, remaining 1/2 teaspoon salt, oil and water in a pan and simmer over low heat until the peppers are tender, about 15 minutes.
3. Add the pieces of brain, cover the pan and simmer over low heat until almost all the liquid has evaporated, another 15 minutes.

Serves 6 with bread and several cooked salads.

SCHEENA DE DOUARA

SABBATH BAKE WITH BEEF INNARDS

This unusual *scheena* was originally put in a pan that was then tightly sealed and taken to a bakery where it was baked slowly, from late Friday afternoon until Saturday at noon, after the end of synagogue. For those who like "variety meats," as they are euphemistically called, this can be prepared on any day and baked in a 325 degree oven for 4 hours or more, which is what I do in New York City. This is an exclusively Jewish dish of Morocco.

*6 pounds beef heart, liver and
  intestine, usually purchased
  clean from the butcher, cut into
  3-inch pieces
2 pounds beef lung (difficult to
  find; optional), cut into 2-inch
  pieces
6 fresh hot green chili peppers*

*10 whole cloves garlic
1/4 cup olive oil
1 teaspoon salt, or to taste
1 teaspoon black pepper
12 sprigs flat-leaf parsley, chopped
4 cups water, or more, to cover the
  meats*

Put all the ingredients in a large pan, cover tightly and bring to a
boil. Place the pan in the oven and bake at 325 degrees for 4 hours.
The pan can be sealed more airtight by putting a sheet of aluminum
foil over the top and pressing the pan cover into that.

Serve warm. Serves 8 with salads and bread.

❖ TAJINE DE VEAU AUX ZEITOUN ❖

VEAL WITH OLIVES AND POTATOES

I was told by a cook that every tagine should contain garlic and so
there is here. This interesting dish may be prepared with veal or beef,
preferred Jewish meats. The potatoes are scooped out with a melon
scooper into round balls about 1 inch in diameter—altogether an attractive and tasty preparation for the Sabbath or any other time.

*1/4 cup olive oil
2 pounds boneless veal, cut into 6
  pieces
1 large onion, chopped (1 cup)
2 cloves garlic, chopped
1/2 teaspoon salt, or to taste
1/2 teaspoon black pepper
1 teaspoon sweet paprika*

*1/2 teaspoon turmeric
3 cups water
2 pounds large potatoes, peeled and
  scooped out into balls with a
  melon baller (use odd pieces for
  another purpose)
1/2 cup green cracked olives, pitted
  and rinsed well in cold water*

1. Heat the oil in a pan and stir-fry the veal, onion and garlic with the
   salt, pepper, paprika and turmeric over moderate heat for 5 minutes.

2. Add the water, potatoes and olives, bring to a boil and simmer, covered, over low heat for 1 hour, or until the veal is tender. There should be ample sauce for all. Should the liquid evaporate too quickly, add another 1/2 cup water.

Serves 6 to 8 with Harissa (see page 89), salads and bread.

❋ QUARE LAHEM BIL JELBANA ❋

MEATBALLS IN CLEAR SAUCE

It is a rule of the Jewish kitchen that when garlic is used, then onion is omitted, and vice versa. This meatball recipe, a basic one that can be used for other recipes with meatballs, has plenty of onion and no garlic. It lends itself to large gatherings such as the Sabbath, when food must be cooked for the after-synagogue lunch on Saturday.

FOR THE MEATBALLS

1 1/2 pounds very lean ground beef
1 1/2 teaspoons lecama (mixed spice)
1/2 teaspoon salt
1/2 teaspoon white pepper
1 medium onion, finely chopped (1/2 cup)
1/4 cup chopped fresh coriander
1/2 cup chopped flat-leaf parsley
1 egg, beaten
2 tablespoons corn oil

FOR THE SAUCE

3 tablespoons corn oil
1 large onion, sliced (1 cup)
1 heart of celery, quartered
1 cup water
1/2 teaspoon salt
1/2 teaspoon white pepper
1/4 teaspoon ground mace
1/2 teaspoon saffron stamen or 1/2 teaspoon turmeric
1 pound fresh or frozen green peas

1. *Prepare the Meatballs:* Mix all the meatball ingredients together and refrigerate for 1 to 2 hours so that the flavors will develop. Shape meatballs each 2 inches in diameter. Set aside. Makes 20 meatballs.

2. *Prepare the Sauce:* Heat the oil in a large pan, add the onion and celery

and stir-fry over moderate heat for 1 minute. Add the water and bring to a boil. Reduce the heat to low and add the salt, pepper, mace and saffron or turmeric. Cover and simmer for 20 minutes.

3. Bring 6 cups of water to a boil and add the meatballs, one by one. Bring to a boil again and remove the pan from the heat. Drain, reserving 1 cup of clear liquid. (This step is taken to remove the impurities of the meat, which discolor the sauce.)

4. Add the meatballs to the sauce and the 1 cup of reserved clear broth. Cover and simmer for 10 minutes. Add the green peas and cook for 15 minutes. Some sauce should remain but the dish is not soupy.

Serve warm with bread and several traditional salads or condiments. Serves 6.

NOTE: *Lecama* is a mixed spice in the spirit of the Indian *garam masala*, but *lecama* produces more dimension of flavor.

❃ DJEDJA BIL BSBAS ❃

CHICKEN AND FENNEL BULBS

Fennel, with its mild sweet anise flavor, is compatible with chicken. This dish has very little sauce and is a clean-tasting, lightly seasoned combination, with the natural flavor and melting texture of the fennel. The pale yellow of the turmeric or, preferably, the saffron stamens is the outstanding characteristic. Arrange the chicken and fennel in the pan; they do not require constant stirring. On the contrary, they should not be disturbed as they cook to assist the visually important presentation. This is a Jewish holiday dish, prepared during the spring, when the fennel is harvested — the same time as Passover.

a 3 1/3-pound chicken, loose skin
    and fat discarded, rinsed well
1 large onion, sliced thin (1 cup)
1/2 teaspoon turmeric or 1/2
    teaspoon saffron stamens
1 teaspoon salt
3/4 teaspoon white pepper

4 tablespoons corn oil
2 large fennel bulbs, quartered
1 1/2 cups water
1/4 cup feathery fennel leaves, torn
    into 2-inch pieces
5 sprigs flat-leaf parsley, coarsely
    chopped

1. Cut the chicken into 8 serving pieces, and combine them with the onion, turmeric, salt, pepper and 3 tablespoons oil. Let stand 1/2 hour.

2. Put the remaining 1 tablespoon oil in a pan, add the chicken and onion mixture, cover the pan and cook over low heat for 20 minutes. Place the fennel bulbs in an organized manner in with the chicken, add the water and bring to a boil. Reduce the heat to low, cover and simmer for 1 hour. Distribute the fennel leaves and parsley over the top of the chicken to flavor and garnish it. Cook for 10 minutes more. There will be almost no sauce but everything will be moist nonetheless.

Serve warm with several condiments and French bread. Serves 6 to 8.

❈ TAJINE JUIVE DE POULET ❈

JEWISH CHICKEN AND COURGETTE TAGINE

This combination of lots of onions, which melt down into a thick sauce, chicken and zucchini can be prepared for the Sabbath or another time as well.

It should be mentioned that Moroccan Jews do not eat duck. In fact, I never saw ducks, either living or ready for the pan, in the public markets. Morocco is desert country and it makes sense that water-loving ducks would not thrive there. (I was curious about ducks as I had originally wanted to prepare this tagine with duck instead of chicken.)

3 tablespoons olive oil
a 3-pound chicken or chicken
* parts, cut into 4 pieces, loose*
* skin and fat discarded*
2 pounds onion, chopped
2 cloves garlic, chopped
1 teaspoon salt, or to taste

1/2 teaspoon black pepper
1/2 teaspoon turmeric
2 cups water
2 pounds courgette (zucchini),
* sliced on the diagonal into*
* 2 inch pieces*

1. Heat the oil in a pan, add the chicken, onion, garlic, salt, pepper and

turmeric and stir-fry over low heat for 5 minutes. Bring to a boil, cover the pan and cook for 1/2 hour.

2. Add the courgette and cook for 15 minutes more. The onion will have melted into a sauce and the chicken will be tender.

Serves 4 with salads and bread.

❈ DJEJA BIL HOUMOUS ❈
SLOW-COOKED CHICKEN AND CHICK-PEAS

This is an old-time traditional Jewish dish—something that can be served any day, but especially in winter. Not excessively heavy, it can be served on cool summer days as well.

2 cups dried chick-peas
1 dried chili guaque, stem pulled off and seeds shaken out (see Note page 84)
a 3 1/2-pound chicken, cut into serving pieces
1 teaspoon salt

3 large cloves garlic, crushed in a garlic press
1 teaspoon turmeric
1 teaspoon ground cumin
1 teaspoon paprika
1/2 teaspoon black pepper
4 tablespoons corn oil

1. *Prepare the Chick-peas:* Cover the chick-peas with water and soak them overnight, about 10 hours. Drain and pull off and discard the loose skins.

2. Cover the chick-peas with lightly salted water, add the dry chili *guaque* and bring to a boil. Cook over low heat for about 1 hour to soften the peas, adding more water as it evaporates during cooking. Do not overcook to a melting state as the chick-peas are more aesthetic when served whole and slightly firm.

3. *Prepare the Chicken:* Rinse the chicken well in cold water and dry. Cut off and discard the loose skin and fat.

4. Add the salt, garlic, turmeric, cumin, paprika, pepper and oil to the

chicken pieces and mix well. Set aside to marinate for 1 hour. Heat a large pan slightly, add the chicken and spices and brown over low heat for 10 minutes. Add the softened chick-peas and chili, which should have about 2 cups liquid. Cover the pan and simmer for 1/2 hour or a bit more, enough to soften the chicken and thicken the sauce.

Serve warm with bread and several condiments. Serves 6.

NOTE: The dried chili *guaque,* sometimes called *ancho*—the names given to them in Central America— is about 4 to 5 inches long and 1 inch wide, and has a tapered end. It is dark red/brown in color and spicy hot. The seeds are extremely hot and are usually discarded, but of course they do not have to be if your tolerance for hot foods is high.

❈ KAPORES ❈

RITUAL CHICKENS

At the holiday of Sukkot, each adult member of a Jewish family has a chicken killed by the ritual slaughterer, the *shiket.* The Moroccans cook the chickens in the simple manner below. I have assumed that five members of a family each has a chicken, but it could be fewer or even one chicken as a symbolic expression.

Note that there is a considerable amount of oil in this recipe—very Moroccan—and I have not reduced the traditional amount. However, one could and should do so.

5 whole chickens, cleaned	*1 teaspoon black pepper*
3 pounds onions, chopped	*1 teaspoon turmeric*
1 teaspoon salt, or to taste	*1 quart olive oil*

1. Put all the ingredients in a roasting pan, cover and bake in a 350 degree oven for 1 1/2 hours. Since no water has been added, the onions provide all the liquid for the sauce. The chickens must be turned 3 or 4 times as they bake for the onions to melt into a yellow sauce.

There is sufficient chicken for a large gathering or for several meals, as the dish is preserved in the sauce. Serve with Salade Khadra (Fresh Salad, see page 89) as an appetizer, followed by the chicken and a substantial amount of bread.

❈ HAMAM MAAMER ❈

STUFFED CEREMONIAL PIGEON

On very special Jewish occasions, stuffed ceremonial pigeon is offered to guests. Weddings are especially auspicious opportunities to serve these pigeons since it is an exotic preparation guaranteed, it is said, to energize the bride and groom for their honeymoon. Pigeon protein, plus honey, sugar and the grandiose mixture of dried fruit and orange juice, provides good taste as well as enough healthful ingredients to revive flagging energy. There are actually two separate recipes that when combined elevate the dish to very special occasions.

Although one can stuff pigeons—4 of them—which is the tradition, I have converted this to 2 Cornish game hens, which are so easily available in the United States.

FOR THE STUFFING

2 tablespoons vegetable oil

2 medium onions, coarsely chopped (1 cup)

1/2 cup rice, well rinsed, half cooked in ample water for 7 minutes and drained

8 sprigs flat-leaf parsley, ends trimmed, chopped

4 dried apricots, covered in water 1 hour, drained and sliced into 4 pieces

4 pitted prunes, covered in water 1 hour, drained and sliced into 4 pieces

4 pitted dates, sliced

1/4 cup white raisins

1/4 pound ground beef

1/2 teaspoon salt

1/2 teaspoon white pepper

1/3 cup chopped blanched toasted almonds

1/2 teaspoon ground cinnamon

1 tablespoon sugar

1/8 teaspoon ground nutmeg

1 egg, beaten

2 Cornish game hens, about 2 1/2 pounds

2 tablespoons vegetable oil
1 medium onion, coarsely chopped
    (1/2 cup)
1/4 cup dark raisins
4 pitted whole dates
4 whole dried apricots, covered in
    water for 1 hour, drained
4 whole pitted prunes, covered in
    water for 1 hour, drained
1 teaspoon sugar, or more to
    taste

1/2 teaspoon salt
1/2 teaspoon turmeric
2 tablespoons honey
1/2 cup fresh orange juice
1/2 teaspoon saffron stamens
1/4 cup blanched almonds, toasted
    and chopped
2 tablespoons pine nuts
1/2 cup water

1. *Prepare the Stuffing:* Heat the oil in a pan, add the onions and stir-fry over low heat for 5 minutes, or until they turn golden with a touch of brown. Set aside.

2. Put the half-cooked rice in a large bowl and add the onions and all the remaining stuffing ingredients, except the hens, and mix well.

3. *Prepare the Sauce:* Heat the oil in a pan, add the onion and stir-fry over low heat for 5 minutes, or until it turns golden with a touch of brown. Add all the other sauce ingredients, bring to a boil and simmer over low heat for 10 minutes to integrate the flavors.

4. Stuff each of the hens but not too firmly, allowing some space for the expansion of the rice.

5. Place the stuffed Cornish hens in a lightly oiled roasting pan and pour the sauce over all. Cover the pan and bake in a 350 degree oven for 1/2 hour. Reduce the heat to 325 degrees and bake for 1/2 hour. Remove the cover, baste the hens well and continue to bake for another 1/2 hour, basting again during this time. The sauce will have reduced to a thick semi-sweet mélange and the hens will be crisp.

Cut each hen in half and serve warm with the fruit and some sauce. Serves 4 with bread and salads.

VARIATION

Use the stuffing and sauce to enhance one or two 3-pound chickens.

Should any stuffing be left over, I simply steam 2 cabbage leaves until soft and flexible, fill them with the stuffing, roll them up and place them in the roasting pan with the hens.

❈ L'QUARE DEL HOUT ❈

FISH BALLS IN SPICED TOMATO SAUCE

These fish balls are prepared with matzoh meal, which allows them to be included in the Passover ritual. However, matzoh meal does not confine this highly spiced creation to that holiday only. In fact, the quantity and variety of spices in this dish is a premier example of the Moroccan genius in combining vivid seasonings with traditional fish dishes.

FOR THE SAUCE

2 tablespoons corn oil
1 medium sweet green pepper,
*   cut into 1-inch cubes (1 cup)*
1 whole semi-hot fresh green chili
*   pepper*
a 2-pound can whole tomatoes
3 cloves garlic, crushed in a garlic
*   press*

2 teaspoons fresh sweet paprika
1/2 teaspoon hot chili powder
1/2 teaspoon salt, or to taste
1/4 teaspoon black pepper
1/2 cup water

FOR THE FISH BALLS

2 pounds fillet of whiting, skin
*   removed*
1 egg white
1 tablespoon fine-ground matzoh
*   meal*
1/4 teaspoon ground mace
8 sprigs flat-leaf parsley, sliced

1/2 teaspoon salt
1/2 teaspoon grated orange peel
1/2 teaspoon white pepper
1 large clove garlic, crushed in a
*   garlic press*
1 teaspoon turmeric

1. *Prepare the Sauce:* Heat the oil in a large skillet, add the green pepper and whole chili and stir-fry for several minutes over moderate heat as the colors change. Add the tomatoes and continue to fry. Add the garlic, paprika, chili powder, salt and black pepper. Add the water and mix well. Cover the skillet and simmer over low heat for 1 hour.

2. *Prepare the Fish Balls:* Put everything into a processor and mix together into a fairly smooth consistency. Form fish balls, each 2 inches in diameter. Makes 8 fish balls.

3. Add the fish balls, one by one, to the simmering tomato sauce. Simmer with the skillet partially covered over low heat for 20 minutes. Turn the balls over once. The sauce will be quite thick.

Serve warm with bread, condiments and salad. Serves 6.

❈ TAJINE DE POIS CHICHE ❈
VEGETARIAN CHICK-PEA STEW

This Jewish side dish was served to me at a Friday evening Sabbath meal. I enjoyed it enormously since the chick-pea skins had been removed by soaking the peas overnight and their texture was melting. In addition, paprika, hot red chili and sweet red pepper created a flavor and color that was unique.

1 pound dried chick-peas
12 sprigs fresh coriander, sliced thin
6 whole cloves garlic, peeled
1 fresh, whole hot red chili
1 large sweet red pepper, cut into 6 equal strips, seeds and stems discarded

1 tablespoon sweet paprika
1/2 teaspoon salt
2 tablespoons olive oil
2 tablespoons vegetable oil
3 cups water

1. Soak the chick-peas in water to cover overnight. Drain and pull off the loose skin—not a difficult task at all.

2. Put the chick-peas and all the remaining ingredients in a pan and bring to a boil. Reduce the heat to low and simmer slowly, covered, for about 1/2 hour. Test the chick-peas for doneness. If too firm, continue to cook another 10 or 15 minutes. The liquid will be almost completely evaporated and the color will have developed a pink shade. The chick-peas are not to melt down but should retain their shape.

Serve as a side dish with fish or meat. Serves 6 to 8.

✳ HARISSA ✳

HOT CHILI SAUCE, JEWISH STYLE

Harissa, known as *schka* by the Jews, is the indispensable fiery-hot condiment that can be used as a table chutney or included in meat and poultry dishes when something dynamic is needed. Here is one recipe from a family that prefers their own combination. There are many variations, depending upon personal preference. In any event, *harissa* can be refrigerated for a month or two without deteriorating. Since the chilies are hot, dangerously so if one rubs the eyes, it is suggested that rubber gloves be worn during the preparation of *harissa.*

1 pound dried red chili peppers (guaque)	*10 cloves garlic*
	1/2 teaspoon salt
1 tablespoon ground cumin	*1/4 cup corn oil*
1/4 cup white vinegar	

1. Soak the chili peppers in water for 2 hours and drain. Open the peppers and remove and discard the seeds and stems.

2. Mix all the remaining ingredients with the peppers in a food processor, grinding until smooth but not excessively so. Store in a glass bottle in the refrigerator.

Makes 2 cups.

✳ SALADE KHADRA ✳

FRESH SALAD

During the many years of my residence in India I discovered that the servants in the Jewish homes were actually the guardians of the cuisine. Most of the cooks were Muslims since their knowledge of kosher (*halal*) fitted in with Islamic as well as Jewish ideals.

I found one man in Fez who had worked in Jewish families for thirty years and knew the cuisine as well as any Jewish homemaker. He was at that time employed in a *cacher* (kosher) restaurant in Fez and it was there we met. Here is one of the several recipes that I tasted and collected from him.

1/2 cup red or white wine vinegar
1 cup vegetable oil
1/2 teaspoon salt
1/2 teaspoon black pepper
3 tablespoons prepared Dijon
mustard

2 large ripe tomatoes (1 pound),
cut into 1-inch cubes
3 young cucumbers, peeled and cut
into 1-inch chunks
1 medium red or white onion, sliced
(1/2 cup)

1. Mix together rather well the vinegar, oil, salt, pepper and mustard to make a sauce.

2. Toss the tomatoes, cucumbers and onion together with the sauce.

Serve at room temperature. Serves 6 as an appetizer with drinks or with foods.

❈ SALADA DIL BATATA UL BEYD ❈

LAYERED SALAD

This is a holiday salad and can be served on Passover. Moroccans have a natural flair, a gift really, for cooking along the lines of their tradition. The salad, prepared in layers, is attractive to look at and has an assortment of flavors and textures from the vegetables. A piquant dressing with black oil-cured olives provides a Moroccan flavor.

FOR THE SALAD

1 pound potatoes, cooked in their
jackets until soft but firm,
peeled
2 ripe tomatoes (1 pound), sliced
3 Kirby cucumbers, trimmed and
sliced

1 medium onion, sliced into rings
(1 cup)
3 hard-cooked eggs, sliced
lettuce leaves
6 sprigs flat-leaf parsley, leaves
only

For the Dressing

2 tablespoons white vinegar
2 tablespoons corn oil
juice of 1 lemon
1/2 teaspoon sugar
1/4 teaspoon salt
1/4 teaspoon white pepper

1 teaspoon prepared Dijon
  mustard
10 oil-cured black olives,
  chopped into 1/4-inch pieces
10 capers, whole

1. *Prepare the Salad:* Slice the vegetables and the eggs in a uniform equal size so they can be assembled in layers.

2. *Prepare the Dressing:* Mix all the ingredients together well.

3. *Assemble the Salad:* Place lettuce leaves on the bottom of a flat serving platter. There should be enough to cover the platter. Two layers are then built as follows: One half of all the ingredients per layer, reserving the other half for the second layer.

   Tomato slices are placed on the lettuce. Over that arrange the potato slices. Cover with slices of cucumber. Then the egg and onion slices over those. Now build up the second layer, but omit the lettuce.

   Pour the well-mixed dressing over all and garnish the salad with the parsley leaves.

Serve cold. Serves 6 to 8.

❊ MATESA FELFLA MECHOUI ❊

Sweet and Hot Roasted Pepper Salad with Tomato

This is another condiment in the firmament of Moroccan Jewish cooking.

2 ripe, firm tomatoes (1 pound)
1 sweet green pepper
1 semi-hot chili pepper
1/2 teaspoon salt

1/4 teaspoon white pepper
1/4 cup coarsely sliced sweet white
  onion
3 tablespoons olive oil

1. Peel the tomatoes with a sharp knife. (Do not use the system of blanching in boiling water.) Cut the tomatoes up coarsely.

2. Char the sweet and hot peppers over charcoal or over an open gas burner. Pull off the burned skins, open them up and discard the stems and seeds. Cut into julienne slices. Do not rinse.

3. In a bowl toss the peppers and tomatoes with the seasonings, onion and oil. Chill in the refrigerator before serving.

Serves 6 as a condiment.

❈ SALADA DEL PORO ❈

LEEK SALAD

Here is another fine salad, with a taste of mustard, that contributes to the medley of Sabbath and holiday foods covering the dining table.

*6 fresh leeks, white part only (2),
   root and green leaves removed
   and halved lengthwise
3 tablespoons corn oil
1 teaspoon white vinegar
juice of 1 lemon
1/2 teaspoon salt*

*1/4 teaspoon white pepper
1 small clove garlic, crushed in a
   garlic press
1 teaspoon prepared Dijon
   mustard
1/4 cup chopped flat-leaf parsley*

1. Cook the leek whites in lightly salted water for about 15 minutes. Drain well and cool.

2. Mix together all the remaining ingredients. Place the leeks in a flat dish and pour the sauce over all. Let stand 3 to 4 hours to marinate before serving.

Serve at room temperature or cold. Serves 4 to 6.

❊ SALADA BIL BARBA ❊

BEET SALAD CONDIMENT

This is a condiment—a very good one for beet lovers—and it is popular with Moroccan Jews. Served on small plates to accompany other condiments that enhance the dining tables, especially for the Sabbath meals, the salad can be refrigerated for a week, which in fact intensifies its flavor.

1 1/2 pounds fresh beets, cooked in their skins until soft
5 sprigs flat-leaf parsley, sliced very thin
1/2 teaspoon ground cumin
1/2 teaspoon salt
2 tablespoons corn oil
1 tablespoon white vinegar
juice of 1 lemon

Peel and slice the beets medium thin. Toss with all the remaining ingredients. Refrigerate.

Serve cool. Serves 8.

THE COOKING OF
ALGERIA

Typical marketplace in Algeria

Oasis in the Sahara

ALGERIA

▓ ALGERIA is one of the largest countries in Africa, with only the Sudan and Nigeria larger. The Algerian Sahara Desert covers 85 percent of the country—one of the driest, hottest and most arid areas on earth. Most Algerians live in a narrow band of land with a subtropical climate that faces the Mediterranean Sea. Most Algerians are Arab, with about 20 percent being of Berber stock. These are the cold facts about this country of the Maghreb.

The history of Algeria is similar to that of its neighbors, Morocco and Tunisia, starting with its conquest by the Romans. The earliest inhabitants were the Berbers, a semi-nomadic people living in what was known as the Kingdom of Numidia. At this time the Jews from the Middle East settled there. Some of the Berber tribes converted to Judaism and one of the historical incidents is that of a Jewish Numidian queen who fought against the Arabs in the 7th century. The Berbers were conquered by the Arabs and converted to Islam.

Most Berbers, a fair-skinned people, live today in the Kabylia, a region just to the east of Algiers, with its own language, customs and cuisine. They have been and continue to be assimilated into the mainstream of Arab/Islamic living. Of note, it was the Berbers who domesticated the camel for transportation and food.

The Turks of the Ottoman Empire arrived in Algeria from the 16th to the 19th centuries and contributed lasting ideas to the cuisine, particularly the sweets and pastries.

The French conquest of Algeria occurred in 1830 and lasted until 1962. It is the crossculture of foreign influences and conquest that from a culinary point of view contributed to the codification of Algerian cuisine as we know it today.

Algeria is the most French of the nations of the Maghreb and French is (or was) the second language. Algerians have invented their own *patois*, a mixture of Arabic and French. An Algerian conversation is interspersed with French words, which can be disconcerting to a listener when the remainder of the sentence is in Arabic. Of course, the emphasis on French ways has influenced the cuisine in a positive manner.

Cereals are the staple of the Algerian diet, with wheat and its products of paramount importance. Rice has never been significant as it cannot be grown in a desert region. The subtropical climate of northern Algeria facing the Mediterranean has been conducive to the growing of wheat since the days of the Romans who used both Algeria and Tunisia as the breadbaskets of the Empire.

Yes, couscous is the national dish of Algeria and a traditional part of the diet. There are several types and like all of the cooking each family has what it considers the perfect couscous. The towns near the Moroccan border in the west are influenced by the cooking of that country. On the east, Tunisia has a similar influence. It is amusing to note that there is a competitive spirit regarding the merits of Maghreb cooking. I have heard Moroccans say that Algerians "don't know how to cook." Tunisians also have their own chauvinistic opinions on the matter.

What the Algerians do have is an idiosyncratic style of cooking. Many of the dishes are inventive and enticing for that reason. I refer, for example, among many to Beyd M'Ghelef (Covered Eggs, page 130) or Djedj Mechoui (Marinated Roast Chicken, page 157), the titles not doing justice to either of these inventive preparations. Algerian cuisine can be characterized as the middle point between the sometimes sweet, aromatic, fruit-filled, ingenious cooking of Morocco and the Tunisian love affair with couscous and the fiery condiment, *harissa*.

Spices are paramount to the Algerian palate. Cumin, coriander, modest amounts of cinnamon, paprika, pepper and caraway are found in many dishes. Garlic is cherished. Flat-leaf parsley is an almost automatic addition to the food. Surprisingly, the hot chili has not taken hold as it has in Tunisia. It is used, but does not have the mystique that the *harissa* of Tunisia enjoys, for example.

Standard vegetables—carrots, turnips, potatoes, fresh tomatoes (or tomato paste) are indispensable to the cuisine. The unconventional fennel, artichoke, cardoon and leek in season find their way into salads, couscous and other cooked dishes. A cornucopia of vegetables derives from that narrow strip of land facing the Mediterranean. Unfortunately, the desert does encroach, moving from the south to the north and reducing the amount of fertile acreage each year.

Algerians dote on salads and have many for the hot desert summers. There are also vegetarian dishes that are so relevant for today's emphasis on good eating with less meat, fat and oil.

Lamb is the most important meat, principally because sheep can thrive in a semi-desert environment. Chicken and beef recipes abound. Many kinds of fish, fresh from the waters of the Mediterranean, are inexpensive and frequently included in the diet.

Traditional spices of The Maghreb

Thanks to the French experience, there is a flair for presenting food in an appetizing manner in Algeria. This adds to the skill of the cook, the appearance of the dish and the enthusiasm of the diner.

One cannot fault the cooking of Algeria, set between two other Maghreb countries that have their own culinary aficionados. A French chef told me once that he considered Algerian cooking a close second to Moroccan cuisine. I do not take sides as for many years I have enjoyed all North African cooking, influenced as it is by the climate and the arrival of newcomers from other places and other times.

COUSCOUS

❋ KESKSOU BIL DJEDJ ❋

Chicken Couscous

This is the principal culinary dish of the Algerians. When plans are being made for a wedding, baptism or other celebration, chicken couscous is *de rigueur*. There are two parts to this classic preparation, the couscous and the chicken and vegetable stew, both of which are prepared in the *couscousier*, or tiered steamer. The couscous is steamed in the top pan, while the stew cooks simultaneously in a bottom pan. Here is how it is done.

a 3-pound chicken, cut into 8 pieces, or 8 chicken parts, dark and light meat, loose skin and fat discarded
2 medium onions, diced (1 1/2 cups)
1/2 cup cooked chick-peas
6 carrots (1 pound), peeled and sliced diagonally 1/2 inch thick
1/2 pound white turnip, peeled and sliced 1/4 inch thick

10 sprigs flat-leaf parsley, chopped
5 sprigs fresh coriander, chopped
1 teaspoon salt, or to taste
1/2 teaspoon black pepper
1/2 teaspoon turmeric
1/4 teaspoon ground cinnamon
1 tablespoon corn oil
8 cups water
2 pounds couscous

1. Put everything, except the water and couscous, in a pan and stir-fry over low heat for 15 minutes. Add the water, bring to a boil and cook over moderate heat for 45 minutes, the time needed to tenderize the chicken and vegetables.

2. Remove the chicken to a separate dish.

3. If you are using precooked couscous, prepare it according to the directions. If you are using the classic method, with the natural pasta, see the directions under the Tunisian directions.

4. To serve, each person will take the amount of steamed couscous wanted. Over this enough sauce and vegetables will be added to moisten the pasta. Add a piece or two of the chicken.

Serve warm. Serves 6.

❈ TAAM BIL LHAM ❈

COUSCOUS WITH LAMB

This is a west coast couscous, with a red sauce and the much used lamb, which can be with or without the bone. The couscous is frequently homemade and has very fine grains, whereas the commercial type, which is satisfactory, is somewhat larger in size. In any event, steaming it in a *couscousier* expands couscous to three times its dry state.

4 teaspoons olive oil
1 pound boneless lamb leg, or shank
  with bone, cut into 2-inch pieces
1 medium whole onion
4 cloves garlic, chopped fine
2 teaspoons salt, or to taste
1/2 teaspoon black pepper
1 teaspoon sweet paprika
1/8 teaspoon ground cinnamon
1 small white turnip, cut into 6
  pieces (3/4 cup)
1/2 pound carrot, cut into 1/2-
  inch-thick rounds (1 cup)

2 small potatoes, peeled and
  quartered (1 cup)
2 ounces whole flat-leaf parsley,
  stems and leaves, tied together
6 cups warm water
6 tablespoons tomato paste
1 teaspoon Harissa (see page 89),
  or to taste
2 zucchini, sliced into 1/2-inch-
  thick rounds (1 cup)
1/4 cup dried chick-peas, soaked in
  water overnight
1/4 cup dark raisins (optional)

1. Put the olive oil, lamb, onion and garlic into a pan with the salt, pepper, paprika and cinnamon. Stir-fry over low heat several minutes to brown the lamb, cover the pan and cook for 10 minutes. Add the turnip, carrot, potatoes and parsley. Cover the pan and continue to cook for 15 minutes.

2. Mix together the water, tomato paste and *harissa* and add to the pan. Simmer for 1 hour.

3. Add the zucchini and chick-peas. Cook for 1/2 hour. Remove the onion and parsley. The total cooking time is 2 hours, enough to soften the lamb and integrate all the flavors.

4. Serve the stew warm with 2 cups of couscous steamed in the traditional manner and garnished with steamed raisins.

Algerians eat bread with almost everything except couscous. Serves 4 to 6.

❁ KESKSOU MERGUEZ ❁

COUSCOUS WITH MERGUEZ

There are two variations in this couscous, one is vegetarian and the other is with meat. Both are, however, garnished with the spiced lamb sausage. The dedicated vegetarian may omit the sausage, but think of what he or she is missing.

3 tablespoons vegetable oil
1 large onion, coarsely chopped (1 cup)
1/2 cup dried chick-peas, soaked overnight in water and drained
1/4 teaspoon ground cinnamon
1 teaspoon black pepper
1/2 teaspoon salt
1 tablespoon sweet paprika

3 tablespoons tomato paste or 2 ripe medium tomatoes, diced
8 cups water
3 medium carrots, cut diagonally into thirds
2 white turnips, cut into 8 quarters
2 potatoes, cut into 8 quarters
2 medium zucchini, cut into thirds
Merguez (see page 134)
1 pound couscous

1. *Prepare the Vegetarian Sauté:* Heat the oil in a pan or *couscousier,* add the onion and chick-peas and stir-fry over moderate heat for 2 minutes. Add the cinnamon, pepper, salt, paprika, tomato paste and water. Bring to a boil and simmer for 5 minutes. Add the carrots, turnips and potatoes and cook for 15 minutes. Add the zucchini and cook for 15 minutes more.

2. *Or, Prepare the Meat Sauté:* Select 2 pounds of lamb from the leg, spine or shoulder, with or without the bone, and cut into 3- to 4-inch

pieces. If you prefer chicken, use 2 pounds of legs, thighs or breast (halved), loose skin and fat discarded.

3. Heat the oil in a pan or *couscousier*. Add the onion, chick-peas and the meat or chicken. Stir-fry for 3 minutes to lightly brown. Add the cinnamon, pepper, salt, paprika, tomato paste and water. Bring to a boil and simmer for 15 minutes. Add the carrots, turnips and potatoes and cook for 15 minutes. Add the zucchini and cook 15 minutes more. Total time for the meat sauté is 1 hour.

4. Using 1 tablespoon vegetable oil, fry 2 or 3 *merguez* for each person over moderate heat for about 4 minutes. This will release the fat and brown the sausage. Drain briefly on paper towels.

5. Prepare the couscous in the traditional manner.

6. Serve the vegetarian or meat stew warm on the pasta. Garnish with the *merguez*.

Serves 6.

❧ KESKSOU BIL HOUT ❧
FISH COUSCOUS

Here is a couscous of the coastal cities on the Mediterranean, made with a red sauce colored with tomato and paprika. Use fish such as *mérou*, cod, scrod or snapper with firm white flesh that will not fall apart when cooked. The entire preparation can be done in a *couscousier*, with the fish stew on the bottom and the couscous on the top.

a 3-pound whole fish, cut into 1 1/2- inch-wide slices, with the bone	*1 tablespoon Harissa (see page 89), or to taste*
4 tablespoons vegetable oil	*1/4 teaspoon ground cumin*
1 medium onion, grated (1/2 cup)	*1 bay leaf*
5 cloves garlic, crushed in a garlic press	*3 ripe medium tomatoes (about 3/4 pound)*
1/2 teaspoon dried thyme	*3 cups water*
1 branch celery, chopped	*3 zucchini (1 pound)*
1 teaspoon salt	*1 tablespoon sweet paprika*
1 teaspoon black pepper	

1. Put the fish in a large pan. Add the oil, onion, garlic, thyme, celery, salt, pepper, *harissa*, cumin and bay leaf. Sauté gently over low heat for several minutes.

2. Drop the tomatoes in boiling water for a minute, remove and peel. Squeeze the seeds out of each and chop the flesh. Add to the fish with the water, bring to a boil and simmer over low heat for 5 minutes.

3. Cut each zucchini lengthwise into 4 pieces. Place on the fish and sprinkle the paprika over all. Simmer, covered, over low heat for 20 minutes.

4. During this time, prepare couscous in the traditional method to create a light fluffy texture.

5. Remove the bay leaf. Serve warm with the pasta and fish stew separately.

Serves 6 to 8.

❋ MESSFOUF ❋

COUSCOUS AND BUTTERMILK

The dedicated vegetarian will appreciate this vegetarian dish. Young fava beans still in their tender pods are preferred; however, the freshly shelled beans can also be used. Favas were known as broad beans during my years of residence in India.

The buttermilk provides an added contrast to the couscous and is served in a glass. Some like to spoon some of the buttermilk over the couscous as they dine.

2 pounds couscous
1 tablespoon vegetable or olive oil
1 cup cold water
1 pound green beans, fresh or frozen

2 pounds fresh young fava beans in pods, cut into 1/2-inch pieces
2 teaspoons salt, or to taste
3 tablespoons butter, melted
1 cup buttermilk per person

1. Prepare the couscous. Rinse the couscous well with cold water, drain and spread it out on a large tray to dry for 20 minutes. Sprinkle on

the oil and toss well to mix. Put the couscous in the top of a *couscousier* filled with 3 to 4 cups boiling water. Steam for 20 minutes without stirring.

2. Turn the couscous out onto the tray again and add the cold water. Toss well to mix and let it dry again, absorbing the water, for 20 minutes.

3. During this time, put the vegetables in the top of the steamer, sprinkle with the salt and steam over moderate heat. Return the couscous to the steamer with the vegetables and steam for 20 minutes more. This will soften the couscous and make it fluffy as it expands to 3 times its original size. Turn the couscous and vegetables out onto the tray, add the butter and toss everything together, which will separate the individual grains.

4. Serve each person buttermilk in a glass.
    Also presented, if desired, is a platter of watermelon and honeydew melon cubes in season.

Serves 6 to 8.

NOTE: Fresh fava beans are best eaten early in the harvesting season, when the pods are 2 to 3 inches in length and the inner beans are soft and tender. If the pods are too tough, shell the beans and use them, discarding the pods. Canned fava beans are available in Middle Eastern groceries and are acceptable if all else fails. Use 1 pound of the canned favas.

❊ MESFOUF BIL ZBID ❊

BUTTERED COUSCOUS WITH RAISINS

This is a snack that is garnished with a generous amount of steamed raisins and sprinkled with sugar, ideal for friends who visit. Algerians would not eat this with meat entrées, as they would not be appropriate with this sweet snack.

1 cup couscous
2 tablespoons butter, in slices

1/2 cup dark raisins, steamed in
the couscousier *for 3 minutes*
2 tablespoons sugar

1. Rinse the couscous briefly in cold water, drain and place in the top of a *couscousier*. Put 4 cups of hot water in the bottom section and bring to a boil. Steam for 1/2 hour over moderate/low heat, which will allow the couscous to expand 3 times its size.

2. Turn the couscous out onto a tray, sprinkle over 1/8 cup cold water and loosen the grains with your fingers or a fork to prevent lumps. Return the couscous to the steamer and steam for about 20 minutes more.

3. Turn the couscous out onto the tray and incorporate the butter. Put into a serving bowl and garnish with the raisins, which have been softened by steaming. Then sprinkle the sugar over all.

Serve warm. Serves 4.

VARIATION

The couscous can also be prepared with dates instead of raisins. Remove the pits, then cut the dates in half. Steam for about 3 minutes, which is enough time to soften them. Add to the couscous as garnish.

⌘ KESKSOU KHEDRA ⌘

VEGETABLE COUSCOUS, OLD STYLE

This is old-style Berber couscous, without cinnamon. (Berbers do not use cinnamon.) The couscous may be prepared in vegetarian style or with the traditional dried lamb or beef pieces added. The solid, firm skinned calabaza, also called Cuban pumpkin, is the one used in Algeria. On the outside the color is a mixture of green and pale gold while the pulp on the inside is orange. It has a sweet melting texture and does not require long cooking.

2 tablespoons vegetable oil
2 medium tomatoes, blanched in
*   boiling water, peeled and chopped*
1 large onion, sliced (1 cup)
1 tablespoon sweet paprika
1 teaspoon salt, or to taste
1/2 teaspoon black pepper

8 cups water
1 1/2 pounds young green cabbage,
*   cut into chunks, and core thinly*
*   sliced*
1 1/2 pounds calabaza, peeled and
*   cut into 2-inch chunks*
couscous, steamed for serving

1. Put the oil, tomatoes, onion, paprika, salt and pepper in a pan and mix them together.

2. Put the water in the bottom of a *couscousier* (the Arabic name is *kadra welkeskes*) and bring to a boil. Add the tomato mixture to the top and cook over moderate heat for 15 minutes to prepare the sauce.

3. In a pan cook the cabbage and the thinly sliced core in boiling water for 10 minutes. Drain. Add to the sauce with the calabaza pieces. Cook for 45 minutes.

4. Serve warm, with couscous steamed in the top of the *couscousier.*

Serves 6.

VARIATION

Old-time Berbers in their desert fastness dried the breast of lamb during the hot dry summers—a method of preserving excess meats. The meat in those days was not cut professionally with any knowledge of style or good taste. Cuts were made in the breast, not all the way through, but enough to allow salt to be rubbed in the incisions. Then it was dried in the sun for one week, sufficient time to preserve it for future use.

To include in the cabbage and calabaza couscous, 3-inch chunks of dried lamb were soaked overnight in water to remove the salt. The lamb was drained and added to the sauce (no salt added) before the cabbage or calabaza was added and cooked for 1/2 hour. The vegetables were added and cooked to completion as described above.

SOUPS

HERIRA (1)

CLASSIC SPICED SOUP OF ALGERIA

Everyone likes Herira, an inspired soup with a wide assortment of spices, seasonings, lamb or chicken and the unique *chamira*—a fermented potion that thickens the soup somewhat and adds characteristic flavor. The recipe follows below.

FOR THE CHAMIRA

4 tablespoons flour
1/2 cup water

2 teaspoons white vinegar

FOR THE SOUP

4 tablespoons corn oil
2 pounds boneless lamb leg, cut
    into 1-inch cubes, or 2 1/2
    pounds chicken parts, leg, thigh,
    breast
1 medium onion, chopped (1/2 cup)
2 ripe tomatoes (1 pound),
    chopped
10 sprigs fresh coriander, chopped
6 sprigs flat-leaf parsley, chopped
4 ribs celery, strings removed and
    sliced
1 teaspoon salt, or to taste
1/4 teaspoon black pepper
1 teaspoon ground caraway

1/4 teaspoon ground cinnamon
1/4 teaspoon hot red chili powder
1/2 teaspoon saffron stamens or
    1/2 teaspoon turmeric
1/2 teaspoon ground anise
7 cups water
1 cup dried chick-peas, soaked
    overnight in water and drained
1/4 cup greenish/brown lentils,
    soaked overnight in water and
    drained
2 tablespoons tomato paste
1/4 cup rice, well rinsed, or 4
    ounces angel hair vermicelli
lemon wedges for serving

1. *Prepare the Chamira:* Mix the flour, water and vinegar together. Cover the bowl and let stand in a warm place in the kitchen overnight or longer to ferment. Add to the soup toward the end of the cooking process.

2. *Prepare the Soup:* Put the oil, lamb and onion in a large pan and stir-fry over low heat for 5 minutes to change the color.

3. Add the tomatoes, coriander, parsley, celery, salt, pepper, 1/2 teaspoon caraway, cinnamon, chili powder, saffron and anise and mix well. Add the water and bring to a boil. Add the chick-peas and lentils and cover the pan. Simmer over low heat for 1 1/2 hours.

4. Add the tomato paste, rice and *chamira* and stir frequently for 15 minutes so that the *chamira* does not stick to the pan. Add the balance of the caraway (1/2 teaspoon) and remove the soup from the heat.

5. Serve warm with lemon wedges and squeeze as much juice into the soup as desired.

    Serves 8 as a first course, to be followed by an entrée, in this particular case, the Covered Eggs and the Marinated Roast Chicken (see pages 130 and 157 respectively).

❖ SOUPE DE POIS CASSÉS ❖

SPLIT GREEN PEA SOUP

This pea soup, not a heavy gruel, is frequently eaten in Algeria as a late-night snack with a light salad, such as one of green peppers. This is for winter, heavy as it is on the amount of garlic.

1/2 pound dried split green peas
5 cups water
1 small onion, chopped (1/3 cup)
4 cloves garlic, chopped fine
5 sprigs flat-leaf parsley, chopped

1 teaspoon ground cumin
1/2 teaspoon black pepper
1 teaspoon salt
2 tablespoons peanut oil

1. Cook the split green peas and water together over low heat for 1 hour, or until the peas begin to disintegrate.

2. Add all the remaining ingredients and cook over low heat for 1/2 hour

more. Adjust the salt and pepper to taste. Should the soup become too thick for your taste, add another 1/2 cup water.

Serve warm with bread and salad. Serves 4 to 6.

❧ HERIRA (2) ❧
SPICY VEGETABLE PURÉE AND BEEF SOUP

The west coast of Algeria abuts the coast of Morocco, and the food in that area is influenced somewhat by Morocco. Herira is from the west coast and is served at the evening meal of Ramadhan. A thick, nourishing soup, it is filled with the natural flavor of vegetables and *rasel hanout,* a mixed spice similar to *garam masala* of India. The soup can be made with beef, lamb and to a lesser extent chicken.

2 tablespoons olive oil
1 medium onion. sliced (1/2 cup)
3 cloves garlic, sliced
2 pounds boneless beef, chuck or steak, cut into 1-inch cubes
1/2 teaspoon salt
1/4 teaspoon black pepper
1/2 teaspoon sweet paprika
1/2 bunch fresh coriander, about 2 ounces, trimmed and rinsed well
1/2 cup dried chick-peas, soaked overnight in water and drained

1 pound carrot, cut into 1-inch pieces
2 pounds potatoes, quartered
6 cups water
1/4 cup tomato paste dissolved in 1/2 cup hot water
1 package dried yeast, 7 grams
1/2 cup flour dissolved in 1/2 cup warm water
3 tablespoons rasel hanout (garam masala)
juice of 1 lemon

1. Heat the oil in a large pan, add the onion, garlic and beef and stir-fry over moderate heat for 2 minutes. Add the salt, pepper and paprika and continue to stir.

2. Tie the coriander up with string and put the bundle in the pan, stirring to combine. Add the chick-peas, carrot, potatoes and water and bring to a boil.

3. Add the tomato paste dissolved in water and continue to cook over moderate heat.

4. Cook the meat and vegetables for about 1 hour, or until the meat is soft. Remove and discard the coriander. Remove the meat and set aside.

5. Mix the yeast and the flour and water mixture into a thick paste. Let it rise in a warm spot for 1 hour.

6. Blend all the vegetables and broth into a purée. Return the purée to the pan with the meat and simmer the soup over low heat. Stir in the *rasel hanout* and juice of 1 lemon and stir in the yeast and flour mixture. Simmer for 10 minutes to integrate all the flavors.

Serve warm with bread. You can also serve a side dish of lemon juice, which is sprinkled to taste on the soup. Serves 10 to 12.

❊ SOUPE B'TCHICHA ❊

LAMB SOUP WITH BULGHUR

Soups are usually the first course in an Algerian meal, followed by the entrée and accoutrements of the meal. However, there is enough substance and nutrition in this soup to make it a one-dish meal, with bread and salads on the side.

Tchicha is a type of Algerian cracked bulghur. The pieces have been cracked in such a way that they are about double the size of a grain of couscous.

4 tablespoons corn oil
1/2 pound lamb shoulder, with or without bone, cut into 4 pieces
1 small onion, chopped (1/2 cup)
1/2 teaspoon salt
1/2 teaspoon black pepper
1/4 teaspoon ground cinnamon
1/4 teaspoon turmeric or saffron stamens
4 cups water
1 carrot, halved

4 ribs celery, strings removed and sliced
1 small potato, peeled and halved
4 sprigs flat-leaf parsley, chopped
4 sprigs fresh coriander, chopped
1 large tomato (1/2 pound), chopped
2 tablespoons tomato paste
1/2 cup tchicha (Algerian cracked wheat)
lemon wedges for serving

1. Heat the oil in a pan, add the lamb and onion and stir-fry over low heat for 5 minutes. Add the salt, pepper, cinnamon, turmeric and water and bring to a boil.

2. Add the carrot, celery, potato, parsley, coriander, tomato and tomato paste. Cover the pan and cook for 30 minutes. Remove the carrot, potato and lamb. Purée the carrot and potato and return the purée to the pan. Separate the meat from the bones and return it to the pan, discarding the bones. Add the *tchicha* and simmer for 15 minutes, stirring frequently. The soup is ready.

Serve warm with lemon wedges. Serves 4 or 5.

❈ SHORBA EL HOUT B'TCHICHA ❈

FISH SOUP WITH BULGHUR

The bulghur enhances the flavor of the fish broth here and provides some thickening.

2 tablespoons butter
1 tablespoon corn oil
1 large onion (1 pound), sliced thin
2 ribs celery, trimmed, strings removed and sliced
1/2 teaspoon salt
1/2 teaspoon white pepper

2 cups water
2 medium potatoes (1/2 pound), cut into 1/4-inch dice
1/2 pound whiting fillets or other white fish, such as flounder, cut into 2-inch pieces
1/4 cup tchicha (small bulghur)

1. Put the butter and oil in a pan over low heat. Add the onion, celery, salt and pepper and stir-fry for 3 minutes. Add the water and potatoes, bring to a boil and cook for 15 minutes.

2. Add the fish and *tchicha* and simmer for 15 to 20 minutes more.

Serve the soup warm as a first course. Serves 6.

❈ SHORBA HAMRA ❈

VEGETABLE SOUP WITH ANGEL HAIR NOODLES

A broth of lamb here is enriched with a selection of vegetables, spices and a little red chili powder to provide more dimension and invigorate the soup. After all the ingredients have softened, the potatoes, carrots and turnip are puréed and returned to the broth to thicken it. Texture is provided by the meat, chick-peas and noodles. A traditional and popular soup for all seasons.

4 tablespoons corn oil
2 pounds lamb shank or boneless leg, cut into 2-inch pieces, fat trimmed
1 large onion, chopped (1 cup)
2 large ripe tomatoes (1 pound), chopped
6 cups water
3 carrots (1/2 pound), halved
2 potatoes (1/2 pound), halved
1 small white turnip, peeled and halved

6 sprigs flat-leaf parsley, chopped
6 sprigs fresh coriander, sliced thin
1 rib celery, sliced
1 teaspoon salt
1/4 teaspoon black pepper
1/4 teaspoon hot red chili powder
1/4 teaspoon ground cinnamon
2 tablespoons tomato paste
1/2 cup cooked chick-peas
1/2 cup broken angel hair noodles

1. Put the oil, lamb, onion and tomatoes in a pan and stir-fry over low heat for 5 minutes. Add the water, bring to a boil and add the carrots, potatoes, turnip, parsley, 3 sprigs of coriander, celery, salt, pepper, chili powder and cinnamon. Simmer over low heat for 1 1/2 hours to soften all the ingredients.

2. Remove the carrots, potatoes and turnip and purée them in a processor with 1/2 cup of the lamb broth. Return the purée to the pan and add the tomato paste and chick-peas and cook for 10 minutes. Add the noodles and the balance of the coriander and cook for 5 minutes more.

Serve warm with bread. Serves 8.

❈ SHORBA ❈

LAMB OR CHICKEN SOUP WITH ORZO

Shorba, often teamed with chicken couscous, is served during celebrations and other festive occasions in Algerian gatherings. Each com-
plements the other. Either chicken or lamb may be used as the meat of
the soup. Vegetables and the well-known "bird's tongue" pasta, which
the Greeks refer to as orzo, is included.

*1 pound lamb, with or without
    bone, cut into 1-inch pieces, or 2
    pounds chicken parts*
1 medium onion, grated (1/2 cup)
1/2 zucchini, grated (1/2 cup)
1/2 small potato, grated (1/2 cup)
*1/4 cup dried chick-peas, soaked
    overnight in water and drained*
1/2 rib celery with leaves, halved
1 carrot, halved
2 teaspoons salt
1/2 teaspoon black pepper

1/2 teaspoon ground cinnamon
1 tablespoon sweet paprika
2 tablespoons tomato paste
1 tablespoon vegetable oil
8 cups water
*1/2 cup orzo or substitute angel
    hair vermicelli*
*1 tablespoon flat-leaf parsley,
    chopped*
1 teaspoon fresh mint, chopped
lemon slices for serving

1. Put the meat, onion, zucchini, potato, chick-peas, celery, carrot, salt,
   pepper, cinnamon, paprika, tomato paste, oil and 1/2 cup of the
   water in a pan and sauté over low heat for 20 minutes. Cover the pan
   during this time. Add the balance of the water, bring to a boil and
   cook for 45 minutes. Add the orzo or the vermicelli and cook for 10
   minutes more. Stir in the parsley and mint.

   Serve hot with lemon wedges on the side. Serves 6 to 8.

NOTE: One should be prepared for variability in the cooking time of
   dried chick-peas. Some take more time to soften than others. It does
   take 1 hour, or thereabouts, even though they have soaked overnight.
   Canned chick-peas can also be used, in which case they can be
   added to the soup at the same time as the pasta.

LENTILLE BIL KHODRA

LENTIL SOUP WITH VEGETABLES

The lentil, which originated botanically in the Mediterranean region, is a frequent visitor to the Algerian table. The green/brown lentil seeds are high in protein and produce a rich, thick soup. Here beef and vegetables are added. This soup can be served as a one-dish lunch with bread and perhaps a salad or two.

1 tablespoon corn oil
1 pound beef chuck, cut into 1-inch cubes
1 small onion, chopped (1/3 cup)
6 cloves garlic, crushed in a garlic press
1/2 teaspoon salt, or to taste
1/2 teaspoon black pepper
1/2 teaspoon ground cumin
1/2 teaspoon ground caraway
1/4 teaspoon hot red chili powder
1/4 teaspoon turmeric

1 large tomato (1/2 pound), chopped
2 large carrots (1/2 pound), cut into 1/2-inch cubes
1 large potato (1/2 pound), cut into 1/2-inch cubes
4 ribs celery, strings removed and sliced
4 springs flat-leaf parsley, chopped
3 1/2 cups water
1 pound lentils, well rinsed in cold water
2 tablespoons tomato paste

1. Heat the oil in a pan, add the beef, onion and garlic and stir-fry over moderate heat for 5 minutes. Add the salt, pepper, cumin, caraway, chili powder and turmeric and cook, stirring, for 5 minutes. Add the tomato, carrots, potato, celery, parsley and water. Bring to a boil and simmer over moderate heat for 15 minutes.

2. Add the lentils and tomato paste and simmer over low heat for 1 hour. The lentils and beef will soften and the soup will thicken. Adjust the salt if necessary.

Serve warm with bread and a salad or two. Serves 8.

❁ SHORBA ADES ❁
VEGETARIAN LENTIL SOUP

2 tablespoons vegetable oil
1 small onion, chopped (1/3 cup)
4 cloves garlic, chopped
1 rib celery and leaves, diced
1 large carrot, diced (1 cup)
1/2 teaspoon salt
1/4 teaspoon black pepper
3 cups water

1 teaspoon sweet paprika
1 tablespoon tomato paste
10 ounces lentils (greenish/brown variety), well rinsed in cold water
1/4 cup vermicelli
1 tablespoon chopped fresh coriander

1. Heat the oil in a pan, add the onion, garlic, celery, carrot, salt and pepper and sauté over low heat for 10 minutes. Add the water, paprika, tomato paste and lentils. Bring to a boil, then simmer over low heat, covered, for 40 minutes. Should the soup become too thick, add 1/2 cup water and continue cooking for the full time.

2. Add the vermicelli and cook 5 minutes more. Remove the pan from the heat and add the coriander.

Serve warm. Serves 6 to 8.

LAMB AND BEEF

LAMB

❖ TAJINE AU CHOU-FLEUR ❖
LAMB WITH CAULIFLOWER FRITTERS

People in western Algeria near the Moroccan border like potatoes very much. The French fried style is especially admired and included in many dishes. This tagine is often served on a bed of round-cut French fried potatoes. Filling and sometimes melting into the sauce, the potatoes are truly compatible. Although the potatoes are not part of the recipe but an optional choice in the presentation of the dish, an Algerian would most certainly include them.

FOR THE LAMB

1 tablespoon butter
1 small onion, chopped (1/3 cup)
2 pounds boneless lamb, cut into
   2-inch cubes
1 large ripe tomato (1/2 pound),
   sliced
1/2 teaspoon salt

1/2 teaspoon black pepper
1/8 teaspoon ground cinnamon
1/2 teaspoon saffron stamens or
   1/2 teaspoon turmeric
1/2 cup dried chick-peas, soaked
   overnight in water and drained
3 cups water

FOR THE CAULIFLOWER

3 cups lightly salted water
1 large cauliflower (2 pounds), cut
   into 3-inch florets
2 eggs, beaten

1/4 teaspoon salt
1/4 teaspoon black pepper
1/4 cup peanut oil for pan-frying

1. *Prepare the Lamb:* Heat the butter in a pan, add the onion and lamb and stir-fry over moderate heat for 5 minutes. Add the tomato, salt, pepper, cinnamon, saffron or turmeric, chick-peas and water. Bring to a boil, then simmer, covered, over low heat for 1 hour, or until the lamb is tender. There is some sauce. Set aside.

2. *Prepare the Cauliflower:* Bring the water to a boil, add the cauliflower and cook over moderate heat for 3 minutes, until tender but still firm. Drain and cool. Beat the eggs with the salt and pepper. Heat the oil until hot in a skillet, dip the florets into the batter and fry them on all sides over moderate heat for 2 or 3 minutes. Drain briefly on paper towels.

3. Serve the warm lamb and sauce on a large platter surrounded by the cauliflower fritters. Frequently, a bed of French fried potatoes sliced in the round is also included.

Serves 8.

NOTE: The tagine is served with the following simple and traditional salad.

1 large ripe tomato (1/2 pound), cut into 1/4-inch dice	*1 medium onion, cut into small pieces (1/2 cup)*
3 young Kirby cucumbers, ends trimmed and cut into 1/4-inch dice	*1/2 teaspoon salt*
	1 tablespoon olive oil
	juice of 1 lemon

Mix everything together. Chill and serve with the tagine.

❧ TAJINE BIL BIRKOOK ❧

SWEET LAMB AND PRUNES

Ramadhan is the time for this most delicious concoction filled with dried prunes and raisins, sweetened with sugar and garnished with crisp fried almond slices. At other times of the year, this is food of the upper classes who have the money for good lamb and the other costly ingredients. For those who cannot afford a lamb during the festival, the tagine can be prepared with chicken—not as good or as prestigious as lamb—but still very fine.

1 tablespoon butter	3 tablespoons sugar
1 whole small onion	1 pound prunes, with or without
2 pounds boneless lamb, cut into	pits
1-inch cubes	1/2 pound dark raisins
1/2 teaspoon salt	a 3-inch cinnamon stick
1/2 teaspoon black pepper	2 tablespoons rosewater
1/4 teaspoon ground cinnamon	1 small drop vanilla
1/2 teaspoon saffron stamens	1/4 cup blanched almond slices,
3 inches lemon peel	lightly fried in oil and lightly
1 cup water	salted

1. Put the butter in a pan, add the onion and lamb and fry over low heat for 5 minutes. Add the salt, pepper, ground cinnamon, saffron, lemon peel and water. Bring to a boil and simmer, covered, over low heat for 1 hour to tenderize the lamb.

2. Add the sugar, prunes, raisins and cinnamon stick and simmer for 15 minutes. Remove from the heat and add the rosewater and the drop of vanilla. Stir a moment.

Serve warm garnished with the almonds. Serves 6 to 8.

VARIATION

Dried apricots may also be included here in place of the prunes or in combination with the raisins. The apricots lend a light tartness that contrasts with the sugar.

❈ TAJINE LOUBIA KHADRA ❈

LAMB AND STRING BEAN RAGOUT

Here is a typical Algerian lamb preparation that includes the very popular green bean, also known as string bean or French bean. Cumin and saffron stamens add character, with a modest amount of hot chili powder as well.

3 tablespoons corn oil

2 pounds boneless lamb shoulder, cut into 1-inch cubes

2 medium onions, 1 chopped and 1 sliced into rounds

4 cloves garlic, chopped

1 teaspoon salt, or to taste

1/4 teaspoon black pepper

2 teaspoons ground cumin

1/2 teaspoon hot red chili powder

1/2 teaspoon saffron stamens or 1/2 teaspoon turmeric

4 cups water

1 1/2 pounds string beans, cut into 2-inch pieces

2 ripe tomatoes (1/2 pound), sliced into rounds

2 sprigs flat-leaf parsley, chopped

1. Heat the oil in a pan and add the lamb, the chopped onion and garlic and stir-fry over low heat for 5 minutes. Add the salt, pepper, 1 teaspoon of the cumin, chili powder, saffron or turmeric and water. Bring to a boil and simmer over low heat for 45 minutes.

2. Add the beans and cook for 15 minutes. Add the sliced onion and tomatoes and sprinkle the remaining 1 teaspoon cumin and the parsley over all. Simmer without stirring for 15 minutes. There will be ample sauce.

Serves 6 to 8 with other dishes.

❈ TAJINE EL BSSEL ❈

LAMB AND LEEK RAGOUT

Western Algeria, in the district of Oran near the Moroccan border, cooks differently from other places in the central and eastern parts of the country. This tagine is a typical western Algerian preparation.

3 tablespoons corn oil

2 large onions (1 pound), sliced

2 pounds lamb shoulder chops, cut into 3-inch pieces

1/2 cup dried chick-peas, soaked in water overnight and drained

1/2 teaspoon salt, or to taste

1/2 teaspoon white pepper

1/4 teaspoon ground cinnamon

2 cups water

6 leek, white part only, left whole but well rinsed in cold water

2 ripe tomato (1 pound), chopped

1. Heat the oil in a pan, add 1 sliced onion, the lamb and chick-peas and stir-fry over low heat for 5 minutes. Add the salt, pepper, cinnamon and water. Bring to a boil, cover the pan and simmer for 1/2 hour.

2. Add the leek, the remaining onion and the tomato and cook for 20 minutes or more, until the meat is tender. There will be little sauce.

   Serve warm with French bread. Serves 6 to 8.

VARIATION

Two pounds chicken parts, thigh, breast and leg, may be used instead of the lamb. Follow the recipe, allowing a little less cooking time perhaps, enough to tenderize the chicken but also soften the chick-peas.

❈ TAJINE BIL BSBAS ❈

RAGOUT OF FENNEL AND LAMB

Fennel has its growing season, and it is in October and November that this ragout is cooked, when the large white fennel bulbs with their feathery green leaves make their appearance in the markets of Algeria. Waiting a year for the fennel to be available sharpens the appetite for it and then it is eaten almost to surfeit. The faint anise flavor marries so well with fresh lamb. This tagine is, therefore, a winter dish.

2 tablespoons butter
2 large onions, sliced (1 1/2 cups)
2 pounds boneless leg of lamb, cut
*   into 2-inch cubes*
1 teaspoon salt, or to taste
1/2 teaspoon black pepper
1/4 teaspoon ground cinnamon
1/2 teaspoon turmeric

2 cups water
1/2 cup dried chick-peas, soaked
*   overnight in water and drained*
2 fennel bulbs (2 pounds), cut into
*   thick slices*
1 pound potato, peeled and sliced
*   1/2 inch thick*

1. Melt 1 tablespoon of the butter in a pan, add the onions and stir-fry over low heat for 2 minutes. Add the lamb, salt, pepper, cinnamon and turmeric. Mix, cover the pan and fry slowly for 10 minutes.

2. Add the water and chick-peas and cook, covered, for 15 minutes. Cover the meat with the fennel slices and arrange the potatoes over the fennel. Cover the pan and cook for 40 minutes. Do not stir. Add the remaining tablespoon of butter, cover the pan and remove from the heat.

Serve warm with bread and salads. Serves 6 to 8.

❈ TAJINE BI ZEITOUN ❈

LAMB, OLIVE AND MUSHROOM STEW

In the Oran district of western Algeria, the food differs from that of the capital city, Algiers, and the eastern part of the country near the border of Tunisia. Those in the huge southern portion of Algeria — the blazing Sahara with its nomadic people — eat their own style of desert food.

This recipe is a stew in the western style of the small agricultural town of Sig near the port city of Oran. The region is known to Algerians in the area for its olive groves and mushroom farms that were developed in caves in the sides of nearby mountains.

2 tablespoons butter
1 large onion, chopped (1 cup)
4 large cloves garlic, chopped
2 pounds lamb shoulder, sliced into
 6 to 8 pieces
1 teaspoon salt, or to taste
1/2 teaspoon black pepper
1/2 teaspoon turmeric
5 cups water

1/2 pound mushrooms, sliced
 medium thick
4 carrots, cut into thumb-sized
 pieces
4 small potatoes (3/4 pound),
 quartered
1 pound pitted ripe black olives
2 tablespoons white vinegar

1. Put the butter, onion, garlic, lamb pieces, salt, pepper and turmeric in a pan and sauté over moderate heat for about 5 minutes, or until the onion turns a rich golden color. Add 4 cups of the water and bring to a boil. Simmer for 45 minutes over low heat to tenderize the lamb.

2. Add the mushrooms, carrots and potatoes and cook for 1/2 hour, until the ingredients are soft.

3. During this time put the olives, vinegar and remaining 1 cup water in a pan and bring to a boil. (This removes the excess salt.) Strain in a colander. Add the olives to the stew during the last 15 minutes of cooking time.

Serve warm with bread and salads. Serves 8.

NOTE: Real saffron is the most expensive of seasonings. Turmeric, which is referred to as French saffron, is used here as it serves only as a coloring agent. The turmeric turns the potatoes golden, enhancing the presentation.

❊ TAJINE KARNOON BIL KUFTA ❊

LAMB-STUFFED ARTICHOKES IN GREEN PEA SAUCE

Artichokes are prepared by the Algerians in numerous ways, but none more delicious than in this tagine. The stuffed hearts, with an inch of the stem remaining, are cooked in a saffron sauce with green peas. The aromatic ground lamb stuffing adds its own seasonings to the sauce.

FOR THE KUFTA

2 pounds ground lamb
1 medium onion, chopped
(1/2 cup)
4 sprigs flat-leaf parsley, chopped
1/2 teaspoon ground cinnamon

1/2 teaspoon black pepper
1 teaspoon salt, or to taste
10 large green artichokes, trimmed
and cleaned (see below for
instructions)

FOR THE SAUCE

3 tablespoons corn oil
1 medium onion, chopped
(1/2 cup)
2 cups water
2 tablespoons tomato paste
1/2 teaspoon salt

1/4 teaspoon black pepper
1/2 teaspoon saffron stamens or
1/2 teaspoon turmeric
1 pound fresh green peas
(or frozen when fresh are not
available)

1. *Prepare the Kufta:* Mix everything together, except the artichokes. Form 10 round meatballs, each to fill 1 artichoke heart tightly. Any *kufta* (filling) left over can be made into 1-inch-in-diameter meatballs and added to the sauce.

2. *Prepare the Sauce:* Heat the oil in a pan, add the onion and stir-fry over moderate heat for 2 minutes. Add the water and bring to a boil. Add the tomato paste, salt, pepper and saffron or turmeric. Simmer over low heat for 20 minutes.

3. Add the stuffed artichokes, one by one, let cook for 10 minutes and add the peas. Cook for 1/2 hour more.

Serve warm with bread. Serves 6 to 8.

NOTE: Some prefer chick-peas to the green peas. In that case, use 1 cup cooked chick-peas and add them instead of the peas.

    Also, to enrich the sauce even more than noted above, you may add one pound of lamb shoulder chops, with or without bone, cut into 3-inch pieces. Stir-fry the lamb with the onion, and proceed to make the sauce as directed.

How to prepare artichokes for the tagine: Remove the scale-like leaves, one by one, with a sharp knife, leaving 1 inch of the stem attached as it is edible. When nearing the heart, cut off the now pointed end of the artichoke leaf bundle and scoop out all the fine hairs. Rub the cut part with white vinegar and water, in equal parts, or pure lemon juice. Discard the leaves.

❈ EL HAM BEL BSEL W-TOMTICH ❈

LAMB STEW WITH ONIONS AND TOMATOES

No water is needed in this stew since the onions and tomatoes provide sufficient liquid. The sauce here is rich and red, with aromatic overtones.

1 pound lamb chops or steak, with
    or without bone, cut into 3-inch
    pieces
2 pounds medium onions, sliced
3/4 pound tomato, blanched in
    boiling water for 2 minutes,
    peeled and cut into slices

3 tablespoons vegetable oil
1 teaspoon salt, or to taste
1/4 teaspoon black pepper
1/4 teaspoon ground cinnamon
1 teaspoon sweet paprika
1/4 cup dried chick-peas, soaked in
    water overnight and drained

Put everything in a large pan and simmer, covered, over low heat for 1 hour. The tomatoes and onions melt down into a jam consistency but do not completely dissolve. The lamb should be tender.

Serve warm. Serves 6 with other dishes.

❁ MOULOUKHIA ❁

LAMB AND OKRA

This is not the *m'loukhia* of Tunisia, Egypt or other Mid-Eastern regions that use the green gummy powder, Jews' mallow and tossa jute, which is the source of burlap, in stew. In western Algeria *mouloukhia* is the name for okra, I suspect because if overcooked it becomes mucilaginous, like its namesake.

In eastern Algeria okra is called *bamiya*, which is the name I knew during my residence in India, where it was also called lady's fingers. It is an acquired taste and texture and this Algerian method derives the best out of an attractive vegetable of the cotton family.

3 tablespoons vegetable oil
2 pounds lamb shank, including
    bone, cut into 2-inch pieces
1 medium onion, chopped (1/2
    cup)
6 cloves garlic, chopped fine
6 sprigs flat-leaf parsley, chopped
    fine

1/2 teaspoon salt
1/2 teaspoon black pepper
1 teaspoon ground cumin
2 large tomatoes, chopped
    (1 1/2 cups)
1 tablespoon tomato paste
4 cups water
1 pound small fresh green okra

1. Heat the oil in a large pan, add the lamb, onion, 3 cloves of the garlic, parsley, salt, pepper, cumin, tomatoes and paste and stir-fry over low heat for 10 minutes.

2. Add the water and simmer slowly, covered, for 1 hour. Add the okra and remaining 3 cloves of garlic and cook for 15 minutes. Do not overcook as the okra might disintegrate into a paste. There is, however, a thick sauce.

Serves 6 to 8 with bread and fresh salad.

❋ MARKA BIL KARNOON ❋

ARTICHOKE HEARTS WITH LAMB

Algerian cooking focuses on an important food, in this case the artichoke, and surrounds it with compatible meat, vegetables and seasonings. The artichokes should be fresh and cleaned, with the stems and thistle-like threads removed. I have never used canned artichokes and do not recommend them for this dish. The cooking is slow. *Marka* means "with sauce."

2 tablespoons vegetable oil	1/2 teaspoon turmeric
2 pounds lamb shoulder, cut into 6 pieces	2 cups water
	1/2 cup dried chick-peas, soaked
1 medium onion, chopped	overnight in water and drained
(1/2 cup)	2 carrots (1/4 pound), sliced into
2 large tomatoes, chopped (1 cup)	rounds
1 tablespoon tomato paste	2 medium potatoes (1/2 pound),
1/2 teaspoon salt	peeled and cut into 6 wedges
1/2 teaspoon black pepper	each
1/4 teaspoon ground cinnamon	6 plump artichoke hearts

1. Heat the oil in a pan, add the lamb, onion, tomatoes and paste, salt, pepper, cinnamon and turmeric and stir-fry over low heat for 10 minutes.

2. Add the water, chick-peas and carrots and cook for 1/2 hour more.

Should the lamb be too firm, cook another 15 minutes to tenderize and to reduce and thicken the sauce.

Serves 6 with bread and salad.

❀ EL HAM LAHLOU ❀
SWEET LAMB FOR RAMADHAN

The holy celebration of Ramadhan is when the Algerian Muslims eat this sweet lamb after a day of fasting. It is almost a dessert meat, with raisins, prunes, sugar, almonds and orange blossom water, and it is cooked without salt, to prevent thirst the next day for those fasting.

3 tablespoons butter
1 pound lamb, leg shank or chops, cut into 3-inch pieces, with or without bone
1/2 teaspoon ground cinnamon
3 cups water
1/4 cup sugar
12 dried prunes soaked in water for 1 hour

2 tablespoons white raisins
2 tablespoons whole blanched almonds
1 firm pear, peeled, cored and cut into wedges
2 tablespoons orange blossom water (available at Middle Eastern groceries)

1. Melt the butter in a pan, add the lamb and sauté over low heat for 5 minutes. Add the cinnamon, water and sugar and mix well. Increase the heat to moderate and cook for about 40 minutes, or until the meat is tender. The sauce will darken.

2. Drain the prunes and add them to the lamb with the raisins, almonds and pear. Simmer for 15 minutes more. Remove the pan from the heat and stir in the orange blossom water.

Serve at room temperature with rice, salad and bread. Serves 4 to 6 with other dishes.

❈ BRANIA ❈

LAMB, EGGPLANT AND CHICK-PEA PLATTER

Here is a traditional Algerian dish in which the lamb and vegetable combination is attractive to look at and generous in serving. The various steps in the preparation are well established as is the presentation.

MARAG (THE SOUP)

Marag is not really a soup, although it is called that. It is essentially a strong, slightly thickened broth that is to be served as a sauce over the *brania*. After the soup has been cooked, there should be from 1 to 1 1/2 cups spiced broth.

2 tablespoons butter or corn oil
2 pounds shoulder lamb chops with bone (8 pieces), fat trimmed
1 large onion, chopped (1 cup)
1/2 teaspoon white pepper
1/2 teaspoon saffron stamens or 1/2 teaspoon turmeric

1 teaspoon salt, or to taste
3/4 cup dried chick-peas, soaked in water overnight and drained
3 cups water
3 large cloves garlic
1 1/2 teaspoons ground caraway

1. Put the butter or oil in a pan with the lamb and onion. Stir-fry over low heat for 5 minutes as the onion changes color.

2. Add the pepper, saffron and salt and continue to fry for 5 minutes. Add the chick-peas and water and bring to a boil. Cook, covered, over low heat for 1 1/2 hours. This will be sufficient time to tenderize the meat and chick-peas. If too much liquid evaporates add another 1/2 cup water.

3. Crush the garlic and caraway together in a mortar and stir it into the soup. Simmer for 5 minutes more and remove from the heat.

THE VEGETABLES

2 or 3 eggplant (2 pounds), sliced crosswise 1/2 inch thick
3 teaspoons salt
1 cup water

4 potatoes (2 1/2 pounds), peeled and sliced into rounds 1/4 inch thick
1/2 cup corn oil for pan-frying

1. Do not peel the eggplant. Dissolve the salt in the water, add the eggplant slices mixing everything together. Let stand for 30 minutes, then drain. Squeeze the slices firmly in a kitchen towel.

2. Put 1/4 cup of the oil in a skillet and brown the eggplant lightly on both sides over moderate heat. Drain on paper towels to absorb the excess oil. Set aside in a warm place.

3. Add the balance of the oil to the skillet and fry the potato slices until crisp. Drain and set aside in a warm place.

THE PRESENTATION

Presentation is important and the following steps should be followed.

1. Place the fried potato slices on the bottom of a large serving platter in a single layer. Arrange the lamb in the center of the platter in a heap. The eggplant slices are placed around the edge of the platter and the chick-peas are scattered over the top of everything, as though they were a garnish.

2. Above 1/2 to 1 cup of the spiced broth is then poured over all the ingredients on the platter.
   The same arrangement can be made on individual plates, but *brania* is more impressive when served in one large platter.

Serve warm with several salads. Serves 6 to 8 persons.

❋ BEYD M'GHELEF ❋

COVERED EGGS

This is an inspired recipe of hard-cooked eggs wrapped with seasoned ground lamb, then deep-fried. This is a good party dish most often served with Marinated Roast Chicken (see page 157) and French fries, but it can also be served alone.

1 pound ground lamb
1 small onion, chopped (1/3 cup)
1 teaspoon salt, or to taste
1/4 teaspoon black pepper
1/4 teaspoon ground cinnamon

1 egg, beaten
6 hard-cooked eggs
corn oil for deep-frying
lemon wedges for serving

1. Mix the lamb, onion, salt, pepper, cinnamon and egg together into a smooth paste. Set aside.

2. Peel the eggs and cut them in half crosswise. Take about 2 heaping tablespoons of the lamb mixture and cover egg half. Wrap lamb mixture around egg to make a ball.

3. Heat the oil in a wok or skillet over moderate heat and fry the eggs for 3 or 4 minutes to brown. Drain briefly on paper towels.

Serve warm with lemon wedges. Makes 12 balls.

❈ FELFEL BIL KIFTA ❈

LAMB-STUFFED FRIED PEPPERS

When the hot, dry summer settles over Algeria, the stuffed sweet peppers make their appearance, served with French fries and salads. The peppers can be prepared in large quantities for parties and family ceremonies. They are easy to eat and seasoned with ample garlic to increase the appetite. Good foods create ebullient moods. The bread crumbs included in the stuffing are always homemade. The homemakers would take day-old French-style bread and pulverize it in a brass mortar and pestle, a common object in the kitchens. No electric processors.

6 sweet green peppers (about 1 1/2 pounds)
1 pound ground lamb
4 sprigs flat-leaf parsley, chopped
1 small onion, chopped (1/3 cup)
3 cloves garlic, chopped fine

1 egg, beaten
1 teaspoon salt, or to taste
1/2 teaspoon black pepper
1/4 cup homemade bread crumbs
1/2 cup vegetable oil

1. For each pepper, cut out a 1-inch disc around the stem, remove the stem and scoop out the seeds and discard. Rinse the peppers out with cold water and drain.

2. Mix together the lamb, parsley, onion, garlic, egg, salt, pepper and bread crumbs. Stuff the peppers with the mixture to the top, but do not pack the stuffing in too firmly.

3. Heat the oil in a skillet large enough to hold the stuffed peppers in one layer. Fry them, uncovered, over low heat for 15 minutes, turning them over several times. Drain briefly on paper towels.

Serves 6 with salads and French fries.

VARIATION

The stuffed peppers may also be served with a well-seasoned tomato sauce. The peppers are stuffed and added directly to the sauce where they poach for 1/2 hour. It is not necessary to fry them first; this step is omitted.

2 tablespoons vegetable oil	*1/4 teaspoon salt*
1 small onion, chopped (1/3 cup)	*1/4 teaspoon black pepper*
2 cloves garlic, chopped fine	*1/4 teaspoon turmeric*
1 tablespoon tomato paste	*1 cup water*
1 large ripe tomato, chopped (1 cup)	*6 stuffed peppers as prepared above*

1. Put all the ingredients, except the peppers, in a pan and simmer, covered, over low heat for 15 minutes. Add the stuffed peppers in a single layer, cover the pan and cook for 1/2 hour.

Serve the warm sauce and peppers with salads and French fries. Serves 6.

▓ DOLMA ▓

STUFFED VEGETABLES

Dolma is a Turkish word and it is logically reasonable to assume that this recipe was a product of the Ottoman Empire, which since the 15th century influenced the food of North Africa.

8 pieces of assorted vegetables, or
all one kind, such as zucchini,
Italian peppers, tomatoes and
potatoes

FOR THE STUFFING

1/2 pound ground beef or lamb
1 tablespoon chopped flat-leaf
   parsley
2 tablespoons raw rice, rinsed in
   cold water

1 tablespoon chopped onion
1 egg, beaten
1 teaspoon salt
1/4 teaspoon black pepper
1/4 teaspoon ground cinnamon

FOR THE SAUCE

2 tablespoons corn oil
1 small onion, chopped (1/3 cup)
1 pound lamb shoulder chops,
   halved, or lamb shanks in 4
   pieces
3 cups water
1/4 cup dried chick-peas, soaked in
   water overnight, drained, then
   cooked until tender

1/2 teaspoon salt
1/4 teaspoon black pepper
1/4 teaspoon ground cinnamon
1 egg, beaten
juice of 1/2 lemon
1 tablespoon chopped flat-leaf
   parsley

1. Scoop out the four or five vegetables of your choice. Cut zucchini about 7 inches long in half horizontally. Scoop out the inside of each piece, leaving a firm wall 1/4 inch thick. For Italian peppers, cut out the stem ends and rinse out the seeds. For medium-size ripe-but-firm tomatoes, cut out stems, then scoop out, leaving a firm wall 1/4 inch thick. For potatoes, select 3-inch-long ones that are about 2 inches thick. Rinse well, peel, then scoop out a V-shaped amount from the long, flat surface of the potato. Save the part removed.

2. *Prepare the Stuffing:* Mix together the ground beef, parsley, rice, onion, egg, salt, pepper and cinnamon. Stuff, but not too tightly, the prepared vegetables.

3. *Prepare the Sauce:* Heat the oil in a pan and sauté the onion and lamb together over low heat for 5 minutes. The lamb is added to enrich the sauce. Add the water and bring to a boil over moderate heat. Add the chick-peas, salt, pepper and cinnamon and simmer over low heat for 20 minutes.

4. Place the stuffed vegetables with the scooped-out potato pieces in the sauce. Cook, covered, for 1/2 hour.

5. Pour the beaten egg and lemon juice over the vegetables and remove the pan from the heat. The sauce will have reduced somewhat. Garnish with the parsley.

Serve warm with bread and salads. Serves 4 to 5.

✸ MERGUEZ ✸

ALGERIAN LAMB SAUSAGE

Algerians like their sausage spicy and with an exceptional array of seasonings. The version that follows can be considered medium hot, with pepper and chili providing the heat, while the garlic adds the aromatic richness.

2 pounds boneless lamb, cut into 2-inch pieces	*1 tablespoon ground cumin*
4 ounces white fat attached to the lamb kidney	*1 tablespoon ground coriander*
	1 tablespoon sumac (see glossary note, page 135)
2 heads garlic (about 12 cloves), peeled	*1 tablespoon red hot chili powder*
1 teaspoon salt, or to taste	*2 tablespoons sweet paprika*
1 teaspoon black pepper	*1 cup cold water*
	1 small lamb intestine

1. Grind the lamb, fat and garlic with the medium-size holes of the grinder, 1/4 inch in diameter. Add all the remaining ingredients, including the water, but not the casing. Test the mixture at this stage by preparing a miniature pattie and frying it in a teaspoon of oil in a skillet. Should it need salt, it can be added at this time.

2. Tie one end of the casing tightly to hold the filling. Fill the casing with the lamb mixture, twisting it around every 4 inches to make individual sausages.

The *merguez* can be eaten in various ways the next day. The simple method of cooking is to fry them in hot vegetable oil until brown and crisp. Very little oil is needed since the sausage contains lamb fat.

Serve warm. Makes about 10 to 12 sausages.

NOTE: Algerians often prepare *merguez* with the cheaper cuts of lamb, especially the scraps left over from trimming the more expensive parts. Meat is expensive and this is one way of reducing the cost. I do not mean to imply that one should do this, since a meaty leg of lamb is an ideal cut that can be used.

GLOSSARY: Sicilian or Tanner's Sumac (Rhus coriaria L.)
Sumac is that rare Mediterranean and Middle East seasoning that was used at one time as a salt substitute. The dried reddish crushed powder has a lemon/salt flavor and is used in meat and chicken dishes. It adds an important flavor to Algerian *merguez.*

❊ SLK FEL KOUSHA ❊

BAKED CHEESE AND SPINACH

A light summer-food dish.

*2 pounds spinach, stems trimmed,
   well cleaned and sliced 1/2 inch
   wide
3 tablespoons vegetable oil
1 medium onion, chopped (1/2 cup)
1/2 pound ground lamb or beef*

*1/2 teaspoon salt, or to taste
1/2 teaspoon black pepper
1/2 cup water
2 ounces Gruyère cheese, grated
2 tablespoons chopped flat-leaf
   parsley*

1. Cook the spinach in a covered pan in a small amount of water over moderate heat for 3 minutes. Drain the spinach and press out the excess liquid firmly.

2. Heat the oil in a pan, add the onion and meat and stir-fry over low heat, adding the salt and pepper, for 3 minutes. Add the water and spinach and cook over moderate heat for 5 minutes, stirring frequently.

3. Put the mixture into a baking dish and sprinkle the grated cheese over all. Bake in a 350 degree oven for 10 minutes, enough to brown the cheese lightly.

Serve warm with bread and salads. Serves 6.

✿ LOOBIA MASHTOU SHTITHA ✿

LAMB WITH STRING BEANS IN RED SAUCE

The string or runner beans preferred for this dish are long and broad, unlike the slim so-called French bean. Runner beans have more texture and cook longer. The hot chili adds another dimension to the dish.

2 tablespoons vegetable oil
1 small onion, chopped (1/3 cup)
4 cloves garlic, chopped
1 pound lean lamb ribs or chops
  with bone
1/2 teaspoon salt, or to taste
1/4 teaspoon black pepper

1/2 teaspoon hot red chili flakes
1 tablespoon tomato paste
1/4 teaspoon sweet paprika
1 cup water
1 pound large string beans or
  runner beans, cut diagonally
  into 2-inch pieces

1. Put the oil, onion, garlic, lamb, salt, pepper and chili flakes in a large pan and sauté over low heat for 5 minutes. Add the tomato paste, paprika and water and bring to a boil.

2. Add the beans, cover the pan and simmer for 40 minutes, during which time the sauce will thicken.

Serve warm with bread and salads. Serves 6.

✿ KOOFTA ✿

MEATBALLS IN TOMATO SAUCE

Not too long ago, during the harvest season of tomatoes, families would prepare tomato paste for the winter months. Refrigeration was limited or nonexistent and homecooking meant exactly that. This recipe has canned tomato sauce, a modern modification and a time-saver in an industrial world.

For the Meatballs

1 pound ground lamb
2 cloves garlic, grated or chopped
*   fine*
1/2 cup dry bread crumbs

2 eggs, beaten
1/2 teaspoon salt
1/4 teaspoon black pepper
1 tablespoon sweet paprika

For the Sauce

6 cloves garlic, grated or chopped
*   fine*
1 cup water
2 tablespoons vegetable oil
1 tablespoon sweet paprika
1/2 teaspoon salt

1/4 teaspoon black pepper
16 ounces canned tomato sauce
1 cup water
2 bay leaves
1 sprig thyme or 1 teaspoon dried

1. *Prepare the Meatballs:* Mix together rather well all of the ingredients. Form the mixture into round balls, each 1 1/2 inches in diameter. Set aside. Makes 20 meatballs.

2. *Prepare the Sauce:* Put the garlic in a pan with 1/4 cup of the water and simmer over low heat 1 minute. Add the oil and all the remaining ingredients, including the balance of the water. Bring to a boil and simmer over low heat for 10 minutes. Add the meatballs, one at a time, gently into the sauce. Cook for 1/2 hour. The sauce will thicken.

Serve warm with bread. Serves 6.

❁ DOLMA KERAMBIT ❁

Stuffed Cabbage

Algerians stuff a number of vegetables such as tomatoes, zucchini and green and red peppers, on occasion all together in one pan. Cabbage leaves, on the other hand, are stuffed and cooked alone, since the characteristic flavor and aroma of the cabbage would interfere with the flavors of the other vegetables.

12 large cabbage leaves	1/4 cup dried chick-peas, soaked
2 tablespoons vegetable oil	overnight in water and drained
8 ounces lamb ribs with bone, halved	3 cups hot water
2 medium onions, chopped	1 pound ground lamb or beef
1 1/2 teaspoons salt	3 tablespoons rice
1/2 teaspoon plus 1/4 teaspoon	1/4 cup chopped flat-leaf parsley
pepper	1 egg plus 1 egg yolk, beaten
1/4 teaspoon plus 1/8 teaspoon	
cinnamon	

1. Cut out the central core of a large cabbage, then remove 12 leaves. Cook them in boiling water for 10 minutes, drain and cool.

2. Put the oil, lamb ribs, 1 onion, 1 teaspoon of the salt, the 1/2 teaspoon pepper, the 1/4 teaspoon cinnamon and chick-peas in a pan and simmer over low heat for 10 minutes. Add the water and cook for 10 minutes more.

3. Mix together rather well the ground lamb or beef, rice, parsley, remaining 1/2 teaspoon salt, 1/4 teaspoon pepper, 1/8 teaspoon cinnamon, onion and egg plus the yolk.

4. Take 2 heaping tablespoons of the mixture and place on the thick end of each well-softened cabbage leaf. Fold the right and left side toward the center, then fold the thick end one turn over to close the bundle.

5. Put all the stuffed leaves in the simmering broth, cover the pan and cook over moderate heat for 45 minutes. The liquid will reduce somewhat.

Serve warm with bread and salads. Serves 6.

❈ CHAKCHOUKA MASHTOU ❈

STRING BEAN, POTATO AND LAMB SAUTÉ

Chakchouka may be prepared with meat or without for those who prefer vegetarian food. Both styles are traditional in Algeria and can be appreciated elsewhere.

1 1/2 pounds string beans, strung
 and halved
2 tablespoons vegetable oil
1 large onion, chopped (1 cup)
4 ounces lamb ribs or chops, halved
4 cloves garlic, chopped
1/2 teaspoon salt

1/4 teaspoon black pepper
1 tablespoon sweet paprika
1 medium fresh ripe tomato,
 chopped (1/2 cup)
1/2 cup water
2 small potatoes, peeled and halved
lemon wedges for serving

1. Cook the string beans in water over moderate heat for 10 minutes. Drain and set aside.

2. Heat the oil in a pan, add the onion, lamb, garlic, salt, pepper and paprika and stir-fry over low heat for 5 minutes. Add tomato, water, string beans and potato halves. Cover the pan and cook over low heat for 45 minutes, or until the meat and potatoes are soft.

Serve warm with lemon wedges. Serves 4 with other dishes.

VARIATION

For vegetarians, prepare *chakchouka* without meat, using the same ingredients and steps.

❖ TAJINE EL KHOUKH ❖

STUFFED "PEACHES"

These are not really stuffed peaches but they are designed to simulate a peach, with mashed potatoes and a nugget of ground meat for the stone. The recipe is a special preparation from the capital city of Algiers.

FOR THE WHITE SAUCE

2 tablespoons vegetable oil
1/2 pound lamb ribs or chops, cut
 into 4 pieces
1 medium onion, chopped (1/2 cup)
1 teaspoon salt
1/4 teaspoon black pepper

1/8 teaspoon ground cinnamon
1 ounce or a small handful of flat-
 leaf parsley, chopped
1/4 cup dried chick-peas, soaked
 overnight in water and drained
2 cups water

For the Meatballs

    1/2 pound ground lamb or beef   *2 sprigs flat-leaf parsley, leaves*
    1/8 teaspoon black pepper   *only, chopped*
    1/2 teaspoon salt   *1 egg, beaten*
    1 small onion, chopped (1/4 cup)

For the Mashed Potatoes

    2 pounds potatoes, peeled and   *1 teaspoon salt*
      halved   *1 tablespoon butter*

For the "Peaches"

    2 eggs   *1 cup vegetable oil for frying*
    1 1/2 tablespoons flour

1. *Prepare the White Sauce:* Heat the oil in a pan, add the lamb, onion, salt, pepper, cinnamon, parsley and chick-peas and sauté over low heat for 5 minutes. Add the water, bring to a boil and cook until the meat is tender, about 45 minutes. This is the white sauce.

2. *Prepare the Meatballs:* Mix everything together. Prepare small balls, each 1 1/4 inches in diameter. Makes about 20.

3. Put the meatballs in the simmering sauce and cook for 15 minutes. Remove from the sauce and cool.

4. *Prepare the Mashed Potatoes:* Cook the potatoes in water and salt until soft. Drain, add the butter and mash well while warm. Set aside.

5. *Prepare the "Peaches":* Beat the eggs and flour together into a smooth batter. Take 2 tablespoons mashed potatoes, push in one meatball and roll into a ball 2 inches in diameter. Roll this in the egg batter and set aside. Prepare all the "peaches" this way.

6. Heat the oil in a skillet and brown the "peaches" over moderate heat. Drain briefly on paper towels. Makes 20 "peaches."

7. Serve warm on a platter and pour the warm sauce over all. Another method is to serve the sauce separately, allowing each diner to take the amount desired.

Serves 6.

NOTE: Peaches have variegated colors on the skins that range from light to dark. Old-time cooks attempt to copy what nature has provided by frying the peaches so that shades of brown appear on the "peach."

⌘ BOUZELLOUF MECHOUI ⌘

ROAST LAMB HEAD

A most popular Algerian dish that combines an economical purchase as well as a ritual food for the Islamic holiday, Id El Adha (The Feast of Sacrifice), when lambs are slaughtered and the heads eagerly desired. Crispy and dry without sauce, the head has various bits of meat around the perimeter as well as the tongue and the tender brain flavored with seasonings. My Algerian friends can quite easily polish off one head per person.

1 lamb head, halved lengthwise
4 large cloves garlic, crushed in a
   mortar
1/2 teaspoon salt, or more to taste
1/2 teaspoon black pepper

1 teaspoon ground cumin
1 teaspoon ground caraway
1/2 cup water
2 tablespoons butter
lemon quarters

1. Request the butcher to halve the lamb head with an electric saw since chopping open would leave small bones imbedded in the meat that would be difficult to remove. Scrub and rinse the head well with cold water to remove hair and other impurities. (In Algeria, the head is purchased from the butcher with the skin and so a complete and arduous cleansing process, including singeing the hair over a charcoal fire, must be accomplished in the home.)

2. Add the garlic, salt, pepper, cumin and caraway to the water and mix well.

3. Preheat the oven to 300 degrees. Melt the butter in a roasting pan large enough to hold the head. Add the lamb head and pour the spiced liquid over it. Cover the pan and roast in the oven at low heat for 2 hours, which is sufficient time to tenderize the head meat, brain and tongue. This is a dry roast, with no sauce, and involves picking out the tender bits with your fingers. Elegant it is not, but a dish of the country.

4. This is usually served with a soup—*herira* or *shorba,* a generous amount of lemon juice and a lettuce salad.

Serves 2.

NOTE: Id El Adha is an important Muslim holiday of Biblical origin, when Abraham was to sacrifice his son Isaac and his hand was stayed. To celebrate this ancient event, a lamb is slaughtered in place of the son.

❀ MOKH ❀

LAMB BRAIN WITH TOMATO

2 lamb brains, well rinsed in cold water, drained and cut into 4 pieces each
1/4 cup water
3 ripe tomatoes (1 pound), peeled and coarsely chopped

1/2 teaspoon black pepper
1 teaspoon ground cumin
1 teaspoon salt
2 teaspoons corn oil

1. Mix the water, tomato, pepper, cumin and salt together.

2. Heat the oil in a skillet, add the spice liquid and simmer over low heat for 10 minutes.

3. Add the pieces of brain and stir everything together, in effect scrambling the mixture. Cover the pan and simmer for 15 minutes. Uncover, mix well and serve warm.

Serves 4 as an appetizer with bread.

❀ BRIK ❀

LAMB-FILLED PASTRY ENVELOPES

Brik is a specialty of eastern Algeria, the cities of Constantine and Annaba, near the Tunisian border. *Brik* is also a popular dish in Tunisia and may have originated there. Old-time cooks even today prepare the *brik* wrapper by mixing a pastry dough and rolling it out in a circle as thin as they are able but still thicker than the commercially made fillo. *Brik* may be deep-fried as in this recipe or baked in a 350 degree oven in a buttered baking pan.

FOR THE STUFFING

1 teaspoon butter	*1/2 teaspoon salt*
1/2 pound ground lamb	*1/4 teaspoon black pepper*
1 small onion, chopped (1/3 cup)	*1/8 teaspoon ground cinnamon*
4 sprigs parsley, chopped	

FOR THE BRIK

6 fillo sheets, each 12 × 17 inches	*6 whole eggs*
1 pound potato, boiled, mashed and cooled	*salt and black pepper*
	1 egg, beaten
3–6 teaspoons Harissa (see page 89), to taste	*oil for deep-frying*
	lemon wedges for serving

1. *Prepare the Stuffing:* Melt the butter in a skillet, add the lamb and stir-fry a minute over low heat. Add the onion, parsley, salt, pepper and cinnamon and fry for 5 minutes. Set aside and cool.

2. *Prepare the Brik:* Put 1 sheet of fillo on a dinner plate. Place 1 heaping tablespoon mashed potato in the center of the fillo and flatten it out into a round disc 3 inches in diameter. Sprinkle 1/2–1 teaspoon *harissa* over the potato. Top with 2 heaping tablespoons lamb stuffing. Spread the stuffing to form a depression in it and crack into it a whole egg. Sprinkle salt and pepper lightly over it.

3. *To Shape the Long Envelopes:* Fold sides of the sheet in to overlap in the center; fold both short ends over to make an envelope 4 × 5 inches in size. Dab the inner edges of the folded fillo with the beaten egg to seal the envelopes.

4. Heat the oil in a wok or skillet over moderate heat and place the envelope, sealed side down, into the hot oil. Fry until brown on both sides, for about 3 minutes. Drain briefly on paper towels. Fry 1 envelope at a time.

   Serve warm as an appetizer. Squeeze the lemon wedges generously over the brik. Makes 6.

❈ BOUREK ❈

Lamb-Filled Pastry Logs

Bourek are ideal appetizers to accompany a lunch or dinner menu. They can be baked as they are in this recipe or deep fried and crispy. Commercial fillo is an easy way to assemble Bourek, but old-time cooks prepare their own wrapper dough with flour, butter, salt and water.

For the Stuffing

1 teaspoon butter
1/2 pound ground lamb
1 small onion, chopped (1/2 cup)
4 sprigs parsley, sliced thin or chopped

1/2 teaspoon salt
1/4 teaspoon black pepper
1/8 teaspoon ground cinnamon
1 hard-cooked egg, cooled and grated

For the Bourek

8 fillo sheets, 12 by 17 inches each
3 tablespoons butter, melted

1 egg, beaten
lemon wedges for serving

1. *Prepare the Stuffing:* Put the butter in a skillet, add the lamb and stir-fry a minute. Add all the remaining ingredients, except the egg, and stir-fry over low heat for 5 minutes. Cool and fold in the grated egg.

2. Take 1 fillo sheet and fold both sides toward the center lengthwise. Sprinkle the sheet lightly here and there with butter. Take 2 heaping tablespoons of the meat stuffing or a bit more and press it into cigar shape. Place it on one end of the folded fillo sheet and fold the dough over 3 times into a 1-inch-wide cylinder. Sprinkle more butter over the fillo, dab beaten egg on the end and fold over to seal the package. Make cylinders with the remaining stuffing and fillo in the same manner.

3. Bake in a buttered baking dish in a 350 degree oven for 15 to 20 minutes to brown on both sides.

Serve warm to accompany any kind of shorba *or* herira *soup. Sprinkle over as much lemon juice as wanted. Makes 8.*

❖ SLK ❖

SPINACH STUFFING

2 teaspoons butter
a 10-ounce package frozen chopped
  spinach, thawed and squeezed
  dry, or the equivalent amount
  fresh spinach, chopped fine

1/2 teaspoon salt
1/4 teaspoon black pepper
1/4 cup mashed potato

1. Melt the butter in a skillet and stir-fry the spinach, salt and pepper over low heat for 5 minutes to reduce and dry the bulk. Cool and stir in the mashed potato. Use this stuffing as you would the meat to stuff *bourek*.

BEEF

❈ BOUREK ❈
BEEF-STUFFED PASTRY ROLLS

When the fast of Ramadhan is broken in the early evening hours, various dishes are considered a traditional part of the meal. This is one of those dishes of the family I cooked with in Tunisia.

1/4 cup vegetable oil	*1 egg, beaten*
1 small onion, chopped (1/4 cup)	*2 tablespoons chopped flat-leaf*
1/2 pound ground beef	*parsley*
1/2 teaspoon salt, or to taste	*6 fillo sheets, each 12 × 17 inches*
1/4 teaspoon black pepper	*lemon wedges for serving*

1. Heat 1 tablespoon of the oil in a skillet, add the onion and stir-fry over moderate heat for 2 minutes. Add the beef, salt and pepper and stir-fry for 5 minutes. Add the egg and parsley and fry for 1 minute more. Cool well.

2. Take 1 fillo sheet and spread it out flat with a short end nearest you. Place 2 heaping tablespoons of the beef mixture 2 inches in from the short edge. Fold both long sides in toward the middle; beginning with the short end roll the fillo to shape a packet 4 inches long and 1 1/2 inches wide. Repeat with all the remaining fillo sheets and stuffing. Set aside.

3. Put the balance of the oil in a skillet over moderate/low heat and add the rolls. Brown on both sides for about 3 minutes; the low heat prevents the very thin pastry sheets from burning. Drain the rolls on paper towels for a minute.

Serve warm with a squeeze or two of lemon juice. Makes 6.

LOUBIA BIL L'HEM BIGRI

WHITE BEANS AND BEEF

Beef is not a popular meat in Algeria. Desert people prefer lamb, which is common and traditional. When beef is cooked, it is often with white beans, and the combination makes a wintertime dish.

1 pound dried white beans (haricots), soaked overnight in water and drained
2 pounds boneless beef chuck, cut into 2-inch pieces
4 cups water
1 large potato (1/2 pound), cut into 1/2-inch cubes
2 carrots (1/4 pound), sliced
2 white turnips (1/2 pound), peeled and cut into 1/2-inch cubes

4 ribs celery, strings removed and cut into 1/4-inch-wide slices
4 sprigs flat-leaf parsley, chopped
4 cloves garlic, chopped fine
1 medium onion, chopped (1/2 cup)
1/2 teaspoon salt
1/2 teaspoon white pepper
1/2 teaspoon ground cumin
1/4 teaspoon ground cinnamon
3 tablespoons tomato paste
1 tablespoon olive oil

Cook the beans and beef in the water over low heat for 1 hour. Add the potato, carrots, turnips, celery, parsley, garlic, onion, salt, pepper, cumin, cinnamon and tomato paste. Bring to a boil and simmer over low heat for 1 hour, which is enough to tenderize the ingredients.

Serve with bread. Serves 8.

LOUBIA BIL MERGUEZ

WHITE BEANS AND SAUSAGE

Merguez are beef sausage of the Maghreb and are one of the ubiquitous sights in the meat markets. When cooked with dried white beans, the combination becomes a tasty and nourishing winter dish for large families.

*1 pound dried white beans
(haricots), soaked overnight
in water and drained*
3 cups water
3 tablespoons corn oil
1 medium onion, chopped (1/2 cup)
5 cloves garlic, chopped fine
3 tablespoons tomato paste

4 sprigs flat-leaf parsley, chopped
*4 ribs celery and leaves, strings
removed and sliced*
1/2 teaspoon salt, or to taste
1/2 teaspoon black pepper
1/2 teaspoon ground cumin
*1 pound merguez (Tunisian beef
sausage), halved crosswise*

1. Cook the beans in 2 cups of the water over low heat for 1 hour until soft. Drain. (This can be done one day in advance.)

2. Heat the oil in a pan, add the onion, garlic, tomato paste, parsley, celery, salt, pepper, cumin and remaining 1 cup water. Simmer over low heat for 10 minutes. Add the beans and *merguez* and cook for 15 minutes more.

Serve warm with Lemon-Carrot Salad (see page 175). Serves 8 with bread.

❈ BATATA MERHIYA ❈ BIL L'HAM MERHY

MASHED POTATOES LAYERED WITH BEEF

1 pound potato, peeled
2 tablespoons butter
1 teaspoon salt
2 teaspoons vegetable oil
1 small onion, chopped (1/2 cup)

1/2 pound ground beef
1/4 teaspoon black pepper
1 egg, beaten
2 ounces Gruyère cheese, grated

1. Cook the potatoes until soft. Drain and mash with 1 tablespoon of the butter and salt.

2. Heat the oil in a skillet, add the onion, beef and pepper. Stir-fry over low heat about 5 minutes.

3. Butter a 1-quart casserole with the remaining tablespoon of butter. Put half of the mashed potatoes in the bottom of the dish. Add all the meat and cover with the balance of mashed potatoes. Smooth the surface.

4. Cover with the beaten egg and sprinkle the cheese over all. Bake in a

350 degree oven until the surface is golden and the cheese melted, about 1/2 hour.

Serve warm. Serves 6 with other dishes.

✷ KEBDA MESHERMELA ✷
FRESH LIVER SAUTÉ

1 tablespoon vegetable oil
2 cloves garlic, chopped
1 tablespoon chopped fresh coriander
1/2 pound beef or lamb liver, cut
  into 1/2-inch cubes

1 small ripe tomato, chopped
  (1/3 cup)
1/4 teaspoon salt
1/4 teaspoon black pepper
1/4 teaspoon sweet paprika

Combine everything together in a skillet. Bring to a simmer and stir-fry over moderate heat for 5 minutes.

Serve warm. Serves 4 with bread and salads.

✷ L'SEN BIGRI BIL HOUMOUS ✷
BEEF TONGUE IN CHICK-PEA SAUCE

Tongue is a substantial meat and when combined with chick-peas is usually served in the winter. A mixture of typical Algerian spices and seasonings contribute to the popularity of this not-too-common delicacy.

a 3-pound beef tongue
3 tablespoons corn oil
1 large onion, chopped (1 cup)
5 cloves garlic, chopped fine
4 sprigs flat-leaf parsley, chopped
2 ribs celery, strings removed and
  chopped
1 cup cooked chick-peas

1 teaspoon salt, or to taste
1/2 teaspoon black pepper
1 teaspoon ground cumin
1 teaspoon ground caraway
1/2 teaspoon hot red chili flakes or
  chili powder
2 tablespoons tomato paste
1 cup water

1. Cover the tongue in water, bring to a boil, cover and cook over moderate heat for 1 hour. (Add 1 cup additional water if it evaporates too quickly. A pressure cooker is a useful kitchen utensil and popular in Algeria.) Drain, cool and skin the tongue, removing all of the tough pieces and small bones. Cut into 1/2-inch-wide slices.

2. Put the oil in a pan, add the tongue and all the remaining ingredients, except the tomato paste and water. Stir-fry over moderate heat for 3 minutes. Add the tomato paste and water. Bring to a boil and simmer, covered, over low heat for 20 minutes. Test to make certain that the tongue is tender. If not, add more water and cook another 20 minutes. Tongue is tough and this is where the pressure (*cocotte minute*) is invaluable.

Serve warm with bread, table condiments and salads. Serves 8.

CHICKEN

❀ TAJINE BERKOUK ❀

CHICKEN WITH AROMATIC SPICES, PRUNES AND ALMONDS

A tagine is a clay cooking pot used in old-time Morocco and Algeria. The pot was filled with whatever food was planned and put into a clay oven above ground. The tandoor is the Indian version, which was sunk in the ground; the Algerian oven, of similar simple construction, stayed above. This tagine, sweet and aromatic, is served on Ramadhan but is delicious served anytime of year.

1 medium onion, grated (1/3 cup)
1/2 teaspoon ground cinnamon
1/4 teaspoon ground nutmeg
2 teaspoons vegetable oil
3 pounds halal chicken, cut into 8 serving pieces, loose skin and fat discarded
2 tablespoons butter

10 ounces pitted dried prunes
1 cup blanched almonds, toasted in the oven to a light brown
1 teaspoon salt
2 tablespoons sugar or 1 tablespoon honey or both, to taste
1/4 cup water

1. Mix the onion, cinnamon, nutmeg and vegetable oil together. Mix this seasoning with the chicken pieces and let stand 10 minutes.

2. Heat the butter in a pan, over low heat, add the chicken and marinade and fry, covered, for 10 minutes.

3. Add the prunes, almonds, salt, sugar or honey and water. Simmer over low heat for 1 hour, or until the chicken is tender. The prunes and seasonings will reduce to a thick mélange, without any sauce.

Serve warm with bread. Serves 6.

DJEDJ M'HAMMAR BIL BATATA

GOLDEN CHICKEN STEW

Marinating the chicken overnight in dry seasonings improves the flavor of our commercial chickens with their meticulously arranged living quarters and feed. *Halal* chickens, that is to say, the fresh and ritually slaughtered, are, of course, the most tasteful ones. The golden color of the turmeric, splashed with ripe tomato pieces and the parsley with several whole leaves remaining, is colorful and appetizing. Very Algerian.

1/2 teaspoon salt
1/2 teaspoon black pepper
1/2 teaspoon turmeric
a 3-pound chicken, cut into
* 6 serving pieces*
2 tablespoons corn oil
1 medium onion, chopped (2/3 cup)
4 cloves garlic, chopped
2 ribs celery, strings removed and
* sliced*

6 sprigs flat-leaf parsley, coarsely
* chopped, plus several leaves for*
* garnish*
2 medium tomatoes (1/2 pound),
* coarsely cut*
2 cups water
3 or 4 potatoes (1 pound), peeled,
* cut into 1-inch cubes and*
* French fried*

1. Mix together the salt, pepper and turmeric. Rub all over the chicken pieces. Refrigerate overnight.

2. Heat the oil in a pan and add the onion and chicken. Brown over low heat for 2 minutes. Add the garlic, celery, parsley and tomatoes and stir-fry for 5 minutes.

3. Add the water and bring to a boil. Cover the pan and simmer over low heat for 35 minutes to establish the sauce. There will be a generous amount of sauce for each diner.

Serve warm with the French fried potato cubes. Serves 4 with table salads and bread.

VARIATION

This M'Hammar can also be prepared with lamb, the most popular meat of the Maghreb. Use slightly different ingredients.

2 1/2–3 pounds shoulder lamb
* chops, trimmed of fat, 8 pieces*
1 large onion, chopped (1 cup)

omit the garlic, but include all
* other ingredients as for the*
* chicken rendition*

Marinate the lamb pieces overnight and prepare the stew in the same manner and sequence as the chicken combination.

❋ DJEDJ BEL BEYD ❋

CHICKEN WITH LEMON EGGS

Whenever a chicken dish was wanted for a celebration or some special occasion, my Algerian family would refer to this chicken as "grandmother's recipe." The phrase indicated the high esteem that grandmother's cooking was held in by the family and friends.

Colors of green and gold are provided by the parsley and turmeric, respectively, although in Algeria most of the households used the true saffron, which is not as prohibitively expensive there as it is in the United States.

a 3-pound chicken, cut into 4 pieces, loose skin and fat discarded
1 small onion, chopped (1/2 cup)
4 cloves garlic, chopped fine
1/2 teaspoon black pepper
3/4 teaspoon turmeric
1/8 teaspoon ground cinnamon
1/2 teaspoon salt, or to taste
2 cups water

1 large tomato (1/2 pound), chopped into small pieces
1 rib celery, strings removed and chopped fine
1 tablespoon butter
2 eggs, beaten
juice of 1 lemon
1/2 cup chopped flat-leaf parsley
lemon wedges for serving

1. Mix the chicken pieces together with the onion, garlic, pepper, turmeric, cinnamon and salt and marinate for 5 to 6 hours.

2. Add the water, tomato, celery and butter and bring to a boil. Cover the pan and cook over low heat for 1 hour.

3. Mix the beaten eggs with the lemon juice and parsley. Pour over the chicken pieces, arranging some of the parsley on the chicken. Simmer over low heat for 5 minutes, shaking the pan several times. The sauce will thicken.

Serve warm with lemon wedges, bread and salad. Serves 4 generously.

❋ DJEDJ B'ZETOUN ❋

Chicken with Green Olives

Algeria is olive country and it is logical that they are included in many preparations. This one is classic. Algerians are not, generally speaking, rice eaters but occasionally they serve it where appropriate, as in this chicken with olives.

2 tablespoons vegetable oil
1 large onion, chopped (1 cup)
a 3-pound chicken, cut into 10 pieces, loose skin and fat discarded

1/8 teaspoon ground cinnamon
1 teaspoon black pepper, or to taste
1 large bay leaf
2 1/2 cups water
2 cups pitted green olives

1. Put the oil in a pan and sauté the onion over low heat until it turns golden. Add the chicken, cinnamon, pepper and bay leaf and sauté for 3 minutes. Add the water. Bring to a boil over moderate heat and cover the pan.

2. In another pan cover the olives with hot water, bring to a boil and drain to remove excess salt. Do this 2 times quickly, then add the olives to the chicken. Cook for 20 minutes, or until the chicken is tender.

Serve with plain white rice and bread. Serves 6.

❋ SHTITHA DJEDJ ❋

Chicken in Red Sauce

a 2-pound chicken, cut into quarters, or equal amount chicken parts
6 medium cloves garlic, chopped fine
1/2 teaspoon salt
1 teaspoon sweet paprika

1/4 teaspoon black pepper
1/2 teaspoon ground cinnamon
2 teaspoons tomato paste
1/4 cup dried chick-peas, soaked overnight in water and drained
2 tablespoons vegetable oil

Put everything in a pan, bring to a boil and cook, covered, over low heat for 45 minutes, which will tenderize the chicken and chick-peas and reduce the liquid to a thick red sauce. Should the liquid evaporate too quickly, add another 1/4 cup water and continue cooking until ready.

Serve warm with bread and salads. Serves 4 to 6 with other dishes.

❈ L'KEBAB ❈

FRENCH FRIES IN WHITE SAUCE

L'Kebab is also known as Algerian kebab, but the resemblance ends there. Perhaps it is the poor man's kebab, but without the barbecue, which is the principal characteristic of a real kebab. What it does have is considerable flavor and substance, prepared in an unconventional fashion.

2 tablespoons plus 1/2 cup vegetable oil
1 medium onion, chopped (1/2 cup)
1 pound chicken parts, loose skin and fat discarded
10 sprigs flat-leaf parsley, leaves only, chopped
1/4 cup dried chick-peas, soaked overnight in water and drained

1 teaspoon black pepper
1 teaspoon salt
1/2 teaspoon ground cinnamon
3 cups water
2 pounds potato, peeled and cut for French fries
1 egg, beaten
lemon wedges for serving

1. Mix together in a pan the 2 tablespoons oil, onion, chicken, 5 sprigs chopped parsley, chick-peas, pepper, salt and cinnamon and fry the mixture, covered, over low heat for 10 minutes. Add the water and bring to a boil. Cook over moderate heat for 40 minutes. This is the white sauce.

2. Heat the 1/2 cup oil in a large skillet, add the potatoes very lightly sprinkled with salt and brown over moderate heat about 10 minutes. Remove and set aside.

3. Add the French fries to the chicken and white sauce. Add the egg,

mix and simmer over low heat for 10 minutes. Garnish with the remaining 5 sprigs of chopped parsley leaves.

Serve warm with the lemon wedges. Serves 6.

❈ DJEDJ MEHSHI ❈

STUFFED CHICKEN

The English title of the recipe is very simple, but the seasoning and stuffing may convert you to this utterly delicious roast.

FOR THE STUFFING

2 tablespoons butter
1 small onion, chopped (1/2 cup)
1/2 teaspoon salt
1/4 teaspoon black pepper
2 fresh chicken livers, cut into
*   1/4-inch cubes*

2 gizzards, meaty lobes only, cut
*   into 1/4-inch cubes*
1 cup cooked rice
2 tablespoons chopped flat-leaf
*   parsley*

FOR THE CHICKEN

a 4-pound chicken, cleaned
2 cloves garlic, halved lengthwise
2 cloves garlic, crushed in a garlic
*   press*
1 teaspoon sweet paprika

1/4 teaspoon black pepper
1/2 teaspoon salt
2 bay leaves
1/2 cup water

1. *Prepare the Stuffing:* Melt the butter in a skillet. Add the onion and stir-fry over moderate heat for 2 minutes. Add the salt, pepper, livers and gizzard and stir-fry until the innards change color. Remove the mixture and add it to the rice. Add the parsley and mix together. Set aside.

2. *Prepare the Chicken:* Cut 4 small incisions in the breast and legs of the chicken. Push in the 4 garlic halves.

3. Rub the chicken all over with the crushed garlic, paprika, pepper

and salt. Stuff the chicken with the prepared stuffing. It is not necessary to sew up the cavity. Place the bay leaves on the breasts.

4. Put the chicken and water into an oiled roasting pan and bake, uncovered, in a 350 degree oven for 1 1/2 hours.

Serve the chicken and stuffing warm. Serves 6 to 8 with salads, bread and vegetable side dishes.

❖ DJEDJ MECHOUI ❖

MARINATED ROAST CHICKEN

Delicately flavored, crisp and fat free, this chicken is most often served with Herira (see pages 109 and 110), Covered Eggs (see page 130) and French fries. Unmistakably Algerian homecooking at its best.

1 teaspoon saffron stamens or 1 teaspoon turmeric
1/4 teaspoon black pepper
1 teaspoon salt
1 small onion, chopped fine (1/3 cup)
6 sprigs flat-leaf parsley, chopped

2 cloves garlic, crushed in a garlic press
juice of 1 lemon
a whole 3-pound chicken, loose skin and fat discarded
1 tablespoon butter

1. Mix together the saffron or turmeric, pepper, salt, onion, parsley, garlic and lemon juice. Rub this into the chicken, both inside and out. Refrigerate overnight to absorb the seasonings.

2. Rub a roasting pan with half of the butter. Add the chicken and dot with the balance of the butter.

3. Roast in a 325 degree oven for 1 1/2 hours. Let stand for 15 minutes. Carve into serving pieces.

Serves 6 with other dishes.

❈ LEMHAWET ❈

CHICKEN IN WHITE SAUCE

The food of the city of Algiers is almost always presented for family style eating or entertaining in a white sauce. That is to say that it does not include tomato and paprika, which would then convert it to a red sauce. Red sauce is for other occasions and times.

2 tablespoons plus 1/4 cup
   vegetable oil
1 medium onion, chopped (1/2 cup)
3 pounds chicken parts or a whole
   chicken, cut into serving pieces,
   loose skin and fat discarded
1/4 cup dried chick-peas, soaked
   overnight in water and drained

1 teaspoon salt
1/2 teaspoon black pepper
1/4 teaspoon ground cinnamon
6 sprigs flat-leaf parsley, leaves
   only, chopped
3 cups water
1 egg, beaten
1 tablespoon flour

1. Mix together in a pan the 2 tablespoons oil, onion, chicken, chick-peas, salt, pepper, cinnamon and parsley and fry over low heat for 10 minutes. Add the water, bring to a boil and cook over moderate heat for 1/2 hour. This is the white sauce. Remove the chicken and set aside.

2. Beat the egg and flour together. Roll the chicken in the batter.

3. Beat the 1/4 cup oil in a skillet and brown the chicken over moderate heat for about 10 minutes. Remove the chicken and return it to the white sauce. Simmer for 10 minutes.

Serve warm. Serves 6.

❈ MAKOUD BIL DJEDJ ❈

CHICKEN-STUFFED POTATO PATTIES

Spiced mashed potatoes, finely chopped chicken formed in the shape of a log, then sliced, floured and deep fried—a very curious and unlikely method for assembling these patties but not surprising when you discover Algerian cuisine.

For the Log

2 pounds potato, peeled and quartered	1/4 teaspoon salt
2 eggs, beaten, with a pinch of salt	1/4 teaspoon turmeric
1 medium onion, chopped fine (2/3 cup)	1/8 teaspoon ground cinnamon
2 cloves garlic, crushed in a garlic press	6 sprigs flat-leaf parsley, chopped fine

For the Chicken

1/2 pound breast of cooked chicken, finely chopped	1/2 cup flour for dusting
1/8 teaspoon ground cinnamon	corn oil for deep-frying
1/8 teaspoon black pepper	

1. *Prepare the Log:* Cook the potatoes in lightly salted water until soft but not overdone. Drain well and mash, keeping some texture. Add the eggs, onion, garlic, salt, turmeric, cinnamon and parsley. Mix well.

2. *Prepare the Chicken:* Mix all the ingredients together and set aside.

3. *To Stuff the Patties:* Spread several tablespoons of flour on a cutting board. Put the mashed potatoes on the board and flatten them into a log 3 inches wide, 2 inches deep and about 12 inches long. Using your fingers, make a trench about 1 inch deep down the length of the log; this will contain all the chicken stuffing. Put the stuffing in the indentation and with well-floured fingers pinch the mashed potato edges together, enclosing it and making certain that the log is sealed with the flour.

4. Cut the log crosswise into 1 1/2-inch-wide rectangles. Dust the pieces in the flour.

5. Heat 1 cup oil for deep-frying in a skillet. Over moderate heat brown the patties, a few at a time, on all sides. Drain on paper towels.

6. Serve as an appetizer with drinks or as a side dish with other foods.

Serve warm. Makes 8 stuffed patties.

FISH

❖ SHTITHA SEPIA ❖

RED SQUID STEW

In Algeria squid and octopus are popular, available and cheap. Here and in the variation that follows are both of these cephalopods in a rich red sauce.

2 tablespoons vegetable oil
1 small onion, chopped (1/3 cup)
6 cloves garlic, chopped
2 pounds squid (medium size, 6 in
    1 pound), cleaned and cut into
    1-inch pieces, including tentacles
1 large bay leaf
1/2 teaspoon dried thyme or 1
    teaspoon fresh chopped

1 teaspoon salt, or to taste
1/4 teaspoon black pepper
1 teaspoon sweet paprika
4 large ripe red tomatoes
    (2 pounds), blanched in boiling
    water, peeled, seeds squeezed out
    and chopped; or two 8-ounce
    cans tomato sauce
1/2 cup water

1. Heat the oil in a pan, add the onion and garlic and stir-fry over moderate heat for 1 minute. Add the squid pieces, bay leaf, thyme, salt, pepper and paprika and continue to stir-fry for 2 minutes more.

2. Add the tomato or the sauce and water. Simmer the mixture, covered, over low heat for 45 minutes.

    Serve warm with plain white rice or, as some Algerians prefer, 1 pound cooked elbow macaroni.

Serves 6 to 8 with other dishes.

VARIATION

    Use 2 pounds octopus. Boil the tentacles over high heat for 10 minutes. Drain and pull off the skin. Cut the meat into 1/2-inch-wide slices.

Prepare the same sauce as in steps 1 and 2 for squid, except increase the water to 1 cup or a bit more. Add the octopus slices, cover the pan and simmer over low heat for 1 1/2 hours. Octopus is very firm-fleshed and requires much more time to soften than does squid. When ready there should be substantial thick sauce; be prepared to add water during the long simmering time.

❀ KELB L'BHAR ❀

SEASONED BABY SHARK STEAK WITH TOMATO SAUCE

Algerians refer to the edible baby shark as dog of the ocean, a derogatory name for a most edible fish and one that in recent years has achieved popularity. This simple preparation involves seasoning the shark, pan-frying it, then serving it with a traditional tomato sauce.

FOR THE SHARK

1 pound baby shark steaks, 1/2 inch thick, sliced horizontally with the bone
2 cloves garlic, crushed in a garlic press

1/2 teaspoon salt
1/4 teaspoon black pepper

FOR THE SAUCE

1 tablespoon vegetable oil
2 cloves garlic, chopped fine
1/4 cup water
2 ripe medium tomatoes, chopped (1 1/2 cups)

1 teaspoon sweet paprika
1/2 teaspoon salt
1/4 teaspoon black pepper
1/4 cup flour
3 tablespoons vegetable oil

1. *Prepare the Shark:* Rub the shark steaks with the garlic, salt and pepper and let stand for 15 minutes or longer.

2. *Prepare the Sauce:* Put the oil, garlic and water in a pan and simmer over low heat for 5 minutes. Add the tomatoes, paprika, salt and pepper and simmer for 20 minutes to thicken.

3. Dredge the shark in the flour. Heat the oil in a skillet until hot and brown it over moderate heat for about 5 minutes on both sides.

4. Serve warm with the sauce spooned over the individual slices.

Serves 4 with other dishes.

❋ DOLMA SARDINE ❋

SARDINE BALLS IN RED SAUCE

Sardines are cooked more ways in Algeria than I have encountered anywhere else. They come in cans, too, but this method of preparing them is far more interesting.

FOR THE SARDINES

1 pound small fresh sardines	*1/8 teaspoon hot red chili flakes*
2 cloves garlic, chopped fine	*1 teaspoon sweet paprika*
1/2 teaspoon salt	*1 large egg white*
1/8 teaspoon black pepper	*1 tablespoon flour*
1/2 teaspoon ground cumin	

FOR THE SAUCE

2 tablespoons vegetable oil	*1/8 teaspoon black pepper*
4 cloves garlic, crushed in a mortar	*2 tablespoons tomato paste*
1 cup plus 2 tablespoons water	*1/4 teaspoon salt*
1 teaspoon sweet paprika	*1/2 teaspoon ground cumin*

1. *Prepare the Sardines:* Cut off the sardine heads, open the stomachs, pull out the soft spines and bones in the stomach and remove any pieces of loose skin as well. Pulverize the flesh coarsely in a processor. (My Algerian teacher squeezed the flesh to a pulp with her hand.)

2. Mix the mashed sardines with all the remaining ingredients. Form fish balls, each 1 1/2 inches in diameter. Makes about 12 balls.

3. *Prepare the Sauce:* Put the oil, garlic and the 2 tablespoons water in a pan and simmer over low heat for 2 minutes. Add all the remaining

sauce ingredients, including the 1 cup water, and simmer over low heat for 10 minutes.

4. Add the fish balls carefully to the sauce, cover the pan and cook for 15 minutes. After 5 minutes of cooking stir once or twice; stirring any earlier may tear apart the fish balls.

Serve warm with bread. Serves 6 with other dishes.

❈ DOLMA BIL SARDINE ❈

SARDINE PATTIES

Sardines in Algeria are plentiful and inexpensive. Since these patties freeze well, they can be prepared in large quantities for festive occasions. They make convenient and tasty morsels with drinks and side dishes with everyday meals, too.

2 pounds fresh sardines, heads and tails removed and cleaned
4 cloves garlic, crushed in a garlic press
4 sprigs flat-leaf parsley, chopped fine
1/4 cup finely chopped onion
1/4 teaspoon salt
1/4 teaspoon white pepper
1/2 teaspoon ground cumin
1/4 cup flour
1/4 cup corn oil for pan-frying

1. Fillet the sardines and remove the flesh. Pull out any visible small bones. Cut the flesh into small pieces. Use the easy traditional method: Mash the pieces with your hand for 2 or 3 minutes. (The flesh is soft and this is easily done.) This is not a smooth purée but a mixture with some texture. Add the garlic, parsley, onion, salt, pepper and cumin and mix well.

2. Form fish balls, each 2 inches in diameter, and flatten each into a pattie 1/2 inch thick. Roll the balls in the flour and shake off the excess.

3. Heat the oil in a skillet and brown the patties over moderate heat on both sides for about 3 minutes. Drain briefly on paper towels.

Serve warm. Makes 15 patties.

SARDINE BEDERSA

Spiced Sardines

7 or 8 large fresh sardines (about 1 pound)
5 cloves garlic, crushedin a garlic press
1 teaspoon hot red chili flakes, more or less to taste
1/2 teaspoon ground cumin
1/2 teaspoon salt
2 tablespoons water
1/2 cup flour
1/4 cup vegetable oil

1. Cut off the sardine heads, open the stomachs and clean them out. Rinse well in cold water. Drain and dry on paper towels.
2. Grind together smoothly in a mortar and pestle or processor the garlic, chili flakes, cumin and salt. Mix in the water to create a paste.
3. Put the sardines in a large bowl with the spice paste. Mix everything together, making certain that some of the seasoning is enclosed in the stomachs.
4. Roll the sardines in the flour. Heat the oil in a skillet until hot and brown the sardines over moderate heat about 2 minutes on each side. Drain briefly on paper towels.

Serves 4 with salads and bread.

SARDINE MEHSHI

Stuffed Sardines

This ingenious preparation for fresh sardines from the Mediterranean converts the small fish into a sandwich, which can be served warm or at room temperature, without a loss of flavor.

2 pound fresh sardines (each about 5 inches in size)

For the Stuffing

1 medium onion, chopped
   (1/2 cup)
2 sprigs flat-leaf parsley, chopped
1/2 teaspoon salt

1/2 teaspoon black pepper
1 egg, beaten
1 cup flour
1/4 cup vegetable oil

1. Cut off the sardine heads, cut open the stomachs and clean them out. Rinse well in cold water and dry on paper towels. Pull out the soft spine of each fish with your fingers, starting from the head to the tail, which should be left intact. Press the clean sardines flat.

2. *Prepare the Stuffing:* Mix the onion, parsley, salt, pepper and egg together. Put 1 heaping tablespoon of the stuffing on the stomach side of a sardine and cover it with another flattened sardine. Coat the sandwich liberally in flour and set aside. Repeat for all the sardines.

3. Heat the oil in a skillet until hot and brown the sandwich over moderate heat on both sides for about 4 minutes. Drain briefly on paper towels. Makes 16 sardine sandwiches.

Serve warm with French fries and salad. Serves 6.

SALADS, VEGETABLE DISHES AND CONDIMENTS

❖

❖ SLATA KARNOON (OR EL GURNE) ❖

FRESH ARTICHOKE SALAD

Most artichoke recipes are prepared with the cooked hearts of the plant, which are really the base of the flower head. Here, though, the choke is trimmed and the thistle-like threads removed, then the heart is rinsed in lemon juice and cut into 1/2-inch pieces. The texture of the uncooked heart is both smooth and crunchy; the dressing pulls it all together.

1 tablespoon white vinegar
1/4 teaspoon black pepper
1/4 teaspoon salt
2 tablespoons olive oil
2 artichokes, trimmed, cleaned and the hearts cut into 1/2-inch pieces

1 small onion, coarsely cut (1/3 cup)
1 semi-hot green chili pepper, seeded and sliced 1/4 inch thick

Mix together vigorously the vinegar, pepper, salt and oil and pour it over the artichokes, onion and chili pepper. Toss well to combine.

Serve at room temperature with other Algerian dishes. Serves 4.

❊ BARBA ❊

BEET SALAD

This is a nationally appreciated salad that is colorful and full of flavor. Its taste intensifies when it is prepared one day in advance and served cold the following day. Or double the recipe, with the intention of serving it again the next day.

1 pound small fresh beets
1/2 teaspoon salt
1/4 teaspoon black pepper
3 tablespoons olive oil
1 tablespoon white vinegar

1 clove garlic, chopped fine
4 sprigs flat-leaf parsley, chopped
10 black olives
2 hard-cooked eggs, sliced

1. Do not peel the beets. Cook them in boiling water to cover until soft, about 45 minutes. Drain, cool and peel. Cut into round slices.

2. Mix the salt, pepper, oil, vinegar and garlic together vigorously. Add the beets and combine. Turn the salad out onto a serving platter. Sprinkle the parsley over all. Place the olives and egg slices around the edge of the salad. Chill until serving time.

Serve cold. Serves 4 to 6.

❊ BETTERAVE SALATA ❊

BEET SALAD WITH LEMON DRESSING

Algerians use a lot of lemon juice, and this salad employs it entirely — to the exclusion of vinegar.

1 pound fresh beets, green tops
* removed, beets halved lengthwise*
* but not peeled*
1/4 cup olive oil

2 tablespoons fresh lemon juice
1/2 teaspoon salt
1/8 teaspoon black pepper
1 clove garlic, chopped fine

1. Cook the beets in boiling water to cover until tender, about 40 minutes. Drain, cool, peel and slice.

2. Mix together the oil, lemon juice, salt, pepper and garlic. Add the beets and mix well. Adjust the lemon juice if desired.

Serve at room temperature. Serves 6.

❈ ZAROUDIA BIL CAMOUN ❈
Cumin-Flavored Carrot Salad

3 tablespoons vegetable oil (not olive)
3 cloves garlic, chopped fine
1 tablespoon freshly ground cumin
1/2 teaspoon sweet paprika

1/2 teaspoon salt
1 cup water
1 pound carrot, peeled and cut into 1/2-inch-wide rounds

Mix together in a pan the oil, garlic, cumin, paprika, salt and 2 tablespoons of the water. Add the carrot rounds and the balance of the water. Simmer, covered, over low heat for about 1/2 hour, or until the water evaporates and the carrots soften.

Serve warm as a salad. Serves 4 to 6.

❈ SALATA EL B'SSEL ❈
Leek Salad with Tomato

1 tablespoon white vinegar
2 tablespoons olive oil
1/4 teaspoon salt
1/4 teaspoon white pepper
3 leek, white part only, sliced thin into rounds and the rounds well rinsed in cold water

1 large ripe tomato (1/2 pound), sliced
1 young Kirby cucumber, sliced thin
12 black olives

1. Mix together the vinegar, oil, salt and pepper.

2. Toss the leek, tomato, cucumber and olives together in a bowl. Pour the dressing over all. Refrigerate.

Serve cold. Serves 6.

❈ KARANTIKA ❈
CHICK-PEA PIE SNACK

These snacks are nationally popular in Algeria, but it is the people in western Algeria who claim that their version is the best. In my opinion, if the cook is good the food is good, which is a safe assumption. I must admit I enjoy this pie prepared with chick-pea flour sprinkled with ground cumin and with a few drops of *harissa* to complete the picture. Algerians dote on their *karantika* since it is filling and flavorful at odd hours when a snack is appropriate.

I first discovered chick-pea flour (*besan*) during my years in India. *Besan* is used as a savory in various snack concoctions. How it got to Algeria is a moot question. Even the word *karantika* has an Indo-European sound — musical, not guttural like Arabic. I leave you pondering that thought.

1 pound chick-pea flour	*1/4 teaspoon black pepper*
4 cups water	*1 egg, beaten*
1/2 cup corn oil or peanut oil	*ground cumin for garnish*
1 tablespoon salt	*Harissa (see page 89) for garnish*

1. Combine the flour, water, oil, salt and pepper in a processor until the mixture is smooth. It will be rather thin. Mixing by hand is infinitely more difficult and time-consuming since a smooth combination of ingredients is essential for the texture of the pie.

2. Pour into a Pyrex or a round metal pan, at least 8 inches in diameter, or a rectangular one, 6 inches by 10 inches or thereabouts. It is not necessary to oil the pan.

3. Pour the beaten egg over all and bake in a 400 degree oven for 1/2 hour. Reduce the heat to 300 degrees and bake for 1 hour more, or until the top of the pie becomes golden brown.

4. Serve hot as a snack, sprinkled with the cumin and *harissa* according to personal preference.

Serves 6 to 8 when cut into generous pieces.

❈ MECHOUI SALATA ❈

GRILLED GREEN PEPPER SALAD

This will taste better the day after it is made.

3 large sweet green peppers
1 tablespoon olive oil
1 small onion, chopped fine
   (1/3 cup)
2 cloves garlic, chopped fine
1/4 teaspoon salt

1/4 teaspoon black pepper
1/2 teaspoon Harissa (see page
   89), or to taste
1 medium ripe tomato, blanched in
   hot water, peeled and chopped
   (1/2 cup)

1. Char the whole peppers over charcoal or in a gas oven broiler until quite black. Cool well, peel off the skins and cut open. Remove and discard the stems and seeds. Cut into 1-inch cubes.

2. Heat the oil in a skillet, add the onion, garlic, green pepper cubes, salt, pepper and *harissa* and stir-fry over moderate heat for 5 minutes. Turn out into a serving bowl and mix in the tomato.

Cool well, then serve. Serves 4 to 6.

❈ SALATA FELFEL ❈

ROASTED GREEN PEPPER SALAD

Algerians and others in the Maghreb prefer to char peppers (and eggplant) over charcoal to cook them. This imparts a smoked flavor, adding another dimension to the taste of this salad.

6 medium sweet green peppers	1/2 teaspoon salt, or to taste
1 ripe tomato, diced (1 cup)	1 tablespoon white vinegar
2 tablespoons chopped onion	3 tablespoons vegetable oil
1 clove garlic, chopped fine	

1. Char the whole peppers over charcoal or in a gas oven broiler until well blackened. Cool, peel off the skins and run the peppers under cold water to remove the fragments. Cut them open and remove and discard the stems and seeds. Cut the pulp into long thin strips.

2. Mix together the peppers, tomato, onion, garlic, salt, vinegar and oil. Toss well. Adjust the salt and vinegar if you wish a more intense flavor.

Serve cool or at room temperature. Serves 6 with other dishes.

❋ SALATA BADENDJEL ❋

GRILLED EGGPLANT SALAD

A number of cultures prepare this type of salad, wherein eggplant is grilled over charcoal until soft, which imparts a smoky flavor that is paramount in the seasoning of the salad. I have eaten a similar traditional salad in Calcutta and Istanbul.

1 pound eggplant	1/2 teaspoon ground caraway
1/2 teaspoon salt	1 tablespoon white or cider vinegar
1/8 teaspoon black pepper	1/4 cup olive oil
1 teaspoon Dijon mustard	1 medium ripe tomato, sliced

1. Grill the eggplant over charcoal or in a gas or electric oven broiler until soft, about 10 minutes, turning the eggplant over several times so that it cooks uniformly.

2. Peel off the charred skin and rinse the pulp briefly in cold water. Dry on paper towels. Cut the pulp into long strips.

3. Whisk the salt, pepper, mustard, caraway, vinegar and oil together until frothy. Arrange the eggplant strips on a serving platter and surround with the tomato slices. Pour the dressing over.

Serve at room temperature. Serves 4 with other foods.

❈ SALADA MEKHALTA ❈

MIXED VEGETABLE SALAD

The dressing in this salad has a touch of France, understandable in that Algeria was a French colony for some years.

FOR THE SALAD

*4 medium potatoes (1 pound),
    cooked in their skins and peeled
2 fresh beets (1/2 pound), cooked
    in their skin and peeled
lettuce leaves
2 medium carrots, grated raw (1
    cup)*

*1 small onion, sliced into thin rounds
10 green or black olives
2 hard-cooked eggs, sliced
2 teaspoons chopped flat-leaf parsley
1 ripe medium tomato, sliced
1 clove garlic, crushed in a garlic
    press*

FOR THE DRESSING

*1 raw egg yolk
1 teaspoon Dijon mustard
2 tablespoons white or red wine
    vinegar
2/3 cup vegetable oil*

*1/4 teaspoon salt
1/8 teaspoon white pepper
1 clove garlic, crushed in a garlic
    press*

1. *Prepare the Vegetables:* Slice the potatoes and beets into rounds. Arrange the salad ingredients on a large oval platter as follows: Cover the platter with the lettuce leaves. Place the grated carrot in a heap in the center of the platter. Arrange in a circle around that the potatoes, then the beets. Scatter the onion and olives over all. Arrange the egg slices in an orderly pattern over all. Sprinkle the parsley and garlic over that.

2. *Prepare the Dressing:* Using a whisk or egg beater, mix together the egg yolk and mustard. Add the vinegar, oil, salt, pepper and garlic, beating as the dressing thickens similar to a consistency similar to mayonnaise. Adjust the salt if desired. Serve the dressing separately. Makes about 1 cup.

3. To serve, each person takes as much salad and dressing as wanted.

Serves 6 or 7.

❈ CHLADA BIL KHODRA ❈

Steamed Vegetable Salad

A summer salad that is cool and filled with flavor, steamed not boiled and of infinite health-giving components, is what conventional wisdom now approves of as sensible.

2 potatoes (1/2 pound), peeled and cut into 1/4-inch dice
3 carrots (1/2 pound), cut into 1/4-inch dice
1/2 cup fresh or frozen green peas
1/2 pound cauliflower, cut into 1-inch florets
1 cup fresh or frozen lima beans

2 tablespoons white vinegar
1/2 teaspoon sugar
1/4 teaspoon salt
1/4 teaspoon white pepper
2 tablespoons corn oil
1 small onion, chopped (1/3 cup)
6 sprigs flat-leaf parsley, chopped
1 hard-cooked egg, chopped

1. In a *couscousier* steam the potato, carrot, peas, cauliflower and lima beans over moderate heat for about 1 hour, or until the vegetables are soft but still firm. Drain and cool well. Put them into a serving bowl.

2. Mix together the vinegar, sugar, salt, pepper and oil. Mix the parsley and onion together and garnish the salad with the mixture. Pour the dressing over the vegetables, then sprinkle the chopped egg over all.

Serve cool. Serves 6.

❈ SALATA ROZ ❈

Desert Rice Salad

Serve this on hot summer days, or anytime, but use a long-grain American rice here. The sticky rice of Asia or Basmati rice of India is not appropriate.

1 cup rice, well soaked in water to
   cover for 30 minutes
4 cups water
1 sweet green pepper
1 sweet red pepper
1 clove garlic, chopped fine
3 tablespoons chopped onion
1/2 teaspoon salt, or to taste
1 medium ripe tomato, diced

2 tablespoons chopped flat-leaf
   parsley
12 green olives, with or without
   pits
2 ounces beef salami, diced into
   1/4-inch pieces
2 tablespoons white vinegar
2 tablespoons olive oil
1 hard-cooked egg, quartered

1. Drain the rice. Bring a pot of water to a boil, add the rice and bring
   back to the boil. Cook over low heat for 7 to 9 minutes, testing for
   doneness. Do not overcook. Drain under cold water. Drain again for
   several minutes.

2. Char the whole green and red peppers over charcoal or in a gas oven
   broiler until well blackened. Cool, peel off the skins and run the peppers under cold water to remove the remaining bit of skin. Remove
   and discard the stems and seeds. Cut into 1/2-inch cubes.

3. Mix together the rice and all the remaining ingredients, reserving the
   hard-cooked egg as a garnish for the serving platter. Adjust the salt
   and vinegar if necessary.

Serve at room temperature or cold. Serves 6.

❈ LEHEMISS ❈

SAUTÉED SALAD OF SWEET PEPPERS AND TOMATOES

Summer food in Algeria is designed not to take up a lot of hot stove
time. This salad is simple to prepare and easy to eat. In earlier times the
chopping for it was often done in a wood bowl with a hand chopper;
now, of course, there are food processors in the kitchen.

4 large sweet green peppers
   (2 pounds)
4–5 Italian plum tomatoes
   (1 pound)
2 tablespoons olive oil

1–2 teaspoons fresh chopped hot
   green chili pepper
1/2 teaspoon salt
1 egg, beaten

1. Char the sweet peppers and tomatoes over charcoal or in gas oven broiler. Peel off and discard the skins. Remove the stem and seeds from the peppers and core and seed the tomatoes. Chop the pulp into pieces, each 1/4 inch in size.

2. Stir-fry the pieces in a skillet over low heat for 2 or 3 minutes to evaporate the liquid. Add the oil, chili and salt and stir-fry for 2 minutes. Add the egg and stir it into the salad until it is well mixed in and cooked.

Serve warm with French fries, other salads and Shorba. Serves 6.

❖ ZRODIYA MESHERMELA ❖

CARROT SIDE DISH

This could be served as a warm salad or a side dish with an Algerian meal. What it really is, however, is summer food, when the heat from the Sahara envelops greater Algeria.

1 pound carrots, sliced into rounds 1/8 inch thick
4 cloves garlic, chopped fine
1/2 teaspoon salt
1/2 teaspoon black pepper
1/2 teaspoon sweet paprika
1/4 teaspoon ground caraway
1 cup water
1 tablespoon white vinegar

Put everything except the vinegar in a pan. Bring to a boil, then simmer over low heat for 1/2 hour to integrate the seasonings. Remove the pan from the heat and stir in the vinegar.

Serve warm with bread and other dishes, including meat and salads. Serves 6.

❖ ZROUDIYA M'HAMDA ❖

LEMON-CARROT SALAD

This is not a real salad, as it starts out marinated in lemon juice and is then cooked. More accurately a table condiment, it can be served with any kind of Maghreb food. Unusual, flavorful and with vivid seasoning, it will grace any table.

1 pound carrots, peeled and cubed
1/2 teaspoon salt
juice of 2 lemons
2 tablespoons olive oil
1 whole leek, green and white parts, trimmed, sliced and well rinsed

4 cloves garlic, crushed in a garlic press
1/2 teaspoon white pepper
1/2 teaspoon ground cumin
1 fresh semi-hot green chili pepper, seeded and sliced (optional)

1. Cook the carrots in water with the salt until soft but still with a firm crunch as they will subsequently be stir-fried. Drain and mix in the lemon juice. Cover and refrigerate overnight.

2. The next day, heat the oil in a skillet and add the lemon-flavored carrots (the lemon juice will have been absorbed), leek, garlic, pepper, cumin and hot chili, if used. Stir-fry for 10 minutes over low heat. Cool and refrigerate.

Serve cold. Serves 6 to 8.

NOTE: The semi-hot green chili is also known as "elephant's trunk" as it is twisted and long. Found in many Asian and Middle East food markets, it may be an optional choice here, but it is most consistently included in Algeria. One should be prepared for the heat variability of fresh chilies; a taste in advance is advisable.

❁ ADGIDGET CHOU-FLEUR ❁

CAULIFLOWER FRITTERS

This is summer fare. The fritters should be crisp on the outside and soft within.

1 head cauliflower (about 2 pounds), cut into florets
1 small onion, chopped (1/3 cup)
8 sprigs flat-leaf parsley, leaves only, chopped
1/2 teaspoon salt

1/4 teaspoon black pepper
1 egg, beaten
1/4 cup flour
1/2 cup vegetable oil
lemon wedges for serving

1. Cook the cauliflower florets in lightly salted boiling water over moderate heat for about 10 minutes, until cooked but still firm. Cool and mash.

2. Mix the mashed cauliflower, onion, parsley, salt, pepper, egg and flour together into a semi-smooth but dense batter.

3. Heat the oil in a skillet. Drop heaping tablespoons of batter in a skillet, flatten them and cook over moderate heat for about 3 to 4 minutes until crisp brown. Drain briefly on paper towels. Makes 14 fritters.

Serve warm with lemon wedges. Serves 6 with other dishes.

❈ BADENDJEL MELOUI ❈

STUFFED EGGPLANT ROLLS

Aside from being an inventive dish, nicely spiced, this *badendjel* is completely vegetarian for those who are committed to that point of view.

2 large eggplants (2 pounds), ends trimmed, but not peeled
1 heaping teaspoon salt
corn oil for pan-frying
2 large potatoes (1/2 pound), peeled and quartered
5 sprigs flat-leaf parsley, chopped fine
4 cloves garlic, crushed in a garlic press

1 small onion, chopped fine (1/2 cup)
1/2 teaspoon salt
1/4 teaspoon white pepper
1/4 teaspoon ground cinnamon
1/4 teaspoon turmeric
1/2 cup tomato purée, fresh or canned
1/4 teaspoon ground caraway

1. Slice the eggplants lengthwise, into about 5 or 6 slices each. Sprinkle the slices with the salt and let stand 30 minutes to make them flexible. Rinse in cold water and press the liquid out firmly in a kitchen towel. Set aside.

2. Heat 3 tablespoons of oil in a large skillet and fry the slices on both sides over moderate heat for 2 minutes. Drain on paper towels and lightly press out the oil. Set aside.

3. Boil the potatoes until soft. Drain well and mash. Add the parsley, garlic, onion, salt, pepper, cinnamon and turmeric. Mix well and set the stuffing aside.

4. In a pan mix the tomato purée, caraway and a few sprinkles of salt and pepper and simmer over low heat for 10 minutes. Set aside.

5. *Prepare the Rolls:* Take 1 heaping tablespoon of the stuffing and press it into a cigar-shaped cylinder. Place it on one end of a slice of eggplant and roll the slice up. Put it into an unoiled baking dish. Repeat with all the rolls and stuffing. Pour the tomato sauce over all and bake in a 350 degree oven for 15 minutes.

Serve warm. Serves 4 or 5 with other Algerian dishes.

VARIATION

The French have left their mark on the cuisine of Algeria and here is one instance. When the eggplant rolls have been placed in a baking dish, pour over the sauce and sprinkle with 1/2 cup coarsely grated mozzarella cheese. Bake as directed above, until the cheese has melted and formed a light brown crust.

❖ SALATA BIL FOUL BACHAR ❖

STEAMED FAVA BEAN SALAD

This is an interesting and tasty fat-free salad with the pronounced flavor of ground cumin.

1 pound fresh young fava beans, in their pods, sliced thin
1 teaspoon salt
1 tablespoon ground cumin, or more to taste

1. Steam the fava beans in the top of a *couscousier* over hot water over low heat for about 1 hour. Sprinkle the salt over all and taste for tenderness. If still too firm, continue to steam the beans until ready. The older the pods, the tougher they will be.

2. Turn the fava beans out into a serving bowl and toss with the cumin.

Serve warm. Serves 4 as a side dish.

BSBAS MUKULI

Slow-Cooked Fennel Slices

The light but unmistakable anise flavor of the fennel bulb and its feathery green leaves are addictive. Since fennel is a seasonal vegetable, one must buy it when available, striking while the iron is hot, so to speak. It is a welcome stranger in my kitchen.

4 tablespoons butter
2 fennel bulbs, sliced
1 medium onion, sliced thin (1/2 cup)
1/2 teaspoon salt
1/4 teaspoon black pepper

Melt the butter in a skillet over low heat. Add the fennel, onion, salt and pepper and cover the pan. Cook slowly for 1/2 hour, or until the fennel is meltingly soft.

Serve warm as a side dish with other foods. Serves 4.

JELBEN BIL BEYD

Green Pea Omelet

This very good omelet is served as a side dish with other foods during the summer. Thick with green peas, it is sometimes referred to as a kind of pie as it can be sliced.

1 tablespoon butter
1 pound sweet green peas, fresh or frozen, cooked lightly and drained
1 small onion, chopped fine (1/3 cup)
1/2 teaspoon salt
1/4 teaspoon black pepper
4 eggs, beaten

1. Heat the butter in an 8-inch skillet. Add the green peas and onion and stir-fry over low heat for 3 minutes. Add the salt and pepper and mix well.

2. Pour the eggs in a stream over all and cover the skillet with a dinner plate. Cook for 3 minutes. Turn the omelet over into the plate—an easy task—then slide it back into the skillet and cover with the plate. Brown the second side for 2 minutes.

Serve warm. Serves 4 as a side dish.

❈ BERKOUKES ❈

PASTA BULLETS WITH VEGETARIAN OR MEAT SAUCE

Berkoukes are small round balls known as *"plombs"* in French. They are like lead bullets, except that these are pasta grains larger than couscous. A commercial variety calls them "barley-shaped pasta." Algerians often make these by hand, forcing the prepared dough through a screen with holes double that in size of couscous.

There are two kinds of sauce for this dish; one is vegetarian and the other contains lamb or chicken. Either sauce can be prepared, according to personal preference. The pasta cooks in it, resulting in a family-style one-dish meal.

VEGETARIAN SAUCE

8 cups water	*1 medium onion, chopped*
2 tablespoons vegetable oil	*(1/2 cup)*
2 ripe medium tomatoes, chopped	*6 cloves garlic, chopped fine*
1 tablespoon tomato paste	*2 tablespoons chopped coriander*
1 zucchini, cut into 1/2-inch cubes	*2 teaspoons dried mint*
1/4 pound string beans, cut into	*1 teaspoon salt*
1-inch pieces	*1/4 teaspoon black pepper*
1/2 cup green peas	*1 tablespoon sweet paprika*
1 medium potato, cut into 1/2-inch	*1 pound* berkoukes
cubes	

1. *Prepare the Vegetarian Sauce:* Bring the water to a boil in a large pan and add all the remaining ingredients, except the pasta. Cook over moderate heat for 1/2 hour.

2. Rinse the paste in cold water, drain and add to the sauce. Cook for

15 to 20 minutes, depending upon whether you like pasta *al dente* or softer.

Serve warm with bread. Serves 6.

MEAT SAUCE

8 cups water
2 tablespoons vegetable oil
1 pound lamb, cut into 6 pieces, or
* 1 pound chicken parts in 6 pieces*
1/4 cup chick-peas, soaked in
* water overnight and drained*
1 cup green peas
2 ripe medium tomatoes, chopped
1 tablespoon tomato paste

1 medium onion, chopped
* (1/2 cup)*
6 cloves garlic, chopped fine
2 tablespoons chopped coriander
2 teaspoons dried mint
1 teaspoon salt
1/4 teaspoon black pepper
1 tablespoon sweet paprika
1 pound berkoukes

1. *Prepare the Meat Sauce:* Bring the water to a boil in a large pan and add all the remaining ingredients, except the pasta. Simmer over moderate heat for 1/2 hour.

2. Rinse the pasta in cold water, drain and add to the sauce. Cook for 15 to 20 minutes, depending upon whether you like pasta *al dente* or softer. The meat will soften during this cooking time.

Serve warm with bread. Serves 6.

NOTE: In a desperate situation, orzo, the Greek rice-shaped pasta, works well.

❈ BATATA GRATIN ❈

POTATO AND CHEESE CASSEROLE

This is a Franco-Algerian dish that has contemporary popularity. Its origin may have been in France, but it has moved into the mainstream in Algerian cities.

2 tablespoons butter
3 eggs, beaten
1 1/4 cups milk
1 teaspoon salt

1/4 teaspoon white pepper
2 pounds potato, peeled and sliced
2 ounces grated Gruyère cheese

1. Butter a 2-quart casserole. Beat the eggs, milk, salt and pepper together.

2. Put 1/3 of the potato slices on the bottom of the baking dish. Pour 1/3 of the milk/egg mixture over them. Sprinkle 1/3 of the cheese over that. Add another layer of potatoes, add 1/3 egg mixture and 1/3 of the cheese. The top layer will be the balance of the potato, the egg mixture and cheese.

3. Shake the casserole lightly to distribute the sauce among the potatoes. Bake in a 350 degree oven for 1 hour.

Serve warm. Serves 6 to 8 with other dishes.

NOTE: Conservative Algerians rinse uncooked eggs in their shells with water as a ritualistic gesture, just as meat is *halal,* or religiously clean.

❈ BATA BIL BEYD ❈

POTATO AND EGG PIE

A vegetarian recipe is effective when you do not even notice the absence of meat or poultry. Is this an omelet or a pan-fried pie? It fills the description for both, no matter what you call it. This is a popular summer dish in Algeria.

1 pound potato, peeled and cut into
    1/2-inch cubes
oil for deep-frying
2 teaspoons butter
2 eggs, beaten
4 sprigs flat-leaf parsley, chopped

1 small onion, chopped fine (1/2
    cup)
1/2 teaspoon salt
1/4 teaspoon black pepper
1/8 teaspoon turmeric

1. Heat the oil in a skillet and fry the potatoes until light brown and soft. Drain briefly on paper towels.

2. Butter an 8-inch skillet. Add the potatoes to cover the bottom of the skillet. Beat the eggs, parsley, onion, salt and pepper together. Pour the egg mixture over the potatoes and fry over moderate heat for 4 minutes to brown the bottom of the pie. Cover the skillet with a dinner plate during this time.

3. Turn the pie over into the plate, then slide the pie back into the skillet to brown the other side. Cover with the plate. Cook for 4 minutes.

4. To serve, turn the pie out into a serving platter and slice in wedges.

Serves 4 with bread as a side dish.

❖ BATATA BIL LOUBIA ❖

POTATO AND STRING BEANS

A lot of potatoes are eaten in western Algeria for reasons that have to do with their availability, price and the people's personal preference. Here two vegetables compatible to Algerian taste combine in a simple manner. Serve as a side dish with other foods.

1 pound string beans, ends trimmed and cut into 3 pieces each	*4 teaspoons olive oil*
	6 cloves garlic, chopped fine
1 pound small potato, peeled and quartered	*1 teaspoon salt, or to taste*
	1/4 teaspoon black pepper

1. Steam the beans in the top of a *couscousière* until tender but still crisp, about 15 minutes. At the same time in the bottom of the steamer cook the potatoes until tender but firm. Drain both vegetables.

2. Heat 2 tablespoons oil in a skillet, add the garlic, beans, salt and pepper and stir-fry over low heat for 10 minutes. The beans will turn a dark green.

3. Separately, brown the potatoes in the remaining 2 teaspoons oil over

low heat for 15 minutes. Add to the beans in the skillet and fry for 5 minutes more.

Serve warm as a side dish. Serves 4 to 6.

VARIATION

Some Algerians prefer less frying and oil in this. If you do, prepare the beans as noted above but transfer them to a baking dish. Add the cooked drained potatoes to the beans. Bake in a 350 degree oven for 15 minutes. This is known as Batata Bil Koucha.

❊ MAKOUD ❊

MASHED POTATO PATTIES

These delicious little patties can be made in any quantity with ingredients that do not challenge the home cook. Serve as a side dish with meat or poultry. They make an ideal appetizer with drinks as well.

2 pounds potato, peeled
2 eggs, beaten
1 medium onion, chopped fine
*   (1 cup)*
2 cloves garlic, crushed in a garlic
*   press*
1/2 teaspoon salt

1/4 teaspoon ground turmeric
1/8 teaspoon ground cinnamon
6 sprigs flat-leaf parsley, chopped
*   fine*
1 tablespoon flour (optional)
corn oil for pan-frying

1. Cut the potatoes into quarters and cook in lightly salted boiling water until soft but still with a touch of firmness. Drain and mash but not a smooth purée; leave some texture. Add the eggs, onion, garlic, salt, turmeric, cinnamon and parsley. Mix well. Should the mixture seem too thin, add the flour and mix well.

2. Form small patties, each 2 inches in diameter and 1/2 inch thick.

3. Heat about 1/4 cup oil until hot in a skillet and brown the patties on both sides over moderate heat. Drain on paper towels.

Serve warm. Makes 25 patties.

CHAKCHOUKA BIL SLK

Spinach Sauté

This spinach dish is one of the popular vegetarian side dishes of Algeria.

1 pound fresh spinach, well rinsed in cold water
3 tablespoons olive oil
1 medium onion, chopped (1/2 cup)
4 cloves garlic, crushed in a garlic press
2 large ripe tomatoes (1 pound), peeled and chopped
1/2 teaspoon salt, or to taste
1/4 teaspoon white pepper

1. Pull off and discard the tough stems of the spinach. Put the spinach in a large pan with 1/4 cup water, cover the pan and steam over moderate heat for 3 minutes to reduce the bulk. Drain, cool and press out the liquid quite firmly. Set the spinach aside.
2. Heat the oil in a skillet, add the onion and garlic and stir-fry a minute. Add the tomatoes, salt and pepper. Cover the skillet and cook for 5 minutes. Add the spinach and mix everything together. Cover the pan again and simmer over low heat for 15 minutes more.

Serve warm as a side dish with other foods. Serves 4.

HOUMOUS BIL CAMOUN

Cumin-Flavored Chick-Pea Snack

1 pound dried chick-peas, soaked overnight in water and drained
2 cups water
3 tablespoons vegetable oil
1 small onion, chopped fine (1/2 cup)
4 tablespoons ground cumin
1 teaspoon salt, or to taste

1. Cook the chick-peas in the water for 20 to 25 minutes until soft. Do not overcook into a mush. Drain.

2. Heat the oil in a pan or skillet, add the onion, chick-peas, cumin and salt and stir-fry for 5 minutes.

Serve warm with bread. Serves 4 to 6 as a snack.

VARIATION

Purée the spiced cooked chick-peas. After they have been prepared as in Step 2 above, purée them to a relatively smooth consistency in a food processor.

✦ OMELETTE DE COURGETTES ✦
ZUCCHINI OMELET

This is not an omelet in the classic sense of the word. It would be more accurate to describe it as a zucchini fry. The function of the eggs is to hold the sliced zucchini together in a firm, round flat loaf. In any event, it is Algerian fast food for hot, summer desert days and it should be liberally splashed with lemon juice.

*2 pounds zucchini, trimmed and
   sliced into rounds 1/4 inch thick
1 cup water
1 1/2 teaspoons salt
1/2 teaspoon black pepper
1/2 cup corn oil for deep-frying*

*2 tablespoons butter
1 medium onion, chopped
   (2/3 cup)
2 eggs, beaten
lemon wedges for serving*

1. Soak the zucchini in the 1 cup water and 1 teaspoon of the salt for 15 minutes. Drain and dry the slices. Toss with the remaining 1/2 teaspoon salt and the pepper.

2. Heat the oil in a skillet and deep-fry the zucchini over moderate heat until light brown, about 5 minutes. Drain in a strainer to remove the oil. Set aside.

3. Melt the butter in an 8-inch skillet and stir-fry the onion over moderate heat for 3 minutes. Add the zucchini and mix well in the skillet for 2 minutes. Pour the eggs over all in a stream and continue to cook for

3 minutes more to set the eggs and brown the bottom of the omelet. Turn the omelet over carefully and brown it lightly for 2 minutes.

4. Slip the omelet out onto a serving platter.

Serve warm with bread and the lemon wedges. Serves 4.

❈ KARAA BEL BESEL TAMATIM ❈
ZUCCHINI, ONION AND TOMATO MÉLANGE

This vegetarian combination is a summer dish filled with the natural flavor of summer vegetables.

4 tablespoons vegetable oil
2 medium onions, sliced (1 cup or more)
2 ripe tomatoes, chopped (1 cup)
2 pounds zucchini, slice 1/4 inch thick

1/2 teaspoon salt
1/2 teaspoon black pepper
2 eggs, beaten

1. Heat 2 tablespoons oil in a skillet, add the onion and tomatoes and cook, covered, over low heat 20 minutes, stirring now and then. This reduces the vegetables to a soft mélange.

2. In another skillet heat the remaining 2 tablespoons oil and stir-fry the zucchini over low heat until light brown, about 10 minutes. Add to the onion and tomato mixture with the salt and pepper. Add the eggs, stirring them into the vegetables and cooking for another 3 minutes to set the eggs.

Serve warm. Serves 6 with other dishes.

VARIATION
Here is a non-squash version. Substitute 1 pound of potatoes cut and cooked as French fries in place of the zucchini and mix with the cooked onions and tomatoes. Add seasonings and the eggs as directed.

CHAKCHOUKA DE COURGETTES

ZUCCHINI STEW WITH TOMATO

Purely vegetarian and chili-hot is the way to describe this typical Algerian concoction. A fresh hot red chili provides the dynamite and it can be according to taste, but the traditional method of preparation is with vivid amounts of chili. This is served as a side dish with meat or chicken dishes.

2 tablespoons olive oil
1 large onion, chopped (2 cups)
4 cloves garlic, crushed in a garlic
    press
2 pounds zucchini, cut into
    1/3-inch dice
2 ripe tomatoes (1 pound), peeled
    and chopped

2 tablespoons tomato paste
4 sprigs flat-leaf parsley, chopped
1/2 teaspoon salt
1/4 teaspoon black pepper
1 fresh hot red chili pepper, chopped
1 cup water
lemon wedges for serving

Heat the oil in a large skillet, add the onion and garlic and stir-fry over moderate heat for 3 minutes. Add all the remaining ingredients, except the water and lemon wedges. Cook, covered, over low heat for 15 minutes. Add the water and bring to a boil. Cover the skillet and simmer for 20 minutes.

Serve warm with the lemon wedges; lemon juice will dilute the chili heat if it is too much. Serves 6.

FELFLA M'CHERMLA

GRILLED SWEET AND HOT PEPPER TOMATO CONDIMENT

A condiment should have vivid seasonings and a character that is assertive. Fresh hot chili pepper, red chili powder and black pepper are guaranteed to galvanize the taste buds and encourage an appetite for Algerian cooking.

4 sweet green peppers (1 1/2 pounds)
1 sweet red pepper (1/2 pound)
2 semi-hot fresh green chili peppers
2 tablespoons corn oil
*4 cloves garlic, crushed in a garlic
    press*

1/2 teaspoon salt, or to taste
1/4 teaspoon black pepper
1/4 teaspoon hot red chili powder
*1 pound ripe tomatoes (2), peeled
    and cubed*

1. Char the sweet and hot peppers over charcoal or over the open flame of a gas burner. Peel off as much as you can of the burned skin. Cut the peppers open and remove the stems and seeds. Cut the pulp into 1/2-inch cubes.

2. Put the oil in a large skillet over low heat. Add all the remaining ingredients and the pepper pieces and stir-fry for 20 minutes to integrate the flavors. The condiment will reduce to a thick jam-like consistency.

Serve warm. Serves 6.

❈ ZALOUK ❈

EGGPLANT AND TOMATO CONDIMENT

Sometimes referred to as a salad, this is really a condiment, to be served with other dishes in an Algerian meal. It could also be used effectively as a spread on crackers or bread as an appetizer with drinks.

*1 large eggplant (1 pound), peeled
    and cut into 1/2-inch cubes*
3 tablespoons olive oil
*2 ripe tomatoes (1 pound), peeled
    and chopped*
*3 cloves garlic, crushed in a garlic
    press*

4 sprigs flat-leaf parsley, chopped
1/2 teaspoon salt
*1/4 to 1/2 teaspoon hot chili
    powder, to taste*
1/4 teaspoon black pepper
*1 tablespoon fresh lemon juice, or
    more to taste*

1. Cook the eggplant in 1/2 cup water for a few minutes to soften. Drain and press out the liquid.

2. Warm the oil in a skillet over low heat. Add the tomatoes, garlic, parsley, salt, chili powder and pepper and simmer for 10 minutes. Add the eggplant, mix well and cook 10 minutes more.

Serve warm or at room temperature; many prefer warm. Serves 4.

❋ SHTITHA BATATA ❋

Vegetarian Potato Stew

This is an inexpensive summer food recipe, easy to prepare and filled with traditional seasoning.

2 tablespoons vegetable oil
5 cloves garlic, chopped or grated
2 cups water
1 teaspoon salt
1/4 teaspoon black pepper

1 teaspoon ground cumin
1 tablespoon sweet paprika
1 tablespoon tomato paste
1 pound potato, sliced into rounds
1/4 inch thick

Heat the oil in a pan, add the garlic and 1/4 cup of the water and simmer for 1 minute. Add the salt, pepper, cumin, paprika, tomato paste and the balance of the water. Bring to a boil, add the potatoes and cook over low heat for about 1/2 hour.

The sauce will thicken and the potatoes soften but they will not disintegrate.

Serve warm. Serves 6.

SWEETS

✴ BEGHRIR ✴

Yeast Pancakes with Honey

These wonderfully tasty pancakes are made with fine semolina flour, which adds to the richness of the flavor. The pancakes are a snack, served with mint tea and buttered honey, devoured by hungry diners. Fried on one side over low heat as bubbles pop up on the surface to resemble a honeycomb, the pancake has a light brown firm bottom that contrasts with the soft honey-soaked top.

For the Batter

1 tablespoon soft bakers' (fresh) yeast	*2 pounds fine-ground semolina flour*
4 cups warm water	*1/4 teaspoon salt*

For the Pancakes

corn oil	*2 tablespoons butter*
1/2 cup honey	

1. *Prepare the Batter:* Dissolve the yeast in 1/2 cup warm water and let it proof for 1/2 hour, or until bubbled well.

2. Put the semolina flour in a flat pan or dish and spread the yeast mixture over all. Add the balance of the water (3 1/2 cups) as you rub the semolina grains, as though they were couscous, with the liquid. (This is to remove any lumps in the flour.) Mix well and let it stand in a warm place for about 1 hour, or until doubled in bulk. The batter will be frothy.

3. *Prepare the Pancakes:* Rub an 8-inch nonstick skillet with a few drops of

oil soaked on a cloth. Stir the batter well and pour 1/2 cup of it into the skillet. Cook over low heat; bubbles will form during this slow frying period. Cook until the entire pancake is covered with bubbles. At this stage, the pancake is ready to eat. It is not turned over and part of the attraction is the bubbles on the top and the brown, chewy texture on the bottom. Make 1 pancake at a time. Makes 10 pancakes.

4. Melt the honey and butter together and pour generously over the pancakes.

Serve warm with mint tea. Serves 6.

❋ TCHEREK ❋

ALMOND HORNS

These are reminiscent of the Moroccan pastry, gazelle horns, except that the Algerians have spiced the filling with aromatic cinnamon.

1/2 cup blanched almonds, chopped fine
2 tablespoons sugar
1 tablespoon orange blossom water plus 1/4 cup orange blossom water, to dip (available at Middle Eastern groceries)

1/2 teaspoon ground cinnamon
1/2 recipe Griwech dough (see page 193)
powdered sugar

1. Mix the almonds, sugar, the 1 tablespoon orange blossom water and cinnamon into a moist paste known as the *akda* in Algeria. Set aside.

2. Roll out the dough into a large thin circle or rectangle 1/8 inch thick. Using a metal cutter or the edge of a glass 2 1/2 inches in diameter, cut out circles, one by one, and set them aside.

3. Take 1 heaping teaspoon or a bit more of the paste and roll it into a 2-inch-long cylinder. Place this near one edge of the pastry circle and fold it over. To seal, use the tines of a fork or moisten a rounded edge of the pastry with a dab of water and pinch the ends tightly. Shape

the sealed horn like a quarter moon. Fill and shape pastries with the remaining dough and paste in the same manner.

4. Place the pastries on a lightly floured cookie sheet and bake in a 350 degree oven for about 17 minutes, just enough to lightly tan the horn. Do not overbake and darken the pastry.

5. Remove the horns from the oven and dip them quickly in the 1/4 cup orange blossom water. Dust immediately with the powdered sugar.

Makes 12 to 14 horns.

❂ GRIWECH ❂

HONEY TWISTS

A rich dough, well kneaded, cut and knotted, deep-fried until light brown, soaked in honey, then sprinkled with toasted sesame seeds. Sounds mouthwatering? It is.

FOR THE GRIWECH DOUGH

3 cups flour
1/4 teaspoon baking powder
1/4 pound butter or margarine, melted
1 tablespoon orange blossom water (available in Middle Eastern groceries)

1 egg, beaten
1/8 teaspoon turmeric, for color
1 cup water
1/8 teaspoon salt

Prepare the Griwech Dough: Put the flour into a large bowl and add all the ingredients. Mix into a dough and knead until smooth. Should it be too moist, dust with flour until the dough ball can be handled with ease. This is a basic pastry dough used in several pastry sweets that follow.

FOR THE GRIWECH

1–2 cups vegetable oil for deep-frying

1 cup honey
toasted sesame seeds

1. *Prepare the Griwech:* Use as much of the dough as you wish to prepare as many honey twists as wanted. I suggest one-half for this recipe. The remainder of the dough can be put into a plastic bag and stored in a freezer for future use.

2. Take half of the dough and roll it out into a rectangle about 1/8 inch thick. Cut a number of thin squares, each 4 inches by 4 inches. Make 4 slashes 3 inches long and equidistant from each other in the center of each square to open it up. Do not cut through to the ends of the squares.

   Lift up, cross and twist together the second and fourth strips. Push the third strip up into the tangle of crossed strips. This requires both hands and several fingers and is not a precise engineering fact. The end result after frying is a browned crisp tangle and this is what is wanted.

3. Heat the oil in a wok or skillet and place 1 twist carefully into it. Let sizzle and brown over moderate/low heat. Turn it over and let it brown, altogether about 3 minutes. Remove and drain for 1 minute on paper towels. Fry 1 twist at a time.

4. Simmer the honey in a saucepan over low heat. Add a twist and let it soak for 1 minute on each side. Remove to a plate and sprinkle with 1/4 teaspoon toasted sesame seeds. Let the twists dry at room temperature.

   Store the twists on a plate covered with plastic wrap since they are sticky and remain so.

Serve when you wish with Fresh Mint Tea (see page 71) or coffee. Makes 8 to 10 twists.

❈ BAKLWA ❈

ALMOND PASTRY PIE

The Algerians do not use the fragile fillo sheets to make their *baklwa*. The Ottoman Empire left its mark with a variety of nut pastry sweets that are similar to those found in Turkey today. In the Algerian version, a simple dough is prepared and thin pastry layers are rolled out to provide substance and replace fillo. What one has is a more substantial pie that is cut into diamond shapes with each diamond decorated with a single almond.

FOR THE AKDA

    1 cup chopped almonds (do not
       chop too fine)
    2 tablespoons sugar
    1 teaspoon ground cinnamon

1 tablespoon orange blossom water
    (available at Middle Eastern
    groceries)

FOR THE PASTRY

    2 cups flour
    1/2 teaspoon baking powder

1/2 cup water

FOR THE PIE

    1 cup butter, melted

1/2 cup whole almonds, not
    blanched

FOR THE SYRUP

    1 cup sugar
    2 cups boiling water

2 tablespoons honey

1. *Prepare the Akda:* Mix everything together as a filling. Set aside.

2. *Prepare the Pastry:* Mix the flour and baking powder together. Add the water, little by little, and mix until a dough forms that can be easily handled. Dust with flour if necessary.

3. *Prepare the Pie:* Butter a round pie pan 8 or 9 inches in diameter. Take about 1/2 cup of the dough and roll out a thin disc that will fit the bottom of the pie pan. Using a pastry brush, smear 1 tablespoon butter over the surface. Do this a total of 3 times—3 thin layers.

4. Press the *akda* in, spreading it almost to the edge of the pan. Cover the *akda* with 3 more layers of pastry, smearing 1 tablespoon butter over each layer, including the top one. If there is pastry left over, put it in a plastic bag and freeze for another occasion.

5. With a sharp knife, cut across the top of the pie diagonally in both directions to form 2-inch-sized diamonds. Cut all the way through the pie to the pan. Push the loose pastry layers into the sides all around the pan. Press 1 almond into the top of each diamond cut-out.

6. Bake in a 350 degree oven for 1 hour, until evenly browned.

7. *Prepare the Syrup:* While the pie bakes, simmer the sugar and water over low heat for 1/2 hour or a bit more to thicken the syrup. Dissolve the honey in the syrup.

8. Remove the Baklwa from the oven and immediately pour 1 cup of the simmering honey syrup over it. The syrup will be absorbed by the pie. Cool well for several hours before cutting, allowing ample time for the syrup to be absorbed.

THE JEWISH CUISINE OF ALGERIA

❋ CHOUCHOUKA ❋

SWEET PEPPER AND TOMATO HORS D'OEUVRE

This may be served as an appetizer or salad with other Algerian dishes.

4 sweet red or green peppers
  (1 pound)
1 tablespoon olive oil
1 head garlic (8 cloves), peeled and
  sliced

1 pound ripe tomato, chopped, or a
  1-pound can
1/2 teaspoon salt, or to taste
1/4 teaspoon black pepper
1 egg, beaten

1. Grill the whole peppers over charcoal or in a gas oven broiler until they are well charred. Cool, rub off the blackened skins, cut open and remove the stems and seeds. Slice into thin strips.

2. Put the oil into a pan, add the garlic, tomatoes, pepper slices, salt and pepper. Simmer, covered, over very low heat for 1 hour.

3. Pour the beaten egg over the vegetables and simmer for 2 minutes more, enough to cook the egg.

Serve warm. Serves 6.

NOTE: Shavuoth is the holiday when no meat is eaten and the family cook relies on vegetarian dishes. This is one of them.

SOUPE DE FÈVETTES

FAVA BEAN SOUP

Fava beans, also commonly known as broad beans, are one of the most ancient food crops and most popular in the Mediterranean region. In this Jewish recipe the broth is enriched with beef and beef bones.

2 cups large dried fava beans
1 pound beef chuck, cut into 6 pieces
several beef bones
6 cups water
1 head garlic (about 8 cloves), peeled
2 teaspoons sweet paprika

1 teaspoon salt, or to taste
1/2 teaspoon black pepper
1 small bunch fresh coriander (2 ounces), rinsed well and sliced
3 zucchini (1 pound), sliced
1 ripe tomato, cubed (1/2 cup)
1/4 to 1/2 cup olive oil, to taste

1. Parboil the beans for 10 minutes and drain. Put all the ingredients into a pan large enough to hold them and bring to a boil. Skim off the foam that rises. Cover the pan and simmer over low heat for 3 hours, which is enough to soften the meat and favas.

2. Remove the meat and bones and set the meat aside. In a food processor process all the vegetables and broth into a moderately thick purée. This is the soup. The meat is served separately.

Serve hot. Serves 6.

COUSCOUS AU BEURRE

BUTTERED COUSCOUS

A complete vegetarian couscous with variety, flavor and ease of service. All the ingredients are served separately on the table and each diner helps him- or herself.

1 pound couscous
6 small zucchini, sliced
1 pound canned or fresh fava beans
(2–3 cups)
1 cup white or dark raisins, rinsed
in cold water

1/4 pound melted butter, or more
as needed
1 quart buttermilk, or more as
needed
1 quart yogurt, or more as needed

1. Steam the couscous in the traditional manner.

2. During that time, cook the zucchini and the fresh favas in a very small amount of water until soft. Or drain the canned fava beans and heat them.

3. Serve all the ingredients separately. The zucchini and fava beans should be served in individual bowls, the raisins in another bowl. The melted butter in a server. The buttermilk and yogurt in their own respective servers.

4. To serve, the diners will help themselves to the couscous and the vegetables, according to personal preference. The raisins are to be sprinkled and the butter poured over the couscous as wanted. The buttermilk is drunk from a glass and the yogurt is spread over the couscous. Serve couscous and vegetables hot.

Serves 6 as a complete vegetarian meal.

NOTE: Fresh fava beans are seasonal and often difficult to find. Canned green fava beans are available in Oriental groceries and are available year round.

COUSCOUS À LA VIANDE

COUSCOUS WITH MEAT AND VEGETABLES

This is a classic style of couscous cooked in Jewish homes. The emphasis is actually on the variety of vegetables while the meat, chicken, beef and lamb, in modest amounts, enrich the broth and provide substance.

1 pound couscous

a 3-pound chicken or equivalent chicken parts, cut into serving pieces, loose skin and fat discarded

1 pound beef chuck

1 large beef bone

1/2 pound lamb, with or without bone

2 medium onions, sliced (1 cup)

1 ripe fresh tomato, cubed (1 cup)

8 cups water

1 cup dried chick-peas, soaked overnight in water and drained

6 small zucchini, cut into 3 pieces each

2 whole leeks, well trimmed and rinsed in cold water

1 pound Savoy-type cabbage, halved

6 carrots, sliced

6 small white turnips, peeled and halved

3 ribs celery, strings removed and cut horizontally into 3 pieces

3 teaspoons sweet paprika

2 bay leaves

1/4 teaspoon dried thyme

1/2 teaspoon black pepper

1 bunch fresh coriander (2–3 ounces), tied in a bundle

1 teaspoon salt, or to taste

1. Steam the couscous in the traditional manner.

2. During this time, put the chicken, beef, beef bone and lamb into a pan large enough to hold them with the onions and tomato. Fry for 5 minutes, turning the meat. Add the water and bring to a boil, removing the foam that rises.

3. Add the chick-peas, zucchini, leeks, cabbage, carrots, turnips and celery. At this time also add the paprika, bay leaves, thyme, pepper, fresh coriander and salt. Cover the pan and cook over low heat for 2 or 3 hours.

4. Remove the chicken when it becomes soft and continue to simmer until the beef and lamb are tender. Remove the meat to one platter for serving. Discard the beef bone.

5. To serve, put all the vegetables and the broth in one serving bowl. You may include the coriander bunch since many like the flavor. Serve the meats on the platter and the couscous in another dish. The diners will help themselves.

Serves 6 to 8.

KUFTA

Broiled Lamb Patties

These are standard, everyday spiced patties that can be grilled over charcoal or in a gas or electric broiler—any way you wish, but the charcoal grill adds another and more authentic flavor.

1 pound ground lamb
4–5 cloves garlic, well chopped
1/2 teaspoon ground bay leaf
1/8 teaspoon ground mace
1/2 teaspoon black pepper
1/8 teaspoon dried thyme
1/2 teaspoon ground cumin
1/4 cup chopped flat-leaf parsley
1 egg, beaten

1. Mix everything together rather well. Form patties by taking 1 heaping tablespoon of the lamb mixture and shaping it into a meatball. Then flatten the meatballs slightly into round patties.
2. Broil over whatever medium you have available for about 3 minutes or a bit more if you prefer meat well done. Makes 8 patties.

Serve warm as an appetizer or one of the dishes at a meal.

TAFINA DE PESACH

Lamb's Head with Spinach and Chick-Peas

A *tafina* (and there are many types) is the one-dish Jewish Sabbath preparation that is cooked slowly from Friday afternoon until noon the next day, Saturday. It is also known as *t'fina* in Tunisia, *scheena* in Morocco and *hameen* in Calcutta, India.

This *tafina* is a specialty of Passover and is served at the seder. Lamb head, the symbolical Pascal Lamb, is combined with spinach and chick-peas. This is a recipe from the town of Batna in the Constantine region of eastern Algeria.

FOR THE LAMB HEAD

1 small lamb head
1/2 teaspoon black peppercorns
4–5 bay leaves

1 tablespoon salt
6–8 cups water

FOR THE TAFINA

3 tablespoons corn or other
    vegetable oil
2 pounds spinach, well rinsed,
    trimmed and tough stems
    discarded
1 cup dried chick-peas, soaked
    overnight in water and drained

1 tablespoon ground coriander
2 teaspoons ground cumin
1/2 teaspoon black pepper
1 teaspoon salt
1 teaspoon sweet paprika
2–3 cups water

1. Have the butcher cut the head into 4 parts. Clean well, pulling off loose hair and skin. Put the head with the seasonings and water in a pan, bring to a boil and simmer over low heat for about 2 hours, or until the meaty parts are tender. Drain well and set aside.

2. Heat the corn or vegetable oil in a large pan (Algerian Jews never cook with olive oil), add the spinach and stir-fry over moderate heat for several minutes to reduce the sheer bulk. Add the chick-peas, coriander, cumin, pepper, salt, paprika and lamb head and mix well.

3. Add the water and bring to a boil. Cover the pan and simmer over low heat for about 3 hours, which is enough time to integrate all the flavors and tenderize the chick-peas.

    Should one wish to follow the *tafina* tradition of preparing this, the head and vegetables should be cooked very slowly all night.

Serve warm. Serves 6.

❊ SALADE DE FENOUIL ❊

FENNEL SALAD

The large, fist-sized bulbs of the fennel plant are the backbone of this salad. The crisp slices are anise flavored, the identifying characteristic of the bulb, which is also a popular vegetable in Italy. This salad is served on Passover but could be served any time that fennel is available.

2 fennel bulbs, cut into thin slices, each 2 inches long
4 tablespoons olive oil

1 teaspoon salt, or to taste
1/4 teaspoon black pepper
juice of 1 large lemon

1. Remove all the leaves on the fennel, except a few feathery green ones next to the bulb, which will add color to the salad. Cut the leaves into 2-inch pieces.

2. Mix everything together and toss well to distribute the seasonings. Let the salad stand, refrigerated, for 1 hour to allow the seasoning to penetrate the fennel slices.

Serve cold during the days of Passover. Serves 6.

✦ COCLO ✦

BIG MEATBALLS

Coclo, an Algerian Jewish preparation, can be added as another ingredient to the Sabbath *tafina*, or it may be prepared as a separate dish and served on the Sabbath, or any other time.

1 pound freshly ground beef
1/2 cup rice, well rinsed
1 head garlic (about 8 cloves), chopped fine in a processor
1 egg, beaten
1/2 teaspoon salt, or to taste
1/2 teaspoon ground bay leaf
1/8 teaspoon ground mace

1/4 teaspoon black pepper
1/8 teaspoon ground thyme
2 tablespoons olive oil
1 medium onion, chopped (1/2 cup)
1/2 bunch (about 6 sprigs) fresh coriander, tied in a bundle
3/4 cup water

1. Mix the beef, rice, garlic, egg, salt, bay leaf, mace, pepper, thyme and olive oil together rather well. Shape the mixture into 2 large meatballs.

2. Put the onion, coriander and water in a pan. Add the meatballs. Cover the pan and simmer over low heat for 2 hours or a bit more. Remove and discard the coriander if you wish, although those who very much like coriander will eat the sprigs with the coclo.

    Reheat if serving on the Sabbath.

Serve warm. Serves 6 with other dishes.

❊ BOULETTES FRITES ❊

MEAT PATTIES IN ZUCCHINI SAUCE

This is daily food that can be served any time of the year except Passover, when the semolina used to enrobe the *boulettes* is not kosher. There are two steps to the preparation—the patties, which are really flattened egg shapes, and the zucchini (*courgette*) sauce. Double the recipe for larger groups.

FOR THE BOULETTES

1 pound ground beef
1 teaspoon ground cumin
1 teaspoon ground coriander
1/2 teaspoon ground black pepper

1 teaspoon salt
1/4 cup fine-ground semolina
2 beaten eggs
1/4 cup corn or vegetable oil

FOR THE SAUCE

1/4 cup corn or vegetable oil
1 medium onion, chopped (1/2 cup)
10 pieces small zucchini (2 pounds), cut into 1-inch-wide pieces

1 teaspoon ground cumin
1 teaspoon ground coriander
1 teaspoon black pepper
1 teaspoon salt
3/4 cup water

1. *Prepare the Boulettes:* Mix the beef, cumin, coriander, pepper and salt together and shape the mixture into egg-sized ovals, flattened slightly to a 1-inch thickness. Makes about 12 pieces.

2. Roll each *boulette* in the semolina and then in the beaten egg.

3. Heat the oil in a large skillet and fry the patties over low heat for 5 minutes, which is enough to cook them.

4. *Prepare the Sauce:* Heat the oil in a pan, add the onion and stir-fry until lightly golden. Add the zucchini, cumin, coriander, pepper and salt. Mix and simmer, covered, over low heat for 15 minutes.

5. Add the fried *boulettes* and 3/4 cup water and simmer slowly for 1 hour.

Serve warm with salads. Serves 6.

❧ YOM KIPPOUR TAJINE ❧

CHICKEN, CHICK-PEA AND ONION STEW FOR YOM KIPPUR

This is served in the evening before the formal beginning of Yom Kippur.

1 pound dried chick-peas, soaked overnight in water and drained	*4 cups water*
	3 teaspoons sweet paprika
4 pounds of chicken parts or two 3-pound chickens, cut into serving portions, loose skin and fat discarded	*2 bay leaves*
	1 teaspoon salt, or to taste
	1/2 teaspoon black pepper
	1/4 to 1/2 cup olive oil, to taste
1 pound onions, chopped	*2 eggs, beaten*

1. Peel off and discard the loosely attached skins of the chick-peas.

2. Arrange the ingredients in layers in a pan large enough to hold all of them. On the bottom place 4 pieces of chicken. Cover these with a portion of the onions and top it with half of the chick-peas. Continue to layer in the same manner, covering the top with chicken.

3. Add the water, paprika, bay leaves, salt, pepper and olive oil. Bring to a boil, skim off the foam and cover the pan. Cook over low heat for about 3 or 4 hours. Slow-cooking is desirable to extract all the flavors.

4. When all the ingredients are softened and the liquid has reduced to a rich sauce, pour the 2 beaten eggs over the surface but do not stir them in. Bake in a 375 degree oven for 15 minutes.

Serve warm with bread and salads. Serves 6 to 8.

❈ SCHEENA ❈

BEEF AND CHICK-PEA SABBATH STEW

This style of *scheena* is prepared on Fridays to be eaten after the morning synagogue service on Saturday. Modern homes will prepare the *scheena* on Friday to be reheated on Saturday.

In old-time Algerian homes the *scheena* was cooked on open charcoal braziers over very low heat all night long so that it could be served warm on Saturday.

1 pound dried chick-peas, soaked overnight in water and drained
1 1/2 pounds chuck or shank beef, divided into 6 portions
1 head garlic (about 8 cloves), peeled

2 teaspoons sweet paprika
1 teaspoon ground coriander
4 cups water
1 pound spinach, well rinsed

1. Put the beef, garlic, paprika, coriander, chick-peas and water into a pan large enough to hold all the ingredients. Bring to a boil and skim off the foam that rises. Cover the pan and cook over very low heat for 3 or 4 hours, enough time for the meat and chick-peas to soften and the liquid reduce

2. Steam the spinach over boiling water for several minutes. Drain, press out the liquid gently, then cover the ingredients in the *scheena* pan. Cook for 2 minutes more.

Serve warm. Serves 6 to 8.

❊ MERGUEZ JUIVE ❊
Jewish-Style Merguez of Algeria

The *merguez* of the Jewish cook is different from that of others. This is not a surprising revelation since family tastes and preferences are universally different. The Jewish community uses kosher meats and the Muslim *halal* meat prepared by their religious members.

Note that there is a considerable amount of spice and when one comes to adding the hot chili judicious consideration should be contemplated.

I suggest taking a teaspoon of the mixture *before* the chili is added and fry a miniature pattie in one tablespoon or corn oil. Taste it, then add the chili according to your preference.

2 pounds ground beef or lamb or
* half and half of each meat*
1 tablespoon ground coriander
1 tablespoon ground cumin
1 tablespoon ground caraway
1 tablespoon black pepper

1 tablespoon sweet paprika
2–3 tablespoons hot red chili pow-
* der, or to taste*
1 teaspoon salt
1 small intestine from a lamb
1 tablespoon corn oil

Mix the first 8 ingredients together and stuff the intestine with the filling. Twist the intestine every 4 inches to separate the individual sausages.

These are best eaten fresh, but may be frozen for future use.

Makes about 20 merguez.

THE COOKING OF TUNISIA

Date palm oasis in Nefta

Bedouin women visiting the Oasis of Nefta

TUNISIA

HECTOR Berlioz's monumental opera, *The Trojans and The Trojans at Carthage* was inspired by Virgil's *Aeneid* and celebrated the love story of Dido and Aeneas and ultimately the destruction of Carthage by the Romans. Carthage, a Phoenician city on the outskirts of modern Tunis, was the home of Hannibal (247–184 B.C.), the most famous of the Carthaginian generals. During one of the Punic Wars against Rome, he left for Europe from the ancient port of Hadrumetum (what is now the modern city of Sousse), leading his troops and a battalion of elephants (what did they eat!) across the Alps. He won a battle but was ultimately defeated when the Romans razed Carthage. He later committed suicide.

When in Tunisia, one is confronted by history and the passage of invaders both benevolent and tyrannical. One should not have high expectations when visiting Carthage of monumental ruins and other architectural clues to the past. Now a few shattered columns and other detritus are all that remain of the glories that were Carthage. Did they leave traces of their cuisine that became incorporated into the foods of Tunisia?

It was the Romans who turned Tunisia into the breadbasket of the Empire and this, no doubt, accounts for the wonderful bread found throughout every village and city in Tunisia. The Romans also found and fought the indigenous people of Tunisia, the Berbers, who used the newly domesticated camel for transportation and food. Some of the Berber tribes had been converted to Judaism, another facet of the cuisine that may or may not contribute to the multitude of ethnic diets.

After the Romans came the Arabs and Islam, with its profound religious contribution and the remarkable proliferation of spices, which left a completely irrevocable imprint on the existing styles of cooking. The indigenous people of the region, Berbers and Jews, benefited from these aromatic additions to the cooking.

The 16th century saw the extension of the Ottoman Empire over Tunisia and Algeria to the border of Morocco, with a brief incursion by the Spanish. Many of the pastries of the Maghreb are of Turkish inspiration as well as the indispensable *malsouka* (pastry leaves) of Tunisia and the *warka* of Morocco.

The French came in the mid-19th century and refined the presentation of food.

But it was the hot chili pepper brought from Mexico to Spain by Columbus and the conquistadores in the 16th century that made its inextinguishable imprint, namely on the classic, fiery condiment *harissa,* without which the Tunisian cuisine would be unthinkable.

Little by little, over the centuries, the Tunisians established their cuisine without forgetting the old ways. Herbs, tubers, fruit and grains were the products of nature in the Tunisian villages. Lentils, sesame, wheat and dates were standard ancestral foods. The Roman overindulgent use of greens in salads plus the use of herbs that were available has continued on into the palates of modern Tunisia.

No cuisine develops in isolation. Tunisia was fortunate to be able to absorb the culinary ideas from the movement of outside forces since the time of the Romans to the end of the French adventure in 1956. There were no cataclysmic upheavals, but a sometimes rocky evolution that brought people and foods together. By about 1850 (my own estimate) an international exchange of vegetables, fruit, grain and even meat from one continent to another had been completed.

The extraordinary group of produce from the Valley of Mexico — corn, the tomato, the hot chili, sweet peppers, squash, pumpkin, beans, the potato and more — had never been seen in the rest of the world. Alternately, from Asia the spices and especially rice, onion, garlic, ginger and the pig were unknown in the western hemisphere. When it all came together and everyone had nearly everything, codified cuisines emerged.

Tunisian cooking has very few complexities that could be discouraging to a cook. The public markets are filled with standard vegetables, such as zucchini, pumpkin, turnips, carrots, eggplant, artichokes, fennel, onion and garlic. Hot chili peppers, both dried and fresh for the famous *harissa,* are always available.

Spices are an indispensable ingredient in the food with cumin, caraway and pepper leading the pack. Fresh flat-leaf parsley and coriander are ubiquitous. Olive oil is one of Tunisia's outstanding products as well as many types of table olives. Miles of olive trees are visible neatly spaced in the countryside. Wheat for the incomparable breads and dates in the desert regions are major agricultural products.

Oranges, lemons, figs, grapes, apricots, melons and pomegranates are all fruit of the Mediterranean region with its salubrious climate that so determines the agriculture. One must consider that the Sahara in the south has been encroaching on the northern part of the three Maghreb

The souk in Tunis

countries under discussion here, reducing the amount of acreage available for agriculture.

So the Tunisian cook must rely on traditional foods to complement what nature has provided. The *marka* are stews with sauce. The *oja* has egg sauces incorporated into frequently vegetarian dishes. The cook uses countless eggs (perhaps too many) for the *brik*, for sauces, garnishes and the baked *tajine*, also called *menina*, which is not quite a soufflé but a baked loaf of chicken or other meats.

Couscous is the national food. Tunisians can count on it when all else fails. *Malsouka* (pastry leaves) is used to envelop stuffings as in the *tajine malsouka* and the *brik*, traditional dishes that exemplify the Tunisian mystique. *Chakchouka*, a Berber word meaning a mélange, is a popular form of fast-food homecooking.

The variety of dishes is large, but uncomplicated—with lamb, beef, poultry and fish from Mediterranean waters incorporated into the diet. A Tunisian friend remarked that one cannot label the cooking *haute cuisine* but, "if the cook is good, the food is good," a truism for a small country with a generous and flavorful table.

COUSCOUS

❖

RANDOM THOUGHTS ABOUT COUSCOUS

Tunisia is couscous country. There are supposed to be an estimated 300 different varieties of couscous throughout the land. Since every family who is devoted to the pleasures, ease or economic advantages of couscous can provide *its own* authentic recipe that has been in *that family* for centuries, the possibility by arithmetic progression is closer to 300,000 different varieties. I would like them all.

The world's largest couscous factory (I refer only to the preparation of pasta, the couscous grains) is situated in Sfax, Tunisian's second city, where there are large vats of semolina flour, miles of tubes and blowers that blow the pasta into the tiny pellets it is destined to be. The smaller the better. When the pasta becomes as large as buckshot, it is called *berkoukes* and is no longer couscous. The people of Sfax have the reputation of being energetic, business-like, hard-working and ethical and it is here that the factory developed into a mega-processor of couscous, producing many thousand tons each day.

At a tasting in the factory precincts one day, the following different types of couscous were set out to be reviewed. There were ten large bowls, sampled at room temperature: shrimp; assorted vegetables—zucchini, potato, carrot, among others; fennel in slivers; couscous salad; mint couscous; diced lamb; mixed nut with pistachio and almond, also known as *masfouf* and a specialty of Sfax; pomegranate; orange; and date. All of them were tasty and illustrated the diversity of the grain and the possibility of modifying traditional combinations into modern taste experiences.

Factory-made couscous has not completely eliminated homemade couscous. Many families still produce couscous at home since they find it has a better flavor as well as perpetuates an ancient tradition. Perhaps these are women of a certain age in smaller towns and villages who move into the kitchen early in the day and do not leave it until much later. These are the women who still prepare couscous, the pasta, at home.

Only rice is as adaptable as couscous is in its ability to combine with what might be considered unconventional ingredients and come up smelling like a rose, as the poets tell us. Persians are the world's greatest rice cookers. One of their most famous combination is a Basmati-type rice seasoned with a sweet sauce of cherries, slivers of dried orange peel and toasted almonds. I believe that couscous is the only national food that could accommodate itself to this Persian idea.

There is a theory circulating that couscous was brought to Morocco and the rest of the Maghreb by Sicilian Muslim families who were forced to flee, having been expelled from the island by a Sicilian king. These incidents are alleged to have occurred after the 15th century. Names such as Couscousi found in Morocco and other names that sound like the word Sicily seem to reveal a Sicilian origin. To my knowledge, this theory has not been documented and is hearsay from cultured Moroccans.

Another theory maintains that couscous is of Berber origin and that the original inhabitants of Morocco originated the preparation of semolina. I am not enthusiastic about this theory either since I find it difficult to believe that the semi-nomadic Berbers living under the Roman Empire would have learned to take the wheat berries (in the desert!), crack them, save the protein-rich siftings, convert them to paste and steam them. No, I am skeptical.

In my opinion the Romans are the answer and much later, the Sicilians who emigrated to the Maghreb. It was the Romans who turned Tunisia into the breadbasket for the Empire by large-scale production of wheat. With the knowledge of the preparation of pasta, from Marco Polo onward, and the explanation that couscous grains are pasta, does this not bend the theory more to Italy/Sicily than to the Berbers? Myth and speculation are frequently the only information we have, but my own conclusion regarding the origin of couscous is that reality is elusive, but how can one accept the Berber theory?

☷ COUSCOUS DE POULET ☷

CHICKEN COUSCOUS

Tunis is the modern capital city of Tunisia, and there one can find this particular couscous in homes and restaurants. On the outskirts of the city, laying in disarray, are the ruins of Carthage on the shore of the Mediterranean. Had couscous been established as a regional food in that era? I do not know.

2 tablespoons olive oil
a 3-pound chicken, cut into 8
   pieces, loose skin and fat
   removed and discarded
1/2 teaspoon black pepper
1 teaspoon salt
2 teaspoons sweet paprika
2 tablespoons tomato paste
1/2 cup cooked chick-peas
4 cups water

2 medium onions, quartered
   (1/4 pound)
2 carrots, quartered (1/4 pound)
2 medium white turnips, peeled
   and quartered (1/2 pound)
1/2 pound cabbage, halved
1 zucchini, quartered (1/2 pound)
2 sweet green peppers, seeded and
   quartered (1 1/2 pound)
couscous

1. Heat the oil in a pan and stir-fry the chicken over moderate heat for 2 minutes. Add the pepper, salt, paprika, tomato paste, chick-peas and water. Bring to a boil and cook, covered, for 20 minutes.

2. Add all the vegetables and cook over low heat for 25 minutes.

3. While the chicken and vegetables cook, steam the couscous in the top *(keskess)* of the *couscousier* in the traditional manner. Total steaming time is 1 hour.

4. To serve, put the couscous in a skillet, add 1/2 of the sauce, strained, and stir gently until the sauce has been incorporated and the couscous has absorbed it.

5. Serve the vegetables, chicken and the balance of the sauce separately. Each diner will add what he or she wants according to personal preference.

   The couscous can also be served in individual bowls, garnished with a variety of the vegetables and the chicken.

Serve warm. Serves 6.

❈ COUSCOUS ZARZIS ❈

COUSCOUS FROM ZARZIS

Zarzis is a peninsula that juts out from the Tunisian mainland, pointing to the island of Jerba nearby. One drives from Jerba to Zarzis over a beautifully constructed causeway crossing a bay in the Mediterranean. Like many foods of Tunisia, regional differences crop up in this couscous, with new taste surprises.

2 pounds boneless leg of lamb, cut into 3-inch pieces	*2 tablespoons finely chopped fresh dill*
2 tablespoons tomato paste	*2 cups water*
2 tablespoons olive oil	*1 teaspoon salt, or to taste*
2 tablespoons Quatre Épices (see page 295)	*2 medium onions, chopped (1 cup)*
	2 pounds couscous

1. Mix everything together, except the couscous in the bottom *(makfoul)* of a *couscousier;* bring to a boil over moderate heat and cook for 1 hour, or until the lamb is tender.

2. Steam the couscous in the *kesskess* (top) of the *couscousier* in the traditional manner. (Note that it must be removed and mixed with hot water twice during the process of steaming to expand the grains.)

3. Serve the couscous separately from the lamb stew.

Serves 6 to 8.

❈ MARKA SFAXIA ❈

FISH COUSCOUS FROM SFAX

Seafood is important in Sfax, and this style of couscous is special to that seaport town. The family that taught me how to prepare this *marka* told me they ate it about three times each week — a good recommendation for those who would enjoy fish with a tang.

1/4 cup olive oil
1 small onion, chopped (1/3 cup)
1 teaspoon hot red chili powder, or
    to taste
1 tablespoon ground cumin
2 cloves garlic, crushed in a garlic
    press
1 tablespoon tomato paste
4 cups water

2 whole small fish (1 1/2 pounds),
    such as red snapper, porgy, or
    your preference
1/2 teaspoon salt
1/4 teaspoon black pepper
1 semi-hot fresh whole green chili
    pepper
1 pound couscous
lemon wedges

1. Heat the oil in the bottom bottom *(makfoul)* of the *couscousier*, add the onion and stir-fry over moderate heat for 2 minutes. Add the paprika, cumin, garlic, tomato paste and 1 cup of the water. Simmer over low heat for 1/2 hour.

2. Add the balance of the water, 3 cups, bring to a boil and add the fish. Cook for 10 minutes. Add the salt, pepper and whole green chili and cook over low heat for 10 minutes more.

3. Steam the couscous in the top *(keskess)* for 45 minutes at the same time as the fish and seasonings are cooking. Steam the couscous in the traditional manner, with oil and water, mixing well to ensure that the grains remain separate.

4. To serve, place the fish in a platter separated from the sauce. Put the couscous in a large bowl. Take half the sauce and pour it over the couscous; let rest for 10 minutes, then mix or toss to integrate the sauce. Put the balance of the sauce in a dish and serve it separately.

Serve warm with the lemon wedges. Serves 6.

❁ JERBIAN MASFOUF ❁

COUSCOUS IN LAYERS

This unusual method of preparing couscous is one of my favorite Tunisian dishes. Arranging everything in layers ensures that the flavors will mix and cook, especially as the meats are cut into small dice.

In the capital city of Tunis, a *masfouf* is a sweet dish with no relationship to the Jerbian idea. Only the names are similar.

FOR THE COUSCOUS

2 pounds couscous
1 cup water

1 teaspoon olive oil

FOR THE MEAT

1 pound boneless lamb, cut into
1/4-inch dice
1/4 pound lamb liver, cut into
1/4-inch dice
2 tablespoons lamb fat, cut into
1/4-inch dice (optional)
1 large onion, chopped (1 cup)
8 sprigs flat-leaf parsley,
chopped

a 6-inch rib celery, with leaves and
stems, chopped
1 teaspoon salt
1/4 teaspoon black pepper

8 cups water
1 tablespoon butter

1. *Prepare the Couscous:* Mix everything together, tossing the mixture to separate the couscous grains. Set aside.

2. *Prepare the Meat:* Mix everything together. Set aside.

3. To assemble, put the 8 cups water in the bottom *(makfoul)* of the *couscousier* and bring to a boil.

4. In the top *(kesskess)* of the *couscousier,* prepare layers as follows: Place 1/2 inch of the couscous in the *kesskess.* Over that put 1/2 inch of the lamb mixture. Continue making layers until the couscous and lamb mixture are finished.

5. Cover the *kesskess* and steam over moderate heat for 30 minutes. Remove the mixture to a bowl and stir in 1/3 cup hot water from the top *(makfoul)* of the courscousier and the butter. Mix well and return the mixture to the *kesskess* to steam 10 to 20 minutes more. Test the meat and couscous to ensure that they are cooked through. If not, simply steam several minutes longer.

Serve hot. Serves 8 to 10.

The walled old city of Kairouan

COUSCOUS BEL HOUSBAN

Couscous with Lamb Offal

The ancient town of Kairouan in Tunisia's central part is known for its magnificent mosques and fortresses, where marble, stone and wood have been carved into powerful aesthetic forms. All this occurred in the 9th century when ruling dynasties of Arabs asserted their power.

It was here in a large garden where a phalanx (it seemed) of women prepared the extraordinary Couscous Bel Housban from the offal of lamb. Tripe, intestines, heart, lung and liver were cleaned and cut up. Spices and seasonings were combined and pockets of tripe were stuffed and tied together. A large *couscousier*, both the top (*keskess*) and the bottom (*makfoul*), were filled and the cooking began.

There is no reason to doubt that this rare couscous can be prepared in your home kitchen with judicious planning and a visit to a Middle East *halal* butcher who will provide all the innards necessary. Try a half recipe; it will not be so intimidating.

For the Stuffing

2 pounds spinach, tough stems trimmed and rinsed very well in cold water, sliced thin
1/2 pound flat-leaf parsley, leaves and young stems, sliced thin
1 large onion, chopped (1 cup)
5 cloves garlic, crushed in a garlic press
2 tablespoons dried mint, crushed
1 teaspoon salt, or to taste
1 teaspoon ground coriander

1 cup cooked chick-peas
1 cup rice, well rinsed
2 tablespoons Harissa (see page 89), more or less to taste
1/2 pound lamb liver, cut into 1-inch cubes
1 lamb heart, veins trimmed and cut into 1-inch cubes
1 lamb lung, cut into 1-inch pieces (4 cups) (optional if not available)

For the Pockets

five 6-inch squares clean tripe
3 feet or more of small lamb intestine, well cleaned
2 large lamb intestines, well cleaned

lamb fat from the tail, cut into 1-inch cubes (optional)
white string
caul fat (optional)

FOR THE MAKFOUL SAUCE

6 cups water
3 tablespoons olive oil
4 tablespoons tomato paste
2 tablespoons Harissa (see page 89)

1 teaspoon black pepper (optional if you use harissa)
2 teaspoons salt
1/2 cup cooked chick-peas
1 small onion, chopped (1/3 cup)

FOR THE COUSCOUS

2 pounds couscous
2 tablespoons olive oil

2 tablespoons water

1. *Prepare the Stuffing:* Mix everything together in a bowl. Set aside.

2. *Prepare the Pockets:* Prepare a ball the size of a large tennis ball using 1 square of tripe: Fill it with 1 cup of the stuffing and wrap it up. Twist about 12 inches of the small intestine around the ball as though it were a rope. Then tie it around with sufficient string to hold it together. (The caul fat, if used, should be wrapped around the ball before the string.) Prepare 5 balls this way.

3. *The Large Intestine:* Fill each large intestine with stuffing, also putting 1 cube of fat at the bottom and top of the intestine. Sew up the opening. Poke about 10 holes into the intestine with a sewing needle so that it does not rupture during cooking. Set aside.

4. *Prepare the Makfoul Sauce:* Put all the *makfoul* sauce ingredients into the bottom (*makfoul*) of a *couscousier.* Bring to a boil over moderate heat, then turn it to low. Add the stuffed tripe balls and the large intestines. Cook for 30 minutes.

5. *Prepare the Couscous:* Mix the couscous, oil and water thoroughly, making certain that everything is well mixed and the grains are separate. The longer one mixes the less likely that lumps will accumulate and more likely that the grains of couscous will remain separate.

6. After the stuffed tripe balls and intestines have cooked for 30 minutes, put the couscous mixture in the top (*kesskess*) of the *couscousier,* cover, and steam it over the vapor rising from the *makfoul* for 1 hour. During this time stir the couscous to ensure that the grains separate. The total time for everything will be 1 1/2 hours.

   Serve the couscous, stuffed items and the sauce separately. Each diner should put a heap of couscous in a soup plate, add slices of the stuffed intestine and tripe balls and pour sauce over all.

Serve warm. Serves 6 to 8.

<small>VARIATION</small>

Another style includes the following in the *makfoul:*

2 ripe tomatoes (1/2 pound), halved	*1/2 pound carrots, cut in half*
1 small onion, chopped (1/3 cup)	*crosswise*
1 teaspoon salt	*1/2 pound white turnips, peeled*
1/2 teaspoon black pepper	*and halved*
8 sprigs flat-leaf parsley, chopped	*1/2 cup cooked fava beans*
1/2 teaspoon ground coriander	*1/2 cup cooked chick-peas*
3 tablespoons olive oil	*4 fresh semi-hot green whole chili*
8 cups water	*peppers*

In the *makfoul* cook the 5 tripe balls and the 2 stuffed intestines with the tomatoes, onion, salt, pepper, parsley, coriander, oil and water for 1 hour. Add the carrots, turnips, fava beans, chick-peas and green chili peppers. Cook over low heat for 1/2 hour more, or until everything is tender and the sauce is reduced somewhat.

Steam the couscous in the *kesskess* for 1 hour. Serve the couscous, stuffed items, sauce and vegetables separately.

Serves 6 to 8.

❈ MASFOUF DE ZARZIS ❈

SPICED SEMOLINA BALLS

This is a Berber recipe from the peninsula of Zarzis, which points at the island of Jerba a few miles off the coast of Tunisia. It is a unique and festive preparation due to the aromatic spices and the technique of putting the *masfouf* together.

Tomato paste is a modern invention of the 1950s and is used with gusto all over Tunisia. Prior to that, quantities of ripe tomatoes were peeled, cooked down and reduced to a purée that now can be purchased at a reasonable price and without the chore of home preparation. Even the Berbers use it.

For the Semolina Balls

6 sprigs flat-leaf parsley, chopped
2 cloves garlic, crushed in a garlic
  press
4 eggs, beaten
1 1/2 cups small-grain semolina
1/4 teaspoon black pepper

1/2 teaspoon salt, or to taste
2 tablespoons olive oil
1 teaspoon ground cinnamon
1 teaspoon ground coriander
1 teaspoon ground caraway
1 teaspoon ground turmeric

For the Couscous

2 pounds couscous
1 cup water

1/2 teaspoon salt
1 tablespoon olive oil

For the Sauce

2 pounds boneless lamb or lamb
  shank, cut into 2-inch pieces
  with bone
2 tablespoons olive oil
2 cloves garlic, crushed in a garlic
  press

2 tablespoons tomato paste
1/2 teaspoon salt
2 teaspoons hot red chili powder or
  Harissa (see page 89)
3 cups water

1. *Prepare the Semolina Balls:* Mix everything together and shape the mixture into 8 small balls. The grains of semolina will expand during steaming. Set aside.

2. *Prepare the Couscous:* Mix everything together very well, tossing and stirring to prevent sticking and ensuring separate couscous grains.

3. *Prepare the Sauce:* Put all the sauce ingredients in the bottom *(makfoul)* of a *couscousier* and bring to a boil over moderate heat.

4. Put 1/2 of the couscous mixture in the top *(keskess)* of the steamer and cover it with the 8 balls of semolina. Cover with the balance of couscous.

5. Steam over low heat for 1 hour, which should be sufficient time to tenderize the lamb, create a potent sauce and steam the couscous and the semolina balls.

6. Serve the couscous and semolina balls on one platter and the lamb and sauce in another. Each diner will fill his or her own plate as desired.

   Serve 6 to 8.

Market in Nefta

❈ COUSCOUS BEDOUI ❈

COUSCOUS OF THE BEDOUIN

The Nefta oasis, where this couscous originated, may have been at one time a Bedouin outpost with a bubbling spring, date palms and camel caravans. This romantic fantasy no longer exists if indeed it ever did. Now a tourist hotel, cars and modern artifacts attest to the 20th century. Yet the dry, desiccating air forcefully reminds you that you are in the Sahara.

1 onion (1 pound), chopped
*10 pounds lamb, leg and shank, cut
    into 3-inch pieces, including bone*
1/4 cup olive oil
1/2 cup tomato paste
2 teaspoons salt, or to taste
1 teaspoon black pepper
about 7–8 cups water
2 pounds Merguez (see page 134)

*2 pounds yellow pumpkin, cut into
    2-inch cubes*
2 pounds small whole carrots
2 pounds small white turnips, peeled
3 pounds cabbage, quartered
2 cups cooked chick-peas
*8 small whole sweet green peppers
    (2 pounds)*
2 pounds couscous

1. In the bottom *(makfoul)* of a *couscousier* fry the onion and lamb in 3 tablespoons of the olive oil over moderate heat for 10 minutes. Add the tomato paste, salt, pepper and enough water to cover the lamb, 7 or 8 cups.

2. Add the *merguez*, pumpkin, carrots, turnips and cabbage and cook for 15 minutes more. Add the chick-peas toward the end of this time.

3. Heat the remaining 1 tablespoon oil in a skillet and fry the whole green peppers over moderate heat for 5 minutes to soften them.

4. While the lamb and vegetables cook, steam the couscous in the top *(kesskess)* of the *couscousier* for 1 hour.

5. To serve, put the lamb, vegetables, couscous and sauce each into a different platter or bowl. The diners help themselves. The center of each plate is garnished with the chick-peas and the green pepper.

Serve warm. Serves 12 gigantic eaters, the Bedouin. (In my opinion the recipe will serve 16 or more diners.)

❖ MASFOUF DE TUNIS ❖

SEMOLINA, RAISIN AND NUT SWEET

Masfouf is a desert snack traditionally served after the fast is broken on Ramadhan evenings. It is, in fact, remarkably like the various *soojee* (cream of wheat semolina) preparations that I have encountered in Kashmir and other parts of India. The techniques of assembling are different, but the idea and ingredients are the same.

1 pound semolina (fine-ground couscous)
1 cup hot water
8 tablespoons (1/4 pound) butter, melted
3 heaping tablespoons white or dark raisins
3 heaping tablespoons blanched

almonds, halved lengthwise and toasted in a 350 degree oven for 10 minutes
3 tablespoons pine nuts
1/2 cup sugar, or more to taste
1/2 pound seedless grapes (optional)

1. Mix the semolina and hot water in a bowl. Put it into the top (*kesskess*) of a *couscousier* or a Chinese-style steamer and steam, covered, over hot water for 10 minutes.

2. Remove the semolina to a bowl and stir in 4 tablespoons of the butter. Mix and toss to separate the grains. Return the semolina to the steamer and steam, covered, for 20 minutes. The semolina will expand and will be cooked through.

3. Soak the raisins in hot water for 5 minutes and drain. Remove the semolina the second time, stir in the balance of the butter, 4 tablespoons, and turn the semolina out on a serving dish. Add the raisins, almonds, pine nuts and mix and toss together. Set aside a few raisins and nuts to decorate the top of the Masfouf. Sprinkle the Masfouf with the sugar and decorate with the raisins and nuts.

Serve at room temperature. Serves 6 or more.

LE BRIK
AND BREAD

❖

❖ MALSOUKA ❖

BRIK PASTRY LEAVES

I saw these pastry leaves made in the famous Tunis pastry shop of Madame Zarrouk, where the *malsouka* were prepared on an inverted convex copper plate lightly heated by gas. The dough was dabbed on and pulled off after seconds of baking on the plate—a slow and rather tedious process when one has to do this all day to prepare hundreds of leaves.

2 pounds very fine semolina   *3–4 cups water*
   (semoule), *ground fine like*
   wheat flour

1. Mix the semolina and as much water as necessary into a sticky paste mixture but firm enough to handle. The mixture will be rather gummy.

2. Wipe a copper skillet clean; do not add oil. Over very low heat take a handful of the sticky dough and dab the skillet quickly all over to shape a round, thin pancake 7 inches in diameter. Loosen the edges quickly and remove the leaf. Make as many leaves as desired as *malsouka* freeze well and can be used at a future date.

    Known as *malsouka*, the leaves are used in *pâtisserie* and the popular brik with egg (Brik à l'Oeuf, see page 229).

Makes about 50 pancackes.

BRIKS À L'OEUF ❀

STUFFED PASTRY LEAVES

Brik a l'Oeuf must be Tunisia's most popular and unique appetizer. It is in several ways related to the spring roll of Vietnam, the Shanghai egg roll and the *martabak* of Indonesia, all of these variations on more or less the same theme, which I have cooked and written about previously. *Brik* is of Turkish inspiration, during the days of the Ottoman Empire when Tunisia was a vassal state from the 13th century to its decline in the 19th century.

It is the Malsouka (page 228), or pastry leaves, that are the limiting factor in preparing *brik*. A thin, white translucent pancake 7 to 8 inches in diameter is prepared from fine semolina flour and water. These are stuffed with a whole egg and special ingredients, depending upon the style, folded over in a half moon and deep-fried for a minute or so in hot vegetable oil.

To cooks in the United States who have access to a Chinatown or other Asian shopping center, there is an easier way. What is known as the Shanghai egg roll wrapper is, in effect, a *malsouka*. It is thin, white, fragile and round and fills all the requirements of an authentic *malsouka*. The purist will want to make the *malsouka* in his or her own kitchen and this is admirable if time-consuming. A recipe that is arduous or intimidating is soon lost or forgotten. By having a readily available source of *malsouka* this ingenious recipe is as easy as falling off a log and will be a continuous and long-time source of pleasure.

The following ingredients are used to make the stuffing for the *brik*.

SHRIMP STUFFING

1/4 teaspoon salt
1/4 teaspoon white pepper
1/2 cup small cooked shrimp, halved lengthwise
4 springs flat-leaf parsley, chopped fine

4 malsouka (pastry leaves)
4 whole eggs
vegetable oil for deep-frying
lemon wedges for serving

1. *Prepare the Shrimp Stuffing:* Mix the salt, pepper, shrimp and parsley together. Spread the *malsouka* out flat. Place 1 heaping tablespoon or a bit more of the shrimp stuffing in the center of the *malsouka*. Spread it out in a circle about 3 inches in diameter, making a small well in the center to hold 1 egg.

2. *To Cook Malsouka:* Heat the oil in a skillet. Add the egg to the well in the stuffing on the *malsouka*. Fold the leaf over carefully into a half moon, keeping a good grip on the folded top. Dip this into the hot oil so that the egg fries first, then lay it flat into the oil. This should be done rapidly since the total frying time is about 1 minute. The *malsouka* will become crisp and golden brown. Remove from the oil and let drain on paper towels briefly.

Serve warm. The exterior should be crisp and the egg yolk inside should still be loose or runny. The trick is to eat your way to the egg by nibbling from one end to the interior, all the while holding the *brik* in both hands. Practice makes perfect.

Serve with lemon wedges. Serves 4.

CHEESE STUFFING

3/4 cup ricotta cheese	*4 malsouka (pastry leaves)*
1/4 teaspoon salt	*4 whole eggs*
1/4 teaspoon white pepper	*vegetable oil for deep-frying*

Mash the ricotta smoothly, mixing in the salt and pepper. Take 1 heaping tablespoon or more of the mixture and spread it out in the center of each *malsouka*, making a well in the center for the egg. Follow the directions for folding and frying as noted above.

VEGETABLE STUFFING (BRIK KEFTAJI)

The key for the perfect vegetarian *brik* is to have a dry cool stuffing. If the stuffing has too much moisture, the *malsouka* will break open in the hot oil.

1 teaspoon vegetable oil	*1/2 cup thinly sliced potato (1 inch*
1 ripe tomato (1/4 pound),	*long slices)*
quartered and seeded, with	*1/4 teaspoon salt*
liquid pressed out	*1/4 teaspoon white pepper*
1 sweet green pepper (1/4 pound),	*4–6 malsouka (pastry leaves)*
quartered and seeded	*4–6 whole eggs*

1. Put the oil in a skillet, add the tomato, pepper and potato and fry over low heat for 5 minutes. Add the salt and pepper during this time. Cool the mixture well and chop all the vegetables together coarsely. Set aside.

2. Take 1 *malsouka* and place 1 heaping tablespoon or more of the mixture in the center. Make a well in the stuffing for the egg and add it. Fold the *malsouka* over into a half moon. Follow the directions for folding and frying as noted on page 230.

Serves 4 to 6.

NOTE: The Algerians have been influenced by the Tunisian invention of the *brik*. It is known as the Brik d'Annaba, an Algerian city near the northern border of Tunisia. The Algerians, however, stuff *brik* with ground lamb and spices, as well as with egg. Fillo sheets are used instead of the round *malsouka* to shape a rectangle 4 × 5 inches, which is deep-fried. It is a grand production (see page 142).

❋ KESRA ❋

BREAD OF THE TROGLODYTES

I visited the troglodyte woman in Matmata with her orange hennaed pigtails, one of the primitive cave dwellers of Fatma. She was grinding the whole wheat on a round stone grinder turned by hand. The wheat was crushed between two stones about 14 inches in diameter and 6 inches thick, just as it had been for centuries before.

3 packages dry yeast (1/4 ounce, 7 grams each)
4–5 cups warm water
3 pounds semolina flour
2 cups whole-wheat flour
1/2 teaspoon salt

1. Proof the yeast in 1 cup warm water.

2. Prepare bread dough in the conventional manner: Mix the flours together with the salt. Add the yeast mixture and enough additional water to form a manageable dough. Knead until smooth. Let rise about 1 hour, or until double in size.

3. Prepare 4 to 6 round loaves, each about 2 inches thick and 10 inches wide. Let rise on oiled cookie sheets for 1/2 hour. Bake in a 375 degree oven for 30 to 40 minutes. Cool on a rack.

Makes 4 to 6 loaves.

SOUPS

SHORBA DE POISSON

FISH SOUP WITH PASTA

Shorba is the name of the pasta the size of a grain of rice. The Greeks refer to this type of pasta as orzo and it is frequently known by that name. *Mérou* is the name of a large white-fleshed Mediterranean fish. I have seen it in the market weighing 10 to 20 pounds, but was told that they reach much larger sizes.

This soup is a specialty of the seaport city of Sfax, where the seafood is exemplary. The basic soup may be prepared in advance and refrigerated until ready to use *before* the pasta is added. Simply bring it to a boil and cook the pasta until *al dente* or softer.

2 tablespoons olive oil
1 small onion, sliced (1/3 cup)
2 cloves garlic, sliced
1/2 teaspoon salt
1/2 teaspoon black pepper
1 teaspoon ground cumin
1 teaspoon sweet paprika
3 tablespoons tomato paste

6 cups water
a 1 1/2-pound whole fish, such as
    sea bass or red snapper
1 large fish head, such as mérou
    or another type of fish
    (optional)
1/2 cup chorba (orzo)
lemon wedges for serving

1. Heat the oil in a large saucepan and fry the onion over moderate heat until golden. Crush the garlic, salt, pepper, cumin and paprika together in a mortar and mix it with the tomato paste. Stir-fry this spice mixture with the onion for 2 minutes.

2. Add the water and bring to a boil. Add the whole fish and the fish head, if used. Cook everything together, covered, over low heat in a pan for 30 minutes.

3. Remove the fish and fish head. Pull off the flesh, discard the bones and return small pieces of the fish to the soup. Bring to a boil and add the orzo. Cook over low heat for 10 minutes for *al dente* or more if you prefer it softer.

Serve hot with lemon wedges. Serves 8.

❀ SHORBA AU POULET ❀

CHICKEN SOUP WITH ORZO

The oasis of Nefta in southern Tunisia prepares its *shorba* with pigeon. One could use as a variation of this two small (one pound each) Cornish hens. However, I have made this *shorba* with chicken, without a drastic modification in the flavor.

Orzo is the rice-shaped pasta that turns up in a number of Tunisian foods. Orzo is actually a Greek word and pasta invention.

2 tablespoons olive oil
1 small onion, chopped (1/3 cup)
3 cloves garlic, crushed in a garlic press
3 tablespoons tomato paste
4 cups water
1 teaspoon salt, or to taste

1/2 teaspoon black pepper
a 3-pound chicken, cut into 8 pieces, loose skin and fat removed and discarded
1 cup orzo
1 lemon, cut into wedges

1. Heat the oil in a pan and fry the onion and garlic over moderate heat for a minute. Add the tomato paste, water, salt, pepper and the chicken pieces. Bring to a boil and cook over low heat for 25 minutes.

2. Add the orzo and cook for 15 minutes until the orzo is *al dente*, or 20 minutes for a softer texture. Should the liquid evaporate too quickly, add 1/2 cup more water. This is, after all, a soup.

Serve warm, chicken and broth, with lemon wedges. Serves 6.

❋ RECHTA ❋

PEASANT SOUP

Rechta is the name of the pasta that we would consider to be a number 17 or 18 commercial flat, thin spaghetti. It is not round but an almost flat noodle.

This is a peasant or farmer's soup that is really a one-dish meal containing, as it does, the substance of the *rechta,* fava and chick-peas, as well as chicken or meat. After a full day's work this "poor man's" food is eaten plain, without embellishment.

*1 tablespoon corn oil
a 3-pound chicken, cut into 8
    pieces, loose skin and fat
    removed and discarded
1 medium onion, coarsely chopped
    (1/2 cup)
2 tablespoons tomato paste
1 rib celery, cut into 4 pieces
6 cups water*

*1/2 pound rechta pasta, broken
    into 1-inch pieces
1 teaspoon salt, or to taste
1–2 teaspoons black pepper, to
    taste
1/4 cup dried skinless cooked fava
    beans
1/4 cup dried chick-peas, soaked
    overnight in water, drained and
    cooked until soft*

1. Heat the oil in a pan and brown the chicken lightly over moderate heat for 3 minutes. Add the onion and fry 1 minute; add the tomato paste, celery and 2 cups of the water. Bring to a boil, reduce the heat to low and cook, covered, for 1/2 hour.

2. Add the balance of the water, 4 cups, bring to a boil and add the pasta, salt and pepper. Add the fava beans and chick-peas and simmer over low heat for 20 minutes more. Adjust the salt and add more pepper if you wish a more intense flavor. Remove the celery.

Serve hot. Serves 6.

VARIATION

Boneless lamb, 1 1/2 pounds, cut into 1-inch cubes can be substituted for the chicken. When using lamb, add 3 cloves garlic, crushed in a garlic press, and add at the same time as the onion. Lamb is a firmer meat than chicken and should be cooked for 45 minutes before the balance of the water and the pasta are added.

※ HASSOO ※

MINIATURE MEATBALL SOUP

When the winter chill arrives in Tunis, the modern capital city of Tunisia, *hassoo* is prepared. It is a winter soup, thick and rich with miniature meatballs added to give additional dimension. The lady of this elegant home where we had been invited on the road to Carthage did not delegate the cooking to a servant, but prepared all the food herself. In this way, she explained, her daughters would be able to duplicate the traditional foods in their own homes and her sons would be familiar with it and demand it in their homes. This way, the tradition would be preserved and continuity would be maintained for another generation.

FOR THE MEATBALLS

1 pound ground lamb
3 cloves garlic, crushed in a garlic
* press*
1 teaspoon dried powdered mint

1/2 teaspoon salt
1/4 teaspoon black pepper
1/4 teaspoon Harissa
* (see page 89)*

FOR THE SOUP

1 tablespoon Harissa (see page 89)
2 tablespoons ground caraway
8 cloves garlic, crushed in a garlic
* press*
1/4 cup tomato paste

1 cup flour
10–12 cups water
2 teaspoons salt, or more to taste
1 tablespoon dried mint leaves,
* crushed*

1. *Prepare the Meatballs:* Mix everything together. Form meatballs, each 1/2 inch in diameter. The balls can be added directly to the soup. Another method is to poach them for 5 minutes in 2 cups boiling water with 2 tablespoons oil added; drain and add to the soup.

2. *Prepare the Soup:* Mix the *harissa,* caraway, garlic and tomato paste together and put it in a large pan.

3. Mix the flour briskly with 3 cups of the water into a smooth paste and rub it through a strainer into the pan. Simmer over low heat, adding 1 cup water every 5 minutes. Stir slowly and continuously with a wooden spoon, ensuring a smooth soup, free of lumps.

4. Add the meatballs, salt and mint and continue to simmer over low heat

for another 10 minutes. Should the soup become too thick, add another cup water. Adjust the salt. Total cooking time about 40 minutes.

Serve warm as a first course during cool days and chilly evenings. Serves 12.

❈ SHORBET HOUT ❈

FISH SOUP FROM ZARZIS

Like much of the cooking in the south of Tunisia, turmeric is added with a generous hand as is the hot chili. You may prefer to adjust the quantities of these two seasonings although this recipe is a reflection of Zarzis cooking. The semolina is of medium coarseness and is not the fine size used to prepare couscous. It is included to give substance to a soup made without vegetables.

2 tablespoons olive oil
1 small onion, chopped (1/3 cup)
6 cloves garlic, crushed in a garlic
  press
2 tablespoons tomato paste
1 teaspoon cumin
1–2 teaspoons hot red chili powder,
  to taste

1 teaspoon turmeric
1 teaspoon salt, or to taste
6 cups water
2 pounds fish, such as mérou, *red*
  snapper or haddock, cut into
  1-inch-wide slices
1/4 cup coarse semolina

1. Heat the oil in a pan, add the onion and stir-fry over moderate heat for 1 minute. Add the garlic and stir a minute; add the tomato paste, cumin, chili powder, turmeric, salt and the water. Bring to a boil and simmer over low heat for 10 minutes.

2. Add the fish slices, cover the pan and cook for 30 minutes. Remove the pan from the heat. Remove the fish slices from the soup and carefully separate the flesh. Discard the bones. Chop the fish pieces coarsely.

3. Return the fish to the soup, bring to a boil and add the semolina. Cook, covered, over low heat for 15 minutes, stirring now and then to keep the semolina moving.

Serve hot. Serves 6 to 8 persons.

❈ DCHICHA AUX CREVETTE ❈

SHRIMP SOUP

Gabès is a seaport, an old town and the gateway to the Sahara towns of Matmata and Douz. It is famous for its shrimp and this soup is typical. There is more than a touch of France here with the wine and the system of putting the soup together. Never mind, it is now from Gabès. The *dchicha* is a thickening agent that gives the soup a more substantial texture.

6 cups water
1/2 cup white wine (optional)
1 pound whole shrimp in the shell
1 pound red snapper, sea bass or
  mérou, sliced
1 rib celery, strings removed and
  sliced
1 whole carrot
1/4 teaspoon dried thyme
1 bay leaf
1 small onion studded with 2 whole
  cloves

1 teaspoon salt
3 tablespoons olive oil
1 small onion, chopped (1/3 cup)
2 tablespoons tomato paste
3 cloves garlic, crushed in a garlic
  press
1/4 teaspoon Harissa
  (see page 89)
1 tablespoon fresh lemon juice
1/4 cup coarse semolina
  (dchicha)
lemon wedges for serving

1. In a pan large enough to hold the ingredients, put the water, wine, if using, shrimp, fish, celery, carrot, thyme, bay leaf, onion with clove and salt. Bring to a boil over moderately low heat. After 15 minutes of boiling remove the shrimp and fish. Cook slowly for a total of 40 minutes.

2. Strain the broth. Peel the shrimp and slice them thin. Remove the flesh from the fish and chop it.

3. Heat the oil in the soup pan. Add the onion and stir-fry over moderate heat for 1 minute. Add the tomato paste and garlic and stir-fry for 1 minute. Add the strained broth and bring to a boil and cook for 10 minutes.

4. Add the *harissa*, lemon juice and semolina and simmer over low heat for 15 minutes. Add the peeled shrimp and chopped fish and simmer for 4 minutes more.

Serve hot with lemon wedges. Serves 6 to 8.

LAMB AND BEEF

LAMB

❖ TAJINE MALSOUKA ❖

Malsouka Pie with Lamb

A *tajine* as used in the cuisine of Tunisia, unlike that of Morocco, is a pie of sorts, with meat, eggs and seasonings, baked very slowly in a low oven. In this case the tagine itself is a round metal pan 14 inches in diameter and about 2 inches deep. The preparation is reminiscent of but not identical to the celebrated Bastilla (see page 34) of the Moroccans. *Malsouka* leaves can now be purchased in food shops in Tunisia and in New York's Chinatown as Shanghai egg roll wrappers. Continuing an age-old tradition, many households and restaurants prepare their own *malsouka* by laboriously tapping an inverted copper bowl set over a steamer with a mixture of flour and water.

FOR THE FILLING

3 tablespoons vegetable oil
1 large onion, chopped (1 cup)
1 pound boneless lamb, cut into very small dice
1 teaspoon salt, or to taste
1 teaspoon black pepper
1 teaspoon crushed saffron stamens

1 teaspoon Quatre Épices (see Note)
1 cup water
10 eggs, beaten
1 cup grated Gruyère cheese
1 teaspoon baking powder
1/4 cup milk

3 tablespoons butter	*18 malsouka (pastry leaves), each about 14 inches in diameter*

1. *Prepare the Filling:* Heat the oil in a skillet, add the onion, lamb, salt, pepper, saffron and spice mixture and stir-fry over low heat for 5 minutes. Add the water and simmer for 20 minutes. Remove the mixture and let it cool for 10 minutes. Stir in the eggs, cheese, baking powder and milk. Set aside.

2. *Prepare the Tagine:* Butter a 14-inch-in-diameter metal pan, about 2 inches deep. Place 4 *malsouka* leaves around the perimeter of the well-buttered pan, covering the bottom and allowing several inches to hang over the sides. Place 8 leaves on the bottom of the pan, fitting them one over the other.

3. Pour in the cooled lamb and egg filling and cover with 4 *malsouka.* Put 2 more *malsouka* on the top and tuck them in around the sides of the pie to seal in the contents.

4. Bake slowly in a 250 degree oven for 45 minutes or a little less so that the color on the top of the pie is pale tan. Turn the pie out upside down so that the bottom, a flat smooth surface, can be presented.

Serve warm, cut into 2- or 3-inch squares as one of the dishes in a complete dinner. Serves 10 to 12.

NOTE: Quatre Épices here should consist of 1 teaspoon each ground coriander, caraway and paprika plus 1 clove garlic crushed in a garlic press, all mixed together. There are many versions of this combination made according to personal preference.

❈ TAJINE AU FROMAGE ❈

LAMB AND CHEESE LOAF

Here the *tajine* is a sort of soufflé, but firmer in texture, containing meat. It may be served hot or cold, with or without the sauce. If served hot, use the sauce.

3 tablespoons olive oil

1 1/2 pounds lamb, cut into
   1/4-inch dice

1 small onion, chopped (1/3 cup)

1 teaspoon salt, or to taste

1/4 teaspoon ground coriander

1/4 teaspoon ground cumin

3 cloves garlic, crushed in a garlic
   press

1/4 teaspoon black pepper

1 teaspoon Harissa (see page 89)

1/4 cup tomato paste

2 cups water

8 eggs, beaten

1/4 cup bread crumbs

1/2 cup grated Gruyère-type cheese

1/4 cup dried white haricot beans,
   soaked overnight in water,
   drained and cooked until soft

1 tablespoon butter, melted

lemon wedges for serving

1. Heat the oil in a pan, add the lamb, onion, salt, coriander, cumin, garlic, pepper, *harissa* and tomato paste and stir-fry over moderate heat for 2 minutes. Add the water and cook for 15 minutes. Strain the mixture through a metal sieve in a bowl. Set the meat mixture aside. Put the sauce in a pan.

2. Mix the eggs, bread crumbs, cheese, beans and the meat mixture together. Add the melted butter to a Pyrex or metal baking dish and add the lamb mixture. Bake in a 350 degree oven for 20 to 30 minutes, or until the loaf is firm but still moist.

3. Bring the sauce to a boil.

4. To serve, slice the loaf into 1-inch-thick slices; serve the sauce separately. If serving cold, simply slice. Serve with lemon wedges.

Serves 10.

❈ VIANDE AU CHOU-FLEUR ❈

LAMB WITH CAULIFLOWER FRITTERS

To enter the old city of Sfax by walking through its ancient walls is to return to a much earlier century. The noises of the new city are stilled and simple tasks become a way of life. Several times I returned to a public restaurant there where the food was of the people, not elitist but aromatic, prepared with care and infinitely delicious. Trust the native is my motto.

FOR THE LAMB

2 tablespoons olive oil
1 large onion, chopped (1 cup)
2 pounds boneless shoulder of
    lamb, cut into 2-inch cubes
1 teaspoon salt, or to taste
1/2 teaspoon black pepper
2 teaspoons ground caraway

1 teaspoon turmeric
1 teaspoon Harissa (see page 89),
    or more to taste
2 cloves garlic, chopped
3 tablespoons tomato paste
1 cup water

FOR THE CAULIFLOWER

1 cauliflower (2 pounds)
2 eggs, beaten with 1/4 teaspoon
    salt

1/2 cup flour, or more if needed
oil for deep-frying

1. *Prepare the Lamb:* Heat the oil in a pan and fry the onion over moderate heat for 2 minutes. Add the lamb and stir-fry 2 more minutes. Add the salt, pepper, caraway, turmeric, paprika, garlic and tomato paste. Stir-fry for 5 minutes.

2. Add the water, cover the pan and cook over low heat for 1 hour or until the lamb is tender. If the liquid evaporates too quickly, add 1 more cup water.

3. *Prepare the Cauliflower:* Cut the cauliflower into 2- or 3-inch florets. Bring water to a boil in a pan large enough to hold the florets and drop them in. Cook rapidly over moderate heat for 3 minutes. Drain and cool.

4. Dip the florets in the eggs, then dredge them in the flour and brown them in moderately hot oil for 2 minutes. Drain on paper towels.

5. When all the cauliflower florets have been browned and the lamb is tender, add the florets to the lamb. Cook for 5 minutes over low heat. Do not stir but shake the pan briskly to mix.

Serve warm with salad and French fried potatoes, the Tunisian way. Serves 8.

VARIATION
Two pounds of boneless beef chuck cut into 2-inch cubes may be substituted for the lamb. The cooking time to tenderize the beef will be about 1 1/2 hours.

❈ MARKA AU CHOU-FLEUR ❈

Lamb with Chick-Peas and Cauliflower Fritters

This recipe is an odd combination that is compatible with the entire character of Tunisian cooking.

For the Lamb

2 tablespoons olive oil
1 small onion, chopped (1/3 cup)
2 pounds boneless lamb, cut into
   3-inch pieces

3 tablespoons tomato paste
1/2 teaspoon salt
1/4 teaspoon black pepper
1 1/2 cups water

For the Cauliflower

1 cauliflower (2 pounds)
4 cups lightly salted water
2 eggs, beaten
2 tablespoons flour

1/2 cup milk
1/2 cup olive oil

1/2 cup cooked chick-peas

1. *Prepare the Lamb:* Heat the oil in a pan and fry the onion and lamb over moderate heat for 5 minutes. Add the tomato paste, salt and pepper and continue to fry for 5 minutes more. Add the water, cover the pan and simmer over low heat for 45 minutes, or until the lamb becomes tender.

2. *Prepare the Cauliflower:* Cut the cauliflower into large florets. Bring the water to a boil over moderate heat and cook the cauliflower for 3 minutes. Drain. (This blanching is intended to remove the strong smell.)

3. Prepare a batter by mixing together the eggs, flour and milk. Dip the florets into the batter. Heat oil until hot and in it brown florets on all sides for 2 minutes.

4. When all the cauliflower has been fried, add it to the lamb mixture with the chick-peas. Simmer over low heat for 10 minutes more. Do not stir—shake the pan to combine. The fritters should not be broken up.

Serve warm with bread and salads. Serves 8.

❖ TAJINE D'ARTICHAUTS ❖ TUNISIENNE

Egg Loaf with Artichokes

There are many variations on the egg loaf, such as with green peas, mushrooms, zucchini, eggplant, spinach, dried white beans, parsley and brain. The list is long, with the possibility of having a combination with and without meat.

6 eggs, beaten	*1/2 teaspoon salt*
1 pound ground beef, lamb or	*1/4 teaspoon black pepper*
chicken	*6 fresh artichoke hearts, halved*
4 sprigs flat-leaf parsley, chopped	*2 tablespoon grated Gruyère-type*
1 medium onion, chopped (1/2 cup)	*cheese*
3 cloves garlic, chopped fine	*a 9 × 5 × 3-inch loaf pan*

1. In a bowl mix together the eggs, meat, parsley, onion, garlic, salt and pepper. Pour into a well-oiled loaf baking dish or Pyrex dish. Arrange the artichokes equally spaced in the meat mixture, pushing them into the mix. Sprinkle the top with the cheese.

2. Bake in a 350 degree oven for 30 minutes, or until the top is light brown.

Serve warm in slices. Serves 6.

❖ RECHDA ❖

Lamb Stew with Noodles

The troglodytes living in their caves in Matmata do have contact with the coastal cities of Tunisia and can therefore prepare food that suits their palates. Above the surface of the caves is a scrub-covered semi-desert with stone walls that are used to trap an unreliable rainfall.

FOR THE STEW

2 pounds boneless lamb, cut into
    3-inch pieces, each 1/2 inch
    thick
2 tablespoons olive oil
3 tablespoons tomato paste
1–2 teaspoons black pepper, to taste

1 teaspoon salt
1 teaspoon Quatre Épices (see
    page 60)
1 medium onion, chopped (2/3 cup)
4 cloves garlic, chopped
8 cups water

FOR THE NOODLES

2 pounds flour
1/2 teaspoon salt

about 2 cups water

1. *Prepare the Stew:* Put all the ingredients in a pan, cover and cook over moderate heat for 1 hour, or until the lamb is tender.

2. *Prepare the Noodles:* Make a dough by combining the flour with almost all the water. Knead until smooth on a floured board.

3. Roll out long strips of dough, 2 inches wide and 1/4 inch thick. Cut the strips into noodles 1 inch square. Toss them in the air to separate them and dry a little. Set aside.

4. After the lamb stew (with a considerable amount of sauce) has cooked for 1 hour and the lamb is tender, add as many noodles as desired for each person and cook another 15 minutes over moderately low heat.

Serve warm with the breads of the Sahara or the French bread of the country. Serves 6 to 8.

❈ MOSLI D'AGNEAU ❈

ROAST LEMON LAMB

Mosli is a popular family and restaurant method for cooking lamb. I have dined on *mosli* prepared from the leg, shank or shoulder of the lamb, cut into generous portions, including the bone. The lemon garnish on the roast provides an influential flavor.

1 teaspoon salt
2 teaspoons black pepper or
   2 teaspoons Harissa
   (see page 89)
1 teaspoon ground cumin
1 cup water
a 4-pound leg of lamb, with or
   without bone, cut into 8 pieces
5 cloves garlic, chopped

1 large onion (1/2 pound), sliced
   into rounds
2 ripe tomatoes (1 pound), sliced
10 potatoes (3 pounds), peeled and
   halved
8 sweet green peppers (2 pounds),
   halved, seeds and stems discarded
2 tablespoons olive oil
8 thin slices lemon

1. Mix the salt, pepper or *harissa* and cumin with the water and in a roasting pan pour it over the lamb. Add the garlic, onion, tomato, potato and green pepper and sprinkle the oil over and around the meat.

2. Bake, uncovered, in a 350 degree oven for 1 1/2 hours, or until the lamb is tender and roasted throughout, basting several times during the roasting. Ten minutes before the lamb is done, scatter the lemon slices over all.

Serve the lamb warm with an assortment of the roasted vegetables and sauce. Serves 8.

❈ GARGOULETTE DES ÉMIRS ❈

LAMB IN A CLAY POT

This recipe was revived by the restaurateur Bechir Ennouri for his restaurant Des Émeris in Souse and has achieved a certain popularity. His hobby, an admirable one, is to bring back recipes that have slipped out of fashion or are of historical importance to a region in Tunisia not visited or available to tourists. The recipe is from his home town in southern Tunisia called Messaina.

There the *gargoulette* is served to celebrate circumcisions and other family ceremonial occasions. The pot (sometimes called a jar) was sealed with clay and baked for about 3 hours in a wood fire. Then before the guests the jar was broken with a wooden hammer, signifying good times, happy times.

The size of the pot determines how many can dine. A large tan clay jar, shaped like a Greek amphora and available, it seems, all over Tunisia, could serve ten people.

2 pounds lamb shank or shoulder, *1/2 teaspoon turmeric*
  cut into 6 pieces *1/2 teaspoon black pepper*
4 cloves garlic, sliced *1 teaspoon salt, or to taste*
1 teaspoon dried rosemary *3 cups water*
1 medium onion, sliced (1/2 cup) *1 clay bean pot with cover*
3 tablespoons tomato paste *aluminum foil*

Mix the lamb, garlic, rosemary, onion, tomato paste, turmeric, pepper, salt and water together in the bean pot. Seal it tightly by first placing the foil over the pot opening, then pushing the cover over it, pressing it in firmly. Bake in a 300 degree oven for 3 hours.

Open the pot and serve warm. Serves 6.

� BROCHETTE D'AGNEAU �
DANS LE SABLE
LAMB BARBECUED IN HOT SAND

Here again the ingenuity of the desert Bedouin and Berber is brought out in the preparation of these brochettes.

Boneless lamb is cut in 1-inch cubes and threaded on metal skewers, alternating with tomato and onion slices. The skewers are sprinkled with salt and pepper.

A hole is dug in the desert sand and a fire built in it. A clay pot (*tajine*) deep enough to hold and support the brochettes upright is placed in the fire. Hot charcoal is heaped around the pot, which operates like an oven. The brochettes are put in the pot, the pot is covered with the lid, then with hot sand and the brochettes inside bake for 1/2 hour.

The tagine is removed from the fire and opened. The lamb is roasted with all the flavor locked in. Simple and effective.

❈ KHUBZ MTABQA ❈

BAKED STUFFED BREAD PANCAKES

A modern stove is not what the Berbers or Bedouin in the desert town of Douz use in baking their bread. When preparing these meat pies, which is what they are, they were baked on a 1/2-inch-thick stone rectangle that had been heated in a modern oven. This would, more or less, equal the simple conditions of a Berber encampment, except for the oven.

FOR THE DOUGH

12 cups flour
2 teaspoons salt

about 2 cups water

FOR THE STUFFING

1 small lamb heart, cut into
   1/4-inch dice
1/4 cup diced lamb fat
1/2 boneless lamb, cut into
   1/4-inch dice
1/2 pound lamb liver, cut into
   1/4-inch dice
2 cloves garlic, chopped fine

5 scallion, sliced thin
6 sprigs flat-leaf parsley, chopped
   fine
1 teaspoon turmeric
1 teaspoon salt
1/2 teaspoon black pepper
2 tablespoons tomato paste

1. *Prepare the Dough:* Mix the flour, salt and enough water together to ensure a firm and smooth but not sticky consistency. Set aside, covered, while you prepare the stuffing.

2. *Prepare the Stuffing:* Put all the ingredients, except the tomato paste, in a skillet and stir-fry over moderately low heat for 10 minutes. Add the tomato paste and continue to fry and stir for 10 minutes more. Remove from the heat and cool.

3. *Prepare the Pancakes:* Roll out the dough on a lightly floured surface into a large thin rectangle 1/8 inch thick. Using a 7- or 8-inch plate as a guide, cut out 2 equal rounds. Cut out 5 more rounds with the remaining dough.

4. Put 4 rounded tablespoons of the stuffing in the center of one of the dough circles. Cover it with another circle and press the edges down all the way with the tines of a fork.

5. Bake the pancakes on an oiled cookie sheet in a very hot oven, 450 degrees, for 15 minutes, or until light brown.

Serve warm, halved, if you wish. Otherwise these are eaten in the round. Makes 7 well-stuffed pancakes.

❋ FELFEL MEHCHI ❋

STUFFED PEPPERS

Many cuisines include stuffed peppers, and in any number of ways. A touch of cheese in this stuffing indicates, perhaps, a French hand, but the method of cooking is Tunisian.

6 medium sweet green or red peppers	*1 cup French bread, soaked in water, squeezed and chopped*
4 tablespoons olive oil	*1/2 teaspoon salt, or to taste*
1 medium onion, chopped (1/2 cup)	*1/4 teaspoon black pepper*
1/2 pound ground lamb	*1/4 cup flour*
5 sprigs flat-leaf parsley, chopped	*2 whole eggs, beaten*
1 hard-cooked egg, chopped	*1 cup water*
1/4 cup grated Gruyère cheese	*2 tablespoons tomato paste*

1. Cut out the stem ends of the peppers and reserve. Discard the seeds and fibers inside. Set the peppers aside.

2. Heat 1 tablespoon of the oil in a skillet and stir-fry the onion and lamb over moderate heat for 5 minutes. Remove the skillet from the heat and cool for 2 minutes. Stir in the parsley, hard-cooked egg, cheese, bread, salt and pepper. Stuff the peppers and replace the stem ends to fit.

3. Dip the stuffed peppers, stem end first, into the flour and coat all over. Then dip the peppers in the beaten eggs to seal the stem ends closed. Heat the remaining 3 tablespoons oil in a skillet and fry the peppers for 3 minutes on all sides. Place them in a pan.

4. Mix together the water and tomato paste. Pour over the peppers, cover the pan and bring to a boil. Reduce the heat to low and cook slowly for 1/2 hour, basting now and then.

Serve warm. Makes 6 peppers as a side dish with other foods.

SFAFID TUNISIENNE

BROILED LAMB BROCHETTE

For this most simple grill, Tunisian lamb is purchased fresh, home grown and full of flavor, with a minimum of fat. The tomato, green pepper and onion are cut slightly larger than the lamb cubes.

I have been served these brochettes without lemon or vegetables but usually with the ubiquitous French fried potatoes and a simple salad of lettuce and tomato slices. Lemon slices are always present.

lemon slices, cut into half moons
1 pound boneless lamb, cut into
  1-inch cubes
1 or 2 ripe tomatoes, cut into
  1/2-inch-thick cubes
2 medium sweet green peppers, cut
  into 1-inch cubes

1 medium onion, cut into 1-inch
  cubes
metal brochettes, each about 8
  inches long
salt, to taste

1. Assemble each brochette in this manner: Begin with a slice of lemon. Follow this with a lamb cube, then a cube of tomato, green pepper and onion and lastly another slice of lemon. Repeat until the brochette is filled but always begin and end with a lemon slice.

2. Sprinkle with salt and broil over charcoal or in a gas or electric broiler until done.

Serve immediately. Serves 6.

BRIK DANNOUNI

LAMB TURNOVERS

Brik are usually prepared with the paper-thin pastry leaves known as *malsouka*. This recipe, from the island of Jerba, the wrapper is hand-made of flour, eggs and olive oil into a rich pastry. Then the turnovers are deep-fried, resulting in a melting meat-stuffed appetizer that is good with drinks or as a first course, preceding more elaborate entrées.

FOR THE DOUGH

3 cups flour
2 egg yolks
3 tablespoons olive oil

1/4 teaspoon salt
about 1/2 cup water

FOR THE STUFFING

1 pound ground lamb
1/3 cup grated Gruyère-style cheese

1/4 teaspoon black pepper

FOR THE TURNOVERS

1 egg yolk, lightly beaten

1 cup corn oil

1. *Prepare the Dough:* Mix the flour, egg yolks, oil and salt together. Add enough water to prepare an easily handled dough. Knead well until smooth. Break the dough into walnut-sized balls and set aside. Makes 12 balls.

2. *Prepare the Stuffing:* Stir-fry the lamb in a skillet over moderate heat for 3 minutes, just enough time to change the color. Cool. Mix the lamb, cheese and pepper together to form the stuffing. Set aside.

3. *Prepare the Turnovers:* Take a ball of the pastry dough and roll it out to a 4-inch circle. Put 1 tablespoon of the stuffing near the bottom edge of the circle. Dab the bottom rim with a little egg to moisten the edge and fold the pastry over to form a half moon. Pinch the edges together with the tines of a fork. Make turnovers with the remaining dough and stuffing in the same manner.

4. Heat the oil in a skillet or wok. Fry the *brik* over moderate heat for about 3 minutes until light brown on each side. Drain on paper towels.

Serve warm as an appetizer or a first course. Makes 12 turnovers.

NOTE: The cooks on Jerba use olive oil (low in cholesterol) for frying the turnovers; however, for our purposes corn oil is perfectly adequate.

BLETTES FARCIES ✿

STUFFED SWISS CHARD

Swiss chard seems to have replaced common spinach on the island of Jerba. In fact, I never saw spinach in the market there. In any event, it is much easier to stuff the large green fronds of chard. The chard balls are easily assembled and full of flavor, and they are steamed over hot water, fulfilling the relevant health criteria of our time.

1/2 pound boneless lamb, chopped
(not ground) into small cubes
1 pound Swiss chard, stems
removed, leaving about 14 fresh
green leaves
1 small onion, chopped (1/3 cup)
6 sprigs flat-leaf parsley, chopped
1 medium potato, peeled and cut
into small cubes (2/3 cup)
2 cloves garlic, chopped fine
1 carrot, peeled and cut into small
cubes (1/2 cup)

1/4 cup berkoukes
(see Note below)
1/4 teaspoon ground cumin
1/4 teaspoon ground caraway
1 tablespoon tomato paste
1 tablespoon olive oil
1/2 teaspoon Harissa
(see page 89)
1/2 teaspoon salt
1/4 teaspoon black pepper

1. Mix everything together except the Swiss chard leaves to form the stuffings.

2. Put 2 chard leaves on a plate and top with 3 tablespoons of the stuffing. Fold the leaves over and around into a ball. Tie the ball up with white string. (On Jerba, long slender strips of palm leaves are used to tie up the chard.)

3. Place the balls in the top (*kesskess*) of a *couscousier.* Fill the bottom (*makfoul*) of the *couscousier* with water and bring to a boil. Steam over low heat for 1 1/2 hours. Do not cover the steamer during this time since it preserves the fresh green color of the chard.

Serve warm. Makes 7 or 8 balls.

NOTE: *Berkoukes* are the very small round balls of pasta. These are known as *m'hammas* in Arabic and *plombs*, round bullets, in French. In the event that neither is available, one could use the rice-shaped orzo.

✸ OJA CERVELLE ✸

LAMB BRAIN IN EGG SAUCE

The *oja* of any combination, and there are many, may be one of the most popular Tunisian dishes, along with *chakchouka*. *Oja* turns up frequently on menus and is convenient for the homecook. It has the principal characteristic of being easy to prepare, quick and economical. It is a first course in a menu for the busy homemaker. Brain prepared any way at all is one of my favorite foods.

1/2 pound lamb brain (1 or 2)
water to cover
1 tablespoon olive oil
3 cloves garlic, chopped fine
2 medium sweet green peppers (1/2 pound), cut into 1/2-inch cubes

1 ripe tomato (1/2 pound), coarsely chopped
1/4 teaspoon black pepper
1/2 teaspoon salt, or to taste
4 whole eggs

1. Cook the brains in the water over moderate heat for 10 minutes. Cool and cut the brains into 1/2-inch cubes. Set aside.

2. Heat the oil in a skillet. Add the garlic and green peppers and stir-fry over moderate heat for 2 minutes. Add the tomato, pepper and salt and cook, covered, for 10 minutes.

3. Add the brains to the sauce, mix well and cook for 5 minutes. Add the eggs and stir them into the sauce. Simmer for 2 minutes for soft and 5 minutes for firm-textured eggs.

Serve warm with French bread. Serves 4.

VARIATION
The following 3 recipes offer a variety of different ways to serve the *Oja*.

❈ OJA MERGUEZ ❈

SAUSAGE IN EGG SAUCE

Merely substitute 1/2 pound *merguez*, cut into 1/2-inch pieces, for the brains. I have also been served *oja* with 2 whole *merguez*, grilled over charcoal and included as a garnish.

❈ OJA BNADEK ❈

MEATBALLS IN EGG SAUCE

Use 1/2 pound ground beef or lamb. Prepare small meatballs, each about 3/4 inches in diameter.

Roll the balls without seasoning tightly in your palms. Cook them in boiling water over moderate heat for 5 minutes. Drain and use them in the same way as the cubes of brain.

❈ OJA AUX CREVETTES ❈

SHRIMP IN EGG SAUCE

Use 1 pound fresh shrimp, peeled, deveined and cut into 1-inch pieces. As in the brain recipe, add the raw shrimp to the tomato and green pepper sauce and cook for 10 minutes. Then stir in the whole eggs and cook for 3 minutes more.

AGNEAU AU FOUR DE SABLE

STUFFED LAMB STOMACH BAKED

This a typical dish of the Bedouin of Douz. The lamb stomach may, however, be stuffed and roasted in an oiled pan in a modern 375 degree oven for 1 hour or more. The tibia allows steam to escape so that the stomach does not break open.

I am including this recipe both for historical purposes as well as for those adventurous souls who wish to try an extremely tasty yet idiosyncratic desert dish.

1 lamb stomach, from your Middle Eastern butcher
2 pounds boneless lamb, cut into 1-inch pieces
1/4 pound lamb fat, chopped (optional)
1 pound potato, peeled and cut into 1-inch pieces
1 large onion, chopped (1 cup)
2 cloves garlic, chopped
4 sprigs flat-leaf parsley, chopped
1 teaspoon turmeric
1 teaspoon salt
1/2 teaspoon black pepper
1 tablespoon tomato paste
1 lamb tibia, hollowed out

1. Rinse the lamb stomach out well to prepare it for the stuffing.

2. Mix all the ingredients together in a bowl, except the tibia. Stuff the lamb stomach with the mixture and sew it up, leaving an opening in which to fit the tibia; this will act as a type of chimney and allow steam to escape.

3. Dig a hole in the sand. (This could be done on a sandy beach.) Build a hot charcoal fire. After it burns for some time and the coals are red hot, move them to the side and put the stomach in upright. Push hot sand around it and cover the sand with the coals of the fire. The lamb tibia should stick out above the level of the coals and sand. Bake for 1 hour.

4. Push aside the fire and sand, remove the stomach and brush off the sand. Pull out the tibia. Cut the stomach into pieces and serve warm.

Serves 6.

✖ ROUZ JERBI ✖

JERBIAN RICE AND LAMB

This is a traditional dish of the island of Jerba. It is a green mixture, due to the Swiss chard and parsley in it. Rice is not grown on Jerba, but has always been imported to prepare this unconventional food of the island.

Canned tomato paste, unlike the homemade concentrate, is far easier to use here. The concentrate may still be prepared in some homes where the old traditions prevail.

2 cups rice, rinsed well
18 sprigs flat-leaf parsley,
  coarsely chopped
1 pound Swiss chard, coarsely
  chopped
1 large onion, chopped (1 cup)
1 pound boneless lamb, cut into
  1/2-inch cubes
1/2 pound lamb liver, cut into
  1/2-inch cubes

2 tablespoons chopped lamb fat
  (optional)
2 tablespoons tomato paste
1 teaspoon sweet paprika
1/2 teaspoon salt, or to taste
1/4 teaspoon black pepper
1 tablespoon olive oil
10 cups boiling water

1. Soak the rice in hot water for 15 minutes. Drain.

2. Mix the rice, parsley, chard, onion, lamb, lamb liver, fat, if used, tomato paste, paprika, salt, pepper and olive oil together. Put the mixture into the top (*keskess*) of a *couscousier*. In the bottom (*makfoul*) of the *couscousier* bring the 10 cups water to a boil. Cover the *couscousier* and steam over moderate heat for 1 hour. Taste the mixture to see if the lamb is tender; if not, steam a few more minutes.

Serve warm with bread and salad. Serves 6 to 8.

BEEF

❈ KAMOUNIA ❈
BEEF RAGOUT WITH CUMIN

I was taught this recipe in a working-class public restaurant in the *souk* of Sfax, which is entered through the gate of the ancient walled city. The kitchen was nothing to write home about but all the equipment was there, including a strongly constructed, blackened gas stove. The menu was of the day, with the carcass of a sheep prominently displayed in the window, looking out into the narrow alley of the souk. Passersby wandered by, making up their minds and pointing out the merits of the lamb. The food was cooked in the traditional manner, no frills but filled with flavor.

This cumin-flavored dish of three meats has several different textures in a lightly spiced, rich and thick, but not hot, sauce.

2 tablespoons olive oil	1/4 teaspoon black pepper
1 large onion, chopped (1 cup)	3 tablespoons tomato paste
2 pounds beef chuck, cut into	1 tablespoon ground cumin
2-inch cubes	1 tablespoon sweet paprika
1 pound heart, trimmed of veins,	1 teaspoon turmeric
cut into 1-inch pieces	3 cloves garlic, crushed in a garlic
1 pound liver, cut into 1-inch pieces	press
1 teaspoon salt, or to taste	3 cups water

1. Heat the oil in a pan and fry the onion over moderate heat for 1 minute. Add the chuck, heart and liver and stir-fry for 5 minutes. Add the salt, pepper, tomato paste, cumin, paprika, turmeric and garlic. Mix well.

2. Add the water and cook, covered, over moderate heat until the beef

is soft, about 1 1/2 hours. Should the liquid evaporate too quickly add another 1/2 cup water.

Serves 8 with bread and salads.

✷ M'LOUKHIA ✷

BEEF IN BLACK SAUCE

M'loukhia is an old-time traditional dish of infinite interest. The Latin name for the plant is *corchorus olitorius,* and it is also known as Jews' mallow or tossa jute. The plant grows from Egypt to Japan but mostly in India and Bangladesh. Jute (burlap) is derived from the mature plant. The green leaves are dried and used.

M'loukhia is one of those idiosyncratic foods that is well known and appreciated by those who are hooked on the black viscous sauce. The Egyptians dote on it and some Tunisians like it very much. Alas, the general public does not find it interesting.

1 cup green m'loukhia *powder*
1/4 cup olive oil
8 cups boiling water
1 pound boneless beef chuck, cut
    into 2-inch pieces
1 tablespoon ground coriander

1 bay leaf
1/2 teaspoon salt, or to taste
2 cloves garlic, crushed in a mortar
    with 1 tablespoon fresh mint
1/2 teaspoon Harissa (optional,
    see page 89)

1. Put the *m'loukhia* and oil in a large pan and mix them into a paste over low heat, stirring continuously, for 2 minutes. Add 6 cups boiling water, stir well, cover the pan and simmer for 2 hours. (Some say 3 hours is better.)

2. Add the beef, coriander, bay leaf, salt and the garlic and mint mixture. Add the balance of the water, 2 cups. Continue to cook over low heat for 1 hour more to tenderize the beef, stirring now and then.

    When the oil has risen to the top, the dish is ready to serve. There is ample sauce.

Serve hot with bread and salads. Serves 6.

❖ KEFTA DE BŒUF ❖

BEEF MEATBALLS

Universally popular meatballs, spiced in the Tunisian manner, are prepared this way in the historically important city of Kairouan. The cheese and bread crumbs indicate a touch of France.

1 pound ground beef
1 small onion, chopped (1/4 cup)
6 sprigs flat-leaf parsley, chopped
2 tablespoons grated Gruyère-type
  cheese
2 teaspoons ground coriander
2 teaspoons Harissa
  (see page 89)

1/2 teaspoon salt
2 egg yolks
1/4 cup bread crumbs
1/2 cup cooked potato, mashed
1/4 cup olive oil

1. Mix everything together, except the oil. Form meatballs using 1 heaping tablespoon of the mixture for each. Makes 10.

2. Heat the oil in a skillet and brown the balls on all sides for about 5 minutes. Drain on paper towels.

3. Serve as an appetizer with drinks or as one of the dishes in a Tunisian lunch or dinner.

Serve warm. Makes 10 meatballs.

❖ OJA KAABER ❖

MEATBALLS IN EGG SAUCE

Meatballs prepared in this manner—prior to adding the sauce—is a way of conserving them. Cook the meatballs in the water and oil, but do not fry them. When the water has evaporated, put the meatballs in a jar with the oil they are in, plus 1/4 cup more oil to cover. On rainy or other non-marketing days, the meatballs are removed from the oil and added to the sauce.

FOR THE MEATBALLS

> 1 pound ground beef
> 1 teaspoon salt
> 1/2 teaspoon black pepper
>
> 2 teaspoons powdered dried mint
> 1/4 cup plus 2 teaspoons olive oil
> 2 cups water

FOR THE SAUCE

> 2 pounds sweet green pepper or peperone chili, seeded and sliced thin
> 2 tablespoons olive oil
> 4 tomatoes (2 pounds), sliced thin
> 2 tablespoons tomato paste
> 1–2 teaspoons Harissa (see page 89), to taste
>
> 1 cup water
> 4 cloves garlic, crushed in a garlic press
> 1/2 teaspoon salt
> 1 teaspoon ground caraway
> 6–8 eggs (usually 1 per person)

1. *Prepare the Meatballs:* Mix the beef, salt, pepper, mint and the 2 teaspoons oil together. Form meatballs, each 1 inch in diameter. Put them in a pan and cover with the water and the remaining 1/4 cup oil.

2. Cook over moderate heat until all the water has evaporated, about 30 minutes. As the water evaporates, do not continue to fry the balls in the oil. Remove them and set aside.

3. *Prepare the Sauce:* Stir-fry the peppers in the oil over moderate heat for 3 minutes. Add the sliced tomato, tomato paste and *harissa* and fry for 5 minutes.

4. Add the water and simmer over low heat for 15 minutes to evaporate some of the liquid. Add the meatballs, removed from the oil, the garlic, salt and caraway. Stir well and simmer for 5 minutes.

5. Beat the eggs very lightly, just enough to break the yolk, and pour them over the surface of the meatballs and sauce. Shake the pan back and forth several times; do not stir the mixture. Allow the eggs to firm up for 3 minutes, but do not let them cook too firm.

Serve hot with bread and salads. Serves 6 to 8.

MACARONI À LA TUNISIENNE

TUNISIAN MACARONI

Tunisian macaroni is a round pellet half the size of the American supermarket variety. In Algeria, it is known as *berkoukes*.

Although this recipe appears on restaurant menus as Tunisian macaroni, which it may be, the inspiration is Italian. One should remember that Italy is only about 70 miles away across the Mediterranean from the shores of Tunisia and also that Tunisia was a vassal state of Rome during the ancient era.

2 tablespoons olive oil	5 sprigs flat-leaf parsley
1 pound boneless beef chuck, cut into 6 pieces	1 teaspoon salt
	1/4 teaspoon white pepper
2 cloves garlic, chopped	3 tablespoons tomato paste
1/4 cup cooked chick-peas	3 cups water
2 ribs celery, strings removed and sliced thin	1 pound macaroni

1. Heat the oil in a pan and add the beef, garlic, chick-peas, celery, parsley, salt, pepper and tomato paste. Stir-fry over moderate heat for 5 minutes. Add 2 cups of the water, cover and cook for 30 minutes to soften the beef.

2. Add the balance of the water, 1 cup, bring to a boil and add the macaroni. Cook for 15 to 20 minutes, stirring frequently, until the meat is soft and the macaroni is *al dente* but not overcooked.

Serve warm with beef, macaroni and sauce for all. Serves 6.

M'BATEN AUX ÉPINARD

BEEF AND SPINACH FRITTERS

M'baten means the lining of a coat—the implication for this dish being, as it was explained to me, that the fritters are lined with the flour, as in enrobed, then fried.

FOR THE FRITTERS

1 pound spinach, blanched in
  boiling water, squeezed dry
  and chopped
2 pounds ground beef
1/2 teaspoon salt
1/4 teaspoon black pepper
2 eggs, beaten
1 tablespoon finely chopped onion

1 cup soft bread, trimmed,
  moistened with water, squeezed
  dry and chopped
1/2 cup flour
1/4 cup olive oil
5 small sweet green peppers
  (1 pound), browned in the oil
  5 minutes

FOR THE SAUCE

2 tablespoons olive oil
1 small onion, chopped (1/4 cup)
4 cloves garlic, crushed in a garlic
  press

1/4 cup tomato paste
3 cups water

1. *Prepare the Fritters:* Mix all the ingredients together except for the olive oil.

2. Prepare patties 3 inches in diameter and almost 1/2 inch thick

3. Pan-fry patties in the olive oil. Drain and add to sauce.

4. *Prepare the Sauce:* Heat the oil in a pan and fry the onion and garlic over low heat for 1 minute. Add the tomato paste and water and simmer over low heat for 15 minutes.

5. Add the prepared lightly browned fritters and cook for 20 minutes, which will reduce the sauce somewhat. Add the green peppers and cook 5 minutes more. Use them as a decorative garnish.

Serve warm with bread and salads. Serves 8.

❊ MERGUEZ ❊
TUNISIAN BEEF SAUSAGE

Merguez, the incomparable lean sausage of Tunisia, are found in butcher shops, hanging in strands by the yard. The beef should be coarsely ground, which adds a firm chewy texture to the finished product. The sausages can be prepared and eaten the same day, and it is recommended that they be used fresh. On the other hand, they can also be refrigerated for 2 or 3 days without any deterioration.

There are those who insist that the real *merguez* are prepared with lamb. Most of my information came from those who insisted that they were prepared with beef. Both types of ingredients are valid.

Merguez may be grilled over charcoal, fried in oil or added to various dishes, including couscous. For my own part, I have prepared them as sausages without casing, not having a sausage machine. Simply shape them in the size noted below and fry or grill them. They are wonderful.

2 pounds lean beef, coarsely ground
2 tablespoons sweet paprika
2 teaspoons black pepper
1 tablespoon olive oil

2 teaspoons ground anise
1 teaspoon dry powdered mint
1 teaspoon salt
2 yards small lamb intestine, well cleaned

Mix everything together well. In a machine prepare cigar-shaped sausages, each 4 inches long and 1/2 inch thick.

Makes about 30.

❊ CHAKCHOUKA AU MERGUEZ ❊
BEEF SAUSAGE IN SAUCE

Merguez are the ubiquitous but infinitely delicious sausage in Tunisia and the other countries of the Maghreb.

Chakchouka is a Berber word, which might lead one to consider the possibility that *merguez* is of Berber origin. The Berbers are the aboriginal people of Tunisia with their own distinctive customs and cuisine.

2 tablespoons olive oil
10 Merguez (see page 261)
2 ripe tomatoes (1 pound), sliced thin
1 or 2 semi-hot fresh green chili peppers, halved, seeded and sliced thin
2 tablespoons tomato paste

1 teaspoon Harissa (see page 89)
4 cloves garlic, crushed in a garlic press
1 teaspoon sweet paprika
1/2 teaspoon salt
1/8 teaspoon ground cinnamon
1/2 cup water
1 whole egg

1. Heat the oil in a pan or large skillet and brown the *merguez* all over for 2 minutes. Add the tomato, hot chili, tomato paste, *harissa*, garlic, paprika, salt and cinnamon. Mix well and fry over low heat for 5 minutes.

2. Add the water and simmer, uncovered, for 10 minutes. Push aside a hollow space in the center of the *merguez* mixture. Break the egg into it and cook for 5 minutes more. (The egg is a decorative device.)

Serve with bread and salads. Serves 6.

❖ LANGUE FARCIE ❖

Stuffed Tongue, Tunis Style

This is probably a Franco-Tunisian invention, but nevertheless popular in Tunis. When a particular recipe is made frequently, even if it is of foreign inspiration, it enters the mainstream and becomes part of the cuisine, as this one has.

1 veal tongue (about 2 pounds)
5 sprigs flat-leaf parsley, chopped
1 medium onion, chopped
   (2/3 cup)
2 tablespoons cooked rice
1/2 teaspoon salt
1/4 teaspoon black pepper
3 cloves garlic, chopped fine

2 hard-cooked eggs, peeled
1 tablespoon olive oil
1 cup water
1/4 teaspoon turmeric
1 tablespoon tomato paste
6 slices of lemon
12 black olives
2 small ripe tomatoes, sliced

1. Cook the tongue, covered, in lightly salted water over moderate heat for 45 minutes. Drain and peel off the skin.

2. Cut the thick part of the tongue halfway down the center and open it up flat. Cut out about 3 tablespoons of the tongue to open a space. Cut off 2 inches of the tip of the tongue and chop it fine with the meat removed from the thick end.

3. Mix the chopped tongue, parsley, onion, rice, salt, pepper and garlic and stuff the tongue. Push the eggs in lengthwise, end to end. Tie the tongue up with string to close it tightly.

4. Oil a baking dish with a cover. Put in the tongue and pour in the water combined with turmeric and tomato paste. Cover the tongue with the lemon slices and place the olives and tomato slices around it.

5. Cover the dish and bake in a 350 degree oven for 30 minutes. Remove the cover and continue to bake until tender, basting now and then, about 20 minutes more. Add more water should the sauce evaporate.

Serve warm. Slice through the egg, and serve with the sauce and vegetables. Or serve cold with mayonnaise, bread and salads. Serves 6.

CHICKEN

 **POULET MEHSHI**

CHICKEN ROAST

This is a typical Jerbian recipe, in which the clay tagine (baking dish) is used. Wandering through the souk of Houmt Souk, the principal town on the island of Jerba, one finds many Berber clay tagines of enchanting quality, painted in black geometrical figures—primitive painting at its best, and utilitarian too.

1 tablespoon olive oil
1 1/2 pounds potato, peeled and cut
   into 2-inch slices
1 large onion, chopped (1 cup)
2 medium tomatoes, chopped
   (1 cup)
2 sweet green peppers (1/2 pound),
   halved, seeded and sliced

1 teaspoon salt, or to taste
1/4 teaspoon black pepper
a 3-pound chicken, cut into 8
   serving pieces, include liver and
   gizzard, loose skin and fat
   removed and discarded
1 cup water
4 sprigs flat-leaf parsley, chopped

1. Rub a tagine or Pyrex baking dish with the oil. Add layers of the following: Line the dish with potato, top with the onion; top the onion with the tomatoes and green peppers and add salt and pepper.

2. Bake in a 375 degree oven for 10 minutes. Remove and place the chicken pieces over all. Return to the oven for 30 minutes.

3. Add the water to prepare the sauce and baste the chicken. Sprinkle with parsley. Return to the oven for 15 minutes.

Serve warm. Serves 6.

✦ TAJINE AU FOIE DE POULET ✦

CHICKEN LIVERS IN A CLAY POT

The traditional method of making this is to use lamb liver, cut it into 1/2-inch cubes and bake it in a clay tagine. A Pyrex dish, well oiled, is a perfectly legitimate substitute for the tagine, although some exoticism is lost.

3 tablespoons olive oil
1/2 pound chicken livers, sliced thick
6 whole eggs, beaten
2 hard-cooked eggs, sliced
1 medium onion, chopped (1/2 cup)
5 sprigs flat-leaf parsley, chopped

1/4 cup grated Gruyère-style cheese
1/2 teaspoon salt, or to taste
1/2 teaspoon black pepper
3 malsouka (pastry wrappers)
tomato slices, black olives, lettuce leaves as garnish

1. Heat 2 tablespoons of the oil in a skillet and stir-fry the chicken livers over moderate heat for 2 minutes to firm them up. Cool.

2. Mix the beaten eggs, hard-cooked eggs, onion, parsley, cheese, salt and pepper together.

3. Oil the tagine with the remaining 1 tablespoon oil and cover the bottom of it with the *malsouka*. Spread the liver mixture over the bottom and pour the egg mixture over all. Lightly move the mixture around so that the egg reaches the *malsouka* on the bottom.

4. Bake in a 350 degree oven for 20 minutes, or until the top is brown. Turn the baked loaf out on a platter and garnish.

Serve warm, sliced. Serves 6 persons as a first course or appetizer.

✦ KLAYIO DE POULET ✦

CHICKEN IN SPICED SAUCE

Here is an everyday chicken dish from a no-frills public restaurant in the walled *souk* of Sfax.

2 tablespoons olive oil
1 medium onion, chopped (1/2 cup)
2 cloves garlic, crushed in a garlic
 press
a 3-pound chicken, cut into 8
 pieces, loose skin and fat
 removed and discarded

1 teaspoon salt
1/4 teaspoon black pepper
1/4 teaspoon turmeric
2 teaspoons sweet paprika
1 teaspoon ground coriander
4 tablespoons tomato paste
2 cups water

1. Heat the oil in a pan and stir-fry the onion over moderate heat for 3 minutes, or until golden. Add the garlic, chicken, salt, pepper, turmeric, paprika and coriander and mix well.

2. Add the tomato paste and water. Simmer over low heat for 40 minutes, or until the chicken is tender and the sauce has thickened.

Serve hot with bread and salads. Serves 4 to 6.

❊ POULET AUX HARICOTS ❊

CHICKEN WITH HARICOT BEANS

The large white haricot bean is substantial and combines well with poultry and meat. In the *souk* of the old city of Sfax I was treated to a large platter of this dish and afterwards a meticulous cooking lesson on how to make it. Outside of the simple restaurant, the clamor of a family haggling over some fruit was all part of the ambience.

1/2 cup dried haricot beans
1 tablespoon olive oil
1 large onion, chopped (1 cup)
a 3 1/2-pound chicken, cut into 8
 pieces, loose skin and fat
 removed and discarded
3 tablespoons tomato paste
1/2 teaspoon salt, or to taste

1/4 teaspoon black pepper
1 teaspoon sweet paprika
2 teaspoons ground caraway
1 teaspoon turmeric
2 cloves garlic, crushed in a garlic
 press
2 cups water

1. Soak the beans overnight covered in water. Drain. The next day cover with water again and simmer over low heat for 45 minutes, until almost soft. Drain and set aside.

2. Heat the oil in a pan and stir-fry the onion over moderate heat for 1 minute. Add the chicken pieces and continue to fry for 5 minutes. Add the tomato paste, salt, pepper, paprika, caraway, turmeric and garlic and stir-fry for 1 minute to combine.

3. Add the water and beans. Cook, covered, for about 45 minutes, or until the chicken and beans are soft and the sauce has thickened.

Serve warm with bread and salad. Serves 6.

❈ POULET ET RIZ À LA VAPEUR ❈

STEAMED CHICKEN AND RICE

Douz is in the Sahara. There was a violent sand storm blowing the day I arrived at the garden-style hotel in the middle of a date oasis. In a matter of seconds my unprotected camera was filled with fine sand, and made inoperable. Hair, nose, eyes and clothes became part of the desert. Nearby, a half dozen supercilious camels remained unperturbed.

For this recipe, rice is brought in from the coast since it obviously could not be grown here. Yet this preparation is traditional of the town. It is a mystery how it started since couscous and bread are the more common foods.

1 pound rice, well rinsed	*2 cloves garlic, chopped*
a 3-pound chicken, cut into 6 or more pieces	*1 medium onion, chopped (1/2 cup)*
2 tablespoons tomato paste	*1 teaspoon turmeric*
2 teaspoons sweet paprika	*1 teaspoon salt*
2 tablespoons olive oil	*1/2 teaspoon black pepper*

1. Cover the rice with warm water and soak it for 10 minutes. Cook it over low heat for 10 minutes. Drain.

2. Mix the rice and all the remaining ingredients together. Put the mixture into the top (*keskess*) of the *couscousier*. Fill the bottom (*makfoul*) with hot water and bring to a boil. Steam the chicken and rice combi-

nation over moderate heat for 1 hour. Test the chicken for tenderness before removing. It may require steaming for 5 or 10 minutes more.

Serve at room temperature. Serves 6.

❊ POULET AU FENOUIL ❊

CHICKEN WITH FRESH FENNEL

Fresh fennel is a popular vegetable during the growing season when it is cooked and often used in salads. The feathery, delicate leaves are included here as a stuffing or garnish.

*a 3-pound chicken, loose skin and
    fat removed and discarded
2 tablespoons chopped fennel leaves
    for stuffing
1 tablespoon olive oil
4 potatoes (1 pound), peeled and
    halved
1 large onion, sliced (1 cup)
2 small tomatoes (1/2 pound),
    halved*

*4 cloves garlic whole
1 fennel bulb, quartered, plus some
    fennel leaves
1 teaspoon salt
1/4 teaspoon black pepper
1 cup water
1/8 teaspoon ground nutmeg
lemon wedges for serving*

1. Stuff the chicken with the 2 tablespoons chopped fennel leaves.

2. Place the chicken in an oiled roasting pan. Scatter around the chicken in layers, first the potato, then onion, tomato, garlic and fennel bulb and leaves. Sprinkle salt and pepper over all. Pour the water around the edge of the dish.

3. Bake in a 350 degree oven for 1 hour, basting now and then as the sauce develops. Five minutes before serving, sprinkle the chicken with the nutmeg and complete the baking.

Serve warm with the sauce, lemon wedges, bread and salad. Serves 4.

❈ MERMEZ AU POULET ❈

Chicken and Chick-Peas

Mermez is an Arabic word that means half cooked and refers to the tomato and green pepper that are added here at almost the last minute of cooking time.

2 tablespoons olive oil
1/2 teaspoon salt
2 teaspoons sweet paprika
1 teaspoon black pepper
a 3-pound chicken, cut into 8
  pieces, loose skin and fat
  removed and discarded
1 tablespoon tomato paste
1/2 cup cooked chick-peas

2 cups water
1 small onion, sliced thin
  (1/3 cup)
3 cloves garlic, crushed in a garlic
  press
1 ripe tomato, quartered
  (1/2 pound)
1 sweet green pepper (1/2 pound),
  seeded and quartered

1. Mix the oil, salt, paprika, pepper, chicken, tomato paste, chick-peas and water together in a pan. Cook the mixture, covered, over moderate heat until half of the liquid has evaporated, about 1/2 hour.

2. Add the onion and garlic and cook for 10 minutes. Add the tomato and green pepper and cook, uncovered, for 10 minutes more.

Serve warm with bread and salads. Serves 6.

❈ CHAKCHOUKA DE FOIE ❈ DE POULET

Chicken Liver and Vegetable Sauté

This very fine dish is a modern recipe in the style of Tunis, utilizing the techniques and seasoning of a *chakchouka* but made with chicken liver. Tunisians usually use the more common lamb liver in their cooking, but this combination cannot be faulted.

3 tablespoons olive oil
2 medium onions (1/2 pound),
   sliced into rounds
2 medium sweet green peppers
   (1/2 pound), seeded and sliced
   into rounds
3 ripe tomatoes (1 pound), sliced
   into rounds

1/2 pound chicken livers, cut into
   lobes
4 cloves garlic, sliced
2 teaspoons Quatre Épices
   (see page 295)
1 teaspoon salt, or to taste
1/4 teaspoon black pepper
6 whole eggs

1. Heat 2 tablespoons of the oil in a skillet and stir-fry the onions over moderately low heat for 2 minutes. Add the green peppers and stir-fry 2 minutes more. Add the tomatoes and continue to fry for 5 minutes but retain the shape of the vegetables.

2. Heat the remaining 1 tablespoon oil in another skillet and stir-fry the chicken livers over moderately low heat for 3 minutes. Add to the tomato mixture and stir together, continuing to fry.

3. Crush the garlic, spice combination, salt and pepper together in a mortar and add it to the liver mixture; stir a minute. Break the eggs over the surface of the *chakchouka.* Cover the skillet and cook for 5 minutes.

Serve warm, one egg per person. Serves 6 with bread.

▩ BRIK AU FOIE DE POULET ▩

CHICKEN LIVERS IN PASTRY LEAVES

Here is another variation of *brik*—the crisply fried, stuffed pastry leaves known as *malsouka.* The liver filling is moist. It is much easier and safer to prepare the *brik* on a flat plate. When stuffed, fold it over and slide it into the hot oil. Should you lift it up the weight of the moist filling may break through.

2 teaspoons olive oil
1/2 pound chicken livers, sliced thin
1 teaspoon chopped onion
1 clove garlic, crushed in a garlic
   press
1/2 teaspoon salt

1 tablespoon finely chopped
   flat-leaf parsley
10 eggs, preferably medium size
6–8 malsouka (pastry leaves)
corn oil for deep-frying
lemon wedges

1. Heat 1 teaspoon of the olive oil in a skillet, add the livers and stir-fry over low heat for 5 minutes. Add the onion, garlic, salt and parsley. Stir-fry 1 minute and remove the skillet from the heat. Cool and add 1 beaten egg to the liver mixture.

2. On a wide plate spread open 1 round *malsouka*. Put 1 heaping tablespoon of the liver mixture in the center in a semicircle. Add 1 whole egg to the center of that. Fold the *malsouka* over.

3. Heat the oil in a deep skillet and fry the *brik* over moderate heat for 2 minutes, or until brown crisp on both sides. Drain briefly on paper towels.

Serve warm with lemon wedges. Makes 6 to 8.

FISH AND SHELLFISH

✦ CHARMOULA ✦

FISH IN SWEET-AND-SOUR RAISIN SAUCE

Charmoula is not a daily preparation. It is, in fact, a ceremonial or festive dish alleged to be special to Bizerte, the seaport in northern Tunisia. Bizerte has a considerable history with the Spanish who occupied the city for some years. The sweet-and-sour sauce appears to be an import from another country, and Spain could be the culprit.

Mérou is a large white-fleshed Mediterranean fish that combines with couscous and is used in *charmoula*. Any large meaty ocean fish could be used to advantage—turbot, cod, haddock or robalo.

FOR THE FISH

> *2 1/2 pounds fish, such as* mérou,　*1 teaspoon black pepper*
> 　*haddock or turbot, cut into*　　*1 teaspoon salt, or to taste*
> 　*1-inch-thick slices*　　　　　*1/4 cup olive oil*
> *1 teaspoon ground cumin*

FOR THE SAUCE

> *3 tablespoons olive oil*　　　*1/2 pound white or dark raisins*
> *2 pounds onions, sliced thin*　*1/4 cup wine or cider vinegar*

1. *Prepare the Fish:* Mix the fish with the cumin, pepper and salt. Heat the oil in a skillet and fry the fish for 2 minutes or so on each side, enough to almost cook it. Remove the slices from the oil and set aside.

2. *Prepare the Sauce:* Heat the oil in a skillet and fry the onions and raisins over low heat until the onions turn golden. Add the vinegar and cook for 5 minutes, stirring frequently.

3. To cook, remove half of the onion/raisin mixture, including the oil, to a baking or Pyrex dish and spread it over the bottom. Place the fish slices over it. Cover with the balance of the onion/raisin sauce. Bake in a 350 degree oven for 25 minutes to integrate all the seasonings and complete cooking the fish.

Serve warm. Serves 4 to 6.

❀ GARGOULETTE DE POISSON ❀

FISH BAKED IN A JAR

A *gargoulette* is an amphora-shaped clay jar that lies on its sides like an abandoned antiquity on a Greek isle. On the island of Jerba in the town of Gellala in the southern part of the island they are used as baking utensils.

4 pounds sea fish, cut into 2-inch-wide pieces	*1 teaspoon ground caraway*
	1 teaspoon ground cumin
6 cloves garlic, chopped	*3 tablespoons olive oil*
1/4 cup ripe tomato, chopped	*1 teaspoon salt*
2 sweet green peppers (1/2 pound), seeded and quartered	*1 cup water*
	aluminum foil

1. Mix all the ingredients together and put them in a clay pot large enough to hold them or a bean pot with a cover. Cover the top tightly with aluminum foil to seal in the liquid.

2. Bake in a 350 degree oven for 1 1/2 hours.

Serve warm. Serves 6 or more.

VARIATION:

Lamb may also be prepared in a *gargoulette*. With lamb the ingredients will be slightly different; principally the cumin is omitted.

2 pounds boneless lamb, cut into
   1 1/2-inch cubes
1/4 teaspoon black pepper
2 tablespoons tomato paste
4 cloves garlic, chopped
2 sweet green peppers (1/2 pound),
   seeded and quartered

1 teaspoon ground caraway
1 tablespoon olive oil
1 teaspoon salt
1 cup water
aluminum foil

1. Prepare the lamb as you would the fish; put everything in a clay pot and seal it well with the aluminum foil.

2. Bake in a 350 degree oven for 2 1/2 hours.

Serve warm. Serves 6.

MARKA BIL HOUT

FISH IN TOMATO SAUCE

The island of Jerba may be cut off from the mainland cities but it nevertheless has a cuisine that now and then resembles the mainstream.

3 tablespoons olive oil
1 large onion, chopped (1 cup)
1 clove garlic, chopped
2 potatoes (1 pound), cut into 6
   pieces each
2 cups water
2 pounds fish, such as sea bass,

mérou *or red snapper, cut into*
   2-inch-wide slices
1/2 teaspoon salt
1/4 teaspoon black pepper
1 large ripe tomato, chopped
   (1 cup)

1. Heat the oil in a pan and stir-fry the onion and garlic over moderate heat for 3 minutes.

2. Add the potato and water, cover the pan and cook over low heat for 15 minutes. Add the fish, salt, pepper and tomato, cover the pan and cook for 20 minutes more.

Serve warm with bread and salads. Serves 6.

MAQUEREAU AU FOUR

BAKED MACKEREL WITH SPICES

The small, silver-skinned mackerel, freshly caught, with its dark, oily flesh is an unexpected pleasure when dining in Tunis. My cooking teacher said that she always included garlic when cooking fish. This recipe also incorporates cumin, caraway and *harissa* in the Tunisian manner—an unbeatable combination.

3 fresh mackerel (about 1 pound each)

2 large ripe tomatoes, peeled and chopped (2 cups), or equal amount canned

2 sweet green peppers (1/2 pound), seeded and julienned

2 cloves garlic, crushed in a garlic press

1/4 cup water

1/2 teaspoon salt, or to taste

1 teaspoon ground cumin

1/2 teaspoon ground caraway

1/2 teaspoon Harissa (see page 89)

2 tablespoons olive oil

6 sprigs flat-leaf parsley, chopped

2 lemons, quartered, for serving

1. Rinse the fish in cold water, drain and place in an oiled baking dish.

2. Mix together in a bowl the tomatoes, green peppers, garlic, water, salt, cumin, caraway, *harissa*, oil and parsley. Pour over the fish. Bake in a 300 degree oven for 40 minutes, basting several times during this period.

Serve warm with bread and lemon quarters. Serves 6.

GAMBRY À LA GABESIENNE

SHRIMP STEW FROM GABÈS

This is a quick stir-fry, a specialty of Gabès, where shrimp is king. The stewed shrimp are eaten one by one, with diners pulling out the seasoned meat and discarding the shells on their plates. This is not an old traditional recipe but one with modern overtones and French influence.

2 tablespoons olive oil
1 tablespoon chopped onion
4 cloves garlic, chopped fine
1/2 teaspoon ground cumin
1 teaspoon Harissa (see page 89),
   or more to taste

3 pounds medium shrimp in the
   shell
1/2 teaspoon salt, or to taste
1/4 teaspoon white pepper
6 sprigs flat-leaf parsley, chopped
2 tablespoons fresh lemon juice

1. Heat the oil in a skillet over moderate heat. Add the onion and garlic and stir-fry for 1 minute. Add the cumin and *harissa* together and stir- fry another minute.

2. Add the shrimp, salt, pepper, parsley and lemon juice, continuing to stir-fry for 2 minutes.

3. Cover the skillet and cook for 10 minutes. Remove the skillet from the heat and serve immediately.

Serve warm as an appetizer. Serves 6 to 8.

❈ OJA AUX CREVETTES ❈

SHRIMP AND GREEN PEPPERS

This recipe is from the capital city, Tunis, where the French presentation of food is more developed than in the smaller towns.

3 tablespoons olive oil
1/2 pound medium shrimp, peeled
   and deveined
3 sweet green peppers (1/2 pound),
   seeded and coarsely cut (2 cups)
2 cloves garlic, crushed in a garlic
   press

2 teaspoons ground coriander
1/2 teaspoon salt
1/2 teaspoon black pepper
2 tablespoons tomato paste
1 cup water
1 egg, lightly beaten

1. Heat the oil over moderate heat and fry the shrimp for 2 minutes. Add the green pepper and stir-fry for 1 minute.

2. Crush the garlic together with the coriander. Add it to the shrimp

mixture with the salt, pepper and tomato paste and mix well. Add the water and simmer over low heat for 10 minutes.

3. Pour the egg over the surface of the mixture and shake the pan several times to integrate the egg and thicken the sauce.

Serve hot. In a separate platter, serve a tablespoon of harissa, *the white parts of scallion and lemon wedges. Diners will help themselves to this assortment.*

❈ FTIRA AUX CREVETTES ❈

BATTER SHRIMP WITH DIP

FOR THE BATTER

2 eggs, separated	*1/4 teaspoon salt*
2 tablespoons flour	*1/4 teaspoon baking soda*

FOR THE DIP

1 tablespoon olive oil	*12 capers*
1/2 teaspoon salt	*3 sprigs flat-leaf parsley, chopped*
1/4 teaspoon black pepper	*fine*
1 ripe tomato, peeled and chopped	*1 tablespoon fresh lemon juice*
fine	
1 clove garlic, crushed in a garlic	*1 cup corn oil for deep-frying*
press	*2 pounds medium shrimp, peeled*
1 small onion, chopped fine (1/3	*and deveined*
cup)	

1. *Prepare the Batter:* Beat the egg whites until stiff. Fold in the lightly beaten egg yolks, flour, salt and baking soda. Set aside.

2. *Prepare the Dip:* Mix everything together briskly. Set aside.

3. *To Serve:* Heat the oil until hot in a wok or skillet. Dip the shrimp, one by one, into the batter and plunge them into the oil, frying over moderate heat for 1 minute. Drain on paper towels. Serve immediately.

Serve at room temperature with the dip (sauce). Serves 6.

✳ CALAMARES FARCIES ✳

STUFFED SQUID

For aficionados of squid, and I am one of them, this recipe from Tunis will fulfill fondest expectations of a Mediterranean favorite.

6 large squid (1 1/2 pounds)
2 tablespoons olive oil, plus oil for
   the baking dish
1 clove garlic, chopped
8 sprigs flat-leaf parsley, chopped
1 medium onion, chopped (1/2 cup)
1/2 teaspoon salt
1/4 teaspoon black pepper

2/3 cup cooked rice
1 medium sweet green pepper
1/4 cup grated Gruyère cheese
1 medium ripe tomato, peeled and
   chopped (1 cup)
2 tablespoons tomato paste
1 1/2 cups water
aluminum foil

1. Clean the squid in the conventional manner. Remove the tentacles and chop them.

2. In a skillet heat the oil over moderate heat, add the squid tentacles, garlic, parsley, onion, salt and pepper. Stir-fry for 2 minutes. Add the rice and mix well.

3. Grill the green pepper in a gas oven broiler for 3 or 4 minutes to char it all over. Remove, peel and cut the pulp into thin strips. Add to the rice mixture. Stir in the cheese and mix well.

4. Stuff each squid with the rice filling but not tightly since the body will shrink in cooking. Place the squid in a well-oiled baking or Pyrex dish. Combine the ripe tomato and paste with the water. Pour it over the squid. Cover the dish with aluminum foil and bake in a 350 degree oven for 1/2 hour. Remove the foil and bake 10 minutes more, basting several times.

Serve warm. Serves 6.

SALADS, VEGETABLE DISHES AND CONDIMENTS

❈ SALADE BLANKIT ❈

SALAD ON FRENCH BREAD

Blankit is the long loaf of well-baked French bread that is a staple in Tunisia. When I was there in recent years, a pound loaf cost about 12 cents.

The secret of this salad, which is very popular in Tunis, is to assemble it just before dining to prevent a soggy mixture on soaked bread. The salad doubles very well as an appetizer with drinks.

FOR THE SALAD

2 medium onions, peeled
   (1/2 pound)
1 pound ripe tomatoes (2 or 3)
1 medium sweet green pepper
   (1/4 pound)

1/2 teaspoon salt
1/4 teaspoon white pepper
2 tablespoons capers

FOR THE BREAD

1/4 cup wine vinegar
1/4 cup olive oil
2 teaspoons Harissa (see page 89)

2 one-day-old loaves French bread,
   cut into 1/2-inch-thick slices

1/2 cup flaked canned tuna
2 hard-cooked eggs, peeled and
   chopped

8 pitted black olives

1. *Prepare the Salad:* Grill the onion, tomatoes and green pepper over charcoal or in a gas or electric broiler to slightly char the surface. (The onion should grill 3 or 4 minutes longer than the others.) Peel the tomatoes and green pepper and chop them coarsely. Chop the onion the same size. Mix the onion, tomatoes, green pepper, salt, pepper and capers together. Set aside.

2. *Prepare the Bread:* Mix the vinegar, oil and *harissa* together.

3. Dip the slices of bread quickly into the mixture or dribble 1 or 2 teaspoons of the dressing on each slice. Moisten the bread, but do not soak it.

4. To serve, cover each dipped slice of bread with 1 heaping tablespoon of the chopped salad. Garnish each slice with a bit of tuna, chopped egg and 1 black olive.

Serves 8.

❊ SALADE DE RADIS ❊

RADISH SALAD

Salads are a way of life in Tunisia. They are always available on the table. Tunisia has a well-established wine industry begun by the French. The wine vinegar is mild, flavorful and recommended.

12 radishes, sliced into rounds	*2 teaspoons salt*
1 rib celery with leaves, string	*2 tablespoons white wine vinegar*
removed and cut into 1/4-inch	*1/8 teaspoon black pepper*
dice	*1 tablespoon olive oil*

1. Mix together the radish, celery and salt. Let stand 1/2 hour. Drain in a metal sieve and lightly press out the liquid.

2. Mix with the vinegar, pepper and oil.

   Serve as a table condiment with meat dishes. Serves 4.

❈ SALADE DE CONCOMBRE ❈

CUCUMBER SALAD

Not quite a salad, this is more of a table condiment that is served with an assortment of foods.

1 large cucumber, peeled (2 cups sliced)
1 tablespoon olive oil
1 tablespoon white vinegar
1/4 teaspoon salt

1/4 teaspoon sugar
1/4 teaspoon white pepper
2 tablespoons scallion, white part only, thinly sliced

1. Cut the cucumber in half lengthwise and scoop out and discard the seeds. Slice into half moons.

2. Mix everything together and refrigerate.

   Serve cold. Serves 4.

❈ HOURIA ❈

CARROT SALAD

Here is a most popular carrot salad that can be prepared either as a smooth purée or coarsely chopped. Some prefer more texture, and the two styles can be alternated.

1 pound carrots, peeled and sliced diagonally
2 teaspoons powered dried mint
1/4 teaspoon white pepper
1 teaspoon Harissa (optional; see page 89)
1 tablespoon olive oil
1 clove garlic, crushed in a garlic press

1 tablespoon wine vinegar
10 capers
1/2 teaspoon salt, or to taste
1 hard-cooked egg, sliced
1 small tomato, sliced
black olives
lettuce leaves

1. Cook the carrots in lightly salted water until soft but still with crunch. Drain well, cool and process them to a smooth purée in a food processor.

2. Add the mint, pepper, *harissa*, if used, oil, garlic, vinegar, capers and salt and mix everything together. Refrigerate.

Serve cool. Garnish the serving dish with the egg, tomato, olives and lettuce. Serves 6.

❖ AUBERGINE MECHOUIA ❖

CHOPPED EGGPLANT SALAD

Eggplant is universally applauded in salads and other combinations. The Tunisian version has more going for it, with capers, olives and good olive oil, among other things. It can be served at room temperature or, better still, slightly chilled.

2 eggplant (1 pound)
1 medium onion, thinly sliced
   (1/2 cup)
2 cloves garlic, crushed in a garlic
   press
1 tablespoon olive oil

1 tablespoon white wine vinegar
1/2 teaspoon salt, or to taste
1/4 teaspoon white pepper
10 capers
black and green olives
lettuce leaves

1. Cut the eggplant in half lengthwise. Spread 1/2 of each eggplant with onion and garlic and cover with the other half. Broil in a gas or electric oven broiler for about 15 minutes, or until soft and lightly charred. Turn the eggplant over once during this process.

2. Peel the eggplant and coarsely chop the pulp with the onion and garlic. Toss the mixture with the oil, vinegar, salt, pepper and capers. Place on a serving dish.
   Garnish the dish with the olives and lettuce leaves.

Serves 6 to 8.

SALADE MECHOUIA

SMOKED SALAD

Mechouia means grilled. The vegetables are grilled, lightly charred to impart a smokey flavor. In some instances small fragments, a few of the charred skins, remain in the salad to intensify the flavor. This salad is a national favorite during the hot summer days and is considered to have a cooling effect.

The texture can vary, from an almost puréed consistency or a coarsely chopped one, which I prefer.

2 medium onions (1/2 pound),
  peeled
1 large ripe tomato (1/2 pound)
1 medium sweet green pepper
  (1/4 pound)
2 tablespoons olive oil
1/2 teaspoon salt

1/4 teaspoon black pepper
1/4 teaspoon ground caraway
1 tablespoon wine vinegar
1 tablespoon capers
2 hard-cooked eggs, quartered
1/4 cup canned tuna

1. Grill the onions, tomato and green pepper over charcoal or in a gas or electric broiler to char the skins and give a smokey flavor. Peel the tomatoes and the green pepper.

2. Chop the onion, tomato and green pepper into 1/4-inch dice. Mix with the oil, salt, pepper, caraway, vinegar and capers.

Serve the salad cold, garnished with the egg quarters and small chunks of tuna. Serves 6.

SALADE DE RIZ D'HAMMAMET

RICE SALAD FROM HAMMAMET

I tasted this salad on the island of Jerba in the town of Hammamet. There may be other combinations on the island, but this is the salad for hot summer days and desert evenings.

1 large navel or other orange	*1 tablespoon white vinegar*
4 cups plain cooked rice, chilled	*1/2 teaspoon salt, or to taste*
1/2 cup green peas, briefly steamed	*lettuce leaves*
1/2 cup small cooked peeled shrimp	*8 scallion, white part only*
1 tablespoon olive oil	*8 small whole cherry tomatoes*

1. Peel the orange and divide into sections. Remove all the membranes and cut the sections into 1/2-inch cubes.

2. Mix the rice, orange, green peas, shrimp, olive oil, vinegar and salt together. Toss the salad to lighten it.

3. Arrange lettuce leaves on one corner of a plate and top with the scallion and tomatoes. Pile the rice salad in the center of the plate.

Served chilled. Serves 6 to 8.

❖ SALADE TUNISIENNE ❖

TUNISIAN SALAD

It is typical for Tunisian salads to be garnished with excellent-quality canned tuna or sardines. This salad is more often than not garnished with tuna.

Note that if the cucumbers are young, then they do not have to be peeled and seeded. Large cucumbers have a thick skin and should be peeled, halved and the seeds scooped out and discarded; then cut the same size as the other vegetables.

1 medium onion, cut into 1/4-inch dice (1/2 cup)	*1 tablespoon white or red wine vinegar*
2 ripe tomatoes (1/2 pound), cut into 1/4-inch dice	*1/4 teaspoon white pepper*
3 young cucumbers (1/2 pound), cut into 1/4-inch dice	*1/2 teaspoon salt*
	1 teaspoon chopped fresh mint
1 sweet green pepper (1/4 pound), cut into 1/4-inch dice	*black olives*
	2 hard-cooked eggs, peeled and quartered
2 tablespoons olive oil	*canned tuna or sardines*

Mix the onion, tomatoes, cucumbers, green peppers, oil, vinegar, pepper, salt and mint together. Toss the salad.

Serve chilled, garnished with the olives, egg quarters and tuna, broken into 1-inch chunks. Serves 6.

❈ KEFTAJI ❈

VEGETABLE FRY WITH VINEGAR

This is a traditional old recipe that sometimes includes *merguez* (sausage). I prefer this vegetarian version, light and piquant, with the inevitable fried egg as garnish. Another homemaker told me in Tunis that vinegar is never used in her kitchen.

4 tablespoons olive oil
8 small potatoes (2 pounds),
  peeled and sliced into rounds
3 zucchini (1 pound), sliced into
  rounds
2 medium sweet green peppers
  (1/2 pound), seeded and sliced
  lengthwise
1 cup water

1/4 cup tomato paste
1 teaspoon salt, or to taste
1/4 teaspoon black pepper
1/2 teaspoon ground coriander
1 tablespoon wine vinegar
1 whole egg per person
1 tablespoon chopped flat-leaf
  parsley

1. Heat 3 tablespoons of the oil in a skillet and fry the potatoes, zucchini and green peppers separately over moderate heat for about 3 minutes. Fry the potatoes first, long enough to soften. Then cut all the softened cooked vegetables into 1/2-inch pieces.

2. Mix the water, tomato paste, salt, pepper and coriander together. Simmer over low heat for 15 minutes to thicken the sauce. Remove from the heat and stir in the vinegar.

3. Put the chopped vegetables on a serving platter. Pour the warm tomato sauce over them.

4. In another skillet heat the 1 tablespoon olive oil. Fry 1 egg for each

person without breaking the yolk. Cover the vegetables with the eggs and sprinkle the parsley over all.

Serve warm. Serves 6.

❖ CHAKCHOUKA SFAXIAN ❖

VEGETABLE MÉLANGE FROM SFAX

Sfax is a seaport, with its old walled town separated from the more modern sections of the city. Sfax is well known for its seafood and for its regional cuisine, a completely vegetarian example of which follows.

Apparently *chakchouka* is a Berber title, neither Arabic nor French.

2 tablespoons olive oil	2 small potatoes (1/2 pound),
1 medium onion, sliced (1/2 cup)	peeled and cut into French fries
1 small ripe tomato, sliced	1 zucchini (1/2 pound), cut into
3 tablespoons tomato paste	1-inch pieces
1 teaspoon Harissa (see page 000)	2/3 cup cooked chick-peas
3 cloves garlic, crushed in a garlic	2/3 cup green peas, fresh or frozen
press	(optional)
1 1/2 cups water with 1/2 teaspoon	3 eggs, lightly beaten
salt added	1 teaspoon powdered dried mint

1. Heat the oil in a pan, add the onion and fry over moderate heat for 2 minutes, or until it turns golden. Add the tomato, tomato paste, *harissa* and garlic and stir-fry for 3 minutes.

2. Add the salted water and bring to a boil. Add the potato slices and cook for 5 minutes. Add the zucchini, chick-peas and green peas, if used. Cook for 15 minutes over low heat to reduce the liquid and soften the potatoes but still retain their shape.

3. Pour the eggs over the mixture and shake the pan several times, rather than stir, to integrate the eggs. Simmer 3 minutes more to firm up the eggs. Scatter the mint over all.

Serve warm. Serves 6 or more.

CHAKCHOUKA DE LÉGUMES

POACHED VEGETABLES

All the world, now, loves vegetarian dishes that have a touch of originality and seasonings. Here is a fine summer dish when the tomatoes are plump, ripe and flavorful (as the seed catalogues promise) and how they generally are when available in Tunisia.

2 tablespoons olive oil
1 medium onion, cut into 1/2-inch cubes (1/2 cup)
2 tablespoons tomato paste
1 teaspoon sweet paprika
1/2 cup water
1/2 teaspoon salt

1 teaspoon ground coriander
2 ripe tomatoes (1 pound), cut into 1/2-inch cubes
2 sweet green peppers (1/2 pound), seeded and cut into 1/2-inch cubes
4 whole eggs

1. Heat the oil in a skillet and stir-fry the onion over low heat until golden brown, about 3 minutes.

2. Combine the tomato paste, paprika, water, salt and coriander. Pour over the onion and simmer, covered, for 15 minutes.

3. Add the tomato and green peppers. Mix well and continue to cook slowly for 15 minutes.

4. Break each egg over the surface of the vegetables, leaving an equal amount of space in between, and cook, uncovered, for 5 minutes. Baste now and then with the cooking juices.

Serve warm with bread. Serves 4.

FTET

FAVA BEANS, NOODLES AND DRY FISH

Douz, in the Tunisian Sahara, is where I spent some time unravelling culinary mysteries. It is hot, sandy, desiccating and fascinating.

Small dried fish are brought in from the seaport of Gabès. They make a surprising yet logical addition to an essentially desert dish, as the fish add protein and provide a taste different from the ubiquitous lamb dishes that prevail.

3 tablespoons olive oil	1/4 pound dried ocean fish, about
1 large onion, chopped (1 cup)	1 1/2 inches long
2 cloves garlic, chopped	1/2 teaspoon sweet paprika
2 tablespoons tomato paste	1/2 teaspoon black pepper
4 cups water	1 teaspoon salt, or more to taste
a 1-pound can cooked fava beans	1 recipe Rechda noodles

1. Heat the oil in a pan and fry the onion and garlic over moderate heat until golden, about 3 minutes. Add the tomato paste and water and cook for 5 minutes. Add the fava beans, dried fish, paprika, pepper and salt. Simmer over moderately low heat for 15 minutes.

2. Prepare a sheet of dough for Rechda, with 2 pounds flour as directed. Roll out the dough to 1/8 inch thick. Cut the strips 1 1/2 inches wide and 2 inches long. Toss the noodles lightly to dry for 15 minutes.

3. When the sauce is ready, add the noodles and let them cook for 10 minutes if you prefer them *al dente* or a little longer for a softer noodle. Stir slowly during this time. Adjust the salt if necessary.

Serve hot with bread. Serves 6 to 8.

❈ DOIGTS DE FATMA ❈

FINGERS OF FATIMA

Fatima was the daughter of Mohammed.

This wonderful appetizer has many aficionados. The stuffings vary from meat to cheese or anything else for that matter. I prefer this cheese stuffing, which is simply seasoned, relying on two cheeses for its impact. *Malsouka,* the incomparable thin white Tunisian pancake, is the wrapper. Although the *doigts* may be prepared with Greek fillo sheets, *malsouka* provide a texture that is chewy rather than crisp.

> 1 cup ricotta cheese
> 1/2 cup grated Gruyère cheese
> 1/2 teaspoon black pepper

> 1/2 teaspoon salt, or to taste
> 1 egg, beaten

FOR THE FINGERS

> 10 malsouka (Tunisian pan-
> cakes), 7 to 8 inches in
> diameter

> 2 hard-cooked eggs, cut lengthwise
> in 6 pieces each
> 2 cups vegetable oil

1. *Prepare the Stuffing:* Mix everything together rather well. Set aside.

2. *Prepare the Fingers:* Take 1 *malsouka* and place the round end near you. Put 2 heaping tablespoons of the cheese filling on it and spread it crosswise into a 4-inch band in the center of the *malsouka*. Top with 1 piece of the hard-cooked egg. Make fingers with the remaining filling and wrappers in the same manner.

3. Fold the sides of the *malsouka* in toward the center. Then fold the package over 3 times, rolling it, to shape a "finger" 4 inches long and 1 inch thick.

4. Heat the oil in a wok or skillet and brown the fingers over moderately low heat for about 1/2 minute. Drain on paper towels.

Serve warm as an appetizer, with or without drinks. Makes 10 fingers.

✦ TAJINE MALSOUKA ✦

HARICOT BEANS, EGGS AND CHEESE BAKED IN PASTRY LEAVES

This *tajine* has all the characteristics of a Tunisian dish, but the general technique of how it is made reveals the hand of France. Like every colonial country, many preparations that have traditional roots have been modified to include the foreign flavors and techniques. I believe that this is a perfectly good example of Europe and Africa.

1 tablespoon olive oil plus	1/2 cup dried white haricot beans,
2 teaspoons for the tagine	soaked overnight in water,
1 tablespoon chopped onion	drained and cooked until soft
2 cloves garlic, chopped fine	6 eggs, beaten
2 tablespoons tomato paste	1/4 cup grated Gruyère-style cheese
1/4 teaspoon black pepper	6 malsouka (pastry leaves)
1/2 teaspoon sweet paprika	10 lemon wedges for garnish

1. Heat the 1 tablespoon oil in a skillet and stir-fry the onion and garlic for 1 minute over moderate heat. Add the tomato paste, pepper, paprika and beans and continue to stir-fry for 3 minutes. Cool the mixture.

2. Mix the eggs and cheese together. Stir into the bean mélange.

3. Rub a tagine or a 1-quart Pyrex dish with the remaining 2 teaspoons oil. Line it with the *malsouka,* covering the bottom and reaching up and over the sides of the dish. Pour in the bean mixture. Fold the overhanging *malsouka* over toward the center. Bake in a 350 degree oven for 20 minutes. Lift the baked loaf out of the dish to a platter and serve.

Serve warm garnished with lemon wedges. Serves 6 as a first course.

❈ DCHICHA ❈

SEMOLINA AND CHICK-PEA MÉLANGE

The troglodytes living in their desert caves in Matmata prepare this nourishing and tasty gruel, which sometimes contains shaved slices of dried preserved lamb, When omitted, this is a completely vegetarian food, a one-dish meal well seasoned with hot chili powder and black pepper.

8 cups water	4 cloves garlic, chopped
1/4 cup olive oil	1 teaspoon salt
2 tablespoons tomato paste	1/4 teaspoon black pepper
1–2 teaspoons hot red chili powder,	1 pound coarse-ground semolina
to taste	(not couscous)
1 medium onion, chopped (1/2 cup)	1 pound cooked chick-peas

Bring the water to a boil and add all the ingredients, except the semolina and chick-peas. Cook over moderately low heat for 1/2 hour. At the end of this time, add the semolina and chick-peas and mix well. Simmer for 5 minutes more, turn off the heat, cover the pan and let stand for 20 minutes.

Serve warm. Serves 6 to 8.

❈ HARISSA DE LA MAISON ❈

HOMEMADE HARISSA (TUNISIAN)

Canned *harissa* is processed to a smooth paste. The homemade variety, which is very hot, is coarsely ground, seasoned with garlic and a little oil. It can be diluted a bit by adding one or two teaspoons of water.

6 dried hot red chili peppers (poivrons), seeds and stems removed and discarded

2 cloves garlic, crushed in a garlic press
2 teaspoons olive oil

1. Rinse the chilies in cold water and break them into pieces. Soak them in cold water for 15 minutes. Drain.

2. Process the chili pieces, garlic and oil into a coarse mixture. Refrigerate.

Serve with any kind of Tunisian food. Harissa is usually presented in a pool of olive oil. Makes about 1/4 cup.

❈ HARISSA (2) ❈

HOT CHILI CONDIMENT (TUNIS)

Harissa is a hot chili condiment used all over Tunisia but less so as one travels south to the Sahara. It is as hot as anything out of Mexico or Sichuan and is used predominantly in the cooking, although it is and can

Chili merchant in El Jem

be served as a table condiment. I prefer *harissa* with a small amount of water added, which dilutes its intensity.

about 12 to 15 hot red dried chili
   peppers (1/4 pound), seeds and
   stems removed and discarded
10 cloves garlic, sliced
1 teaspoon ground coriander

1 teaspoon ground caraway
1/2 teaspoon salt
1 tablespoon olive oil
cold water

1. Break the chilies into pieces and rinse them in cold water.

2. Put all the ingredients in a food processor and grind into a smooth paste. Add 1 or 2 teaspoons cold water to lubricate the process. The more water you use, the thinner the *harissa* becomes. But this is essentially a thick paste.
   Store in a glass jar with a tight cover in the refrigerator.

Makes about 2/3 cup.

❈ HARISSA (3) ❈
NATIONAL HOT SAUCE

The long (4 to 5 inches), maroon-colored, dried hot chili of Tunisia is found all over the country, drying on long strings in shops and markets. The chili is, in fact, an import from the valley of Mexico, having been brought to Spain by Columbus. Then onward it went to Tunisia. It is the *chile guaque* found in Guatemala, also known as *chile guajillo* in Mexico.

1/4 pound dried chili, broken in
   half, seeds and stems removed
   and discarded
1/3 cup water

1 tablespoon ground coriander
1 tablespoon ground caraway
8 cloves garlic, chopped
1/2 teaspoon salt

Soak the chilies in the water for 1/2 hour. Put everything into a processor and grind to a purée, either smooth or with some texture.
   Serve with any kind of Tunisian food. It is also used in cooking.

Makes 1/2 cup.

❊ QUATRE ÉPICES ❊
FOUR SPICES

Many cultures have their spice mix, a combination of 4 to 10 and even more spices, which are used in various dishes. There is the Chinese five-spice powder, *garam masala* of India as well as the curry powder. The Tunisians have four spices. The mixture that follows is the most authentic as well as popular mix. Other mixtures use turmeric in various amounts (see the second recipe), primarily in the desert of Tunisia. I noticed in the market at Houmt Souk on the island of Jerba that there were large burlap bags filled with the four spices. The marvelous aroma permeated the market. The preparation of that amount for sale is an enormous undertaking, especially the drying in the sun.

2 tablespoons ground coriander
1 teaspoon dried mint, crushed to a powder
1/2 teaspoon black pepper

1 teaspoon dried rose buds or 1 teaspoon rose water
2 cloves garlic, crushed in a mortar

Mix everything together and dry in the sun on a clean white cloth for 3 or 4 days. Then grind it all together in a food processor. Store in a jar with a tight cover.

Makes 1/4 cup.

❊ QUATRE ÉPICES (2) ❊
FOUR SPICES (TUNISIA)

Four spice mixtures differ from one region to another and sometimes from one family to another. This mixture from Zarzis in the south of Tunisia includes turmeric in some quantity, which colors the food.

4 tablespoons hot red chili powder
2 tablespoons turmeric

6 tablespoons coriander
1 tablespoon black pepper

Mix everything together. Store in a jar with a tight cover.

Makes about 3/4 cup.

NOTE: With chili powder and pepper, the mixture is a tongue tingler. Use with care.

❋ NAVETS ❋

WHITE TURNIP PICKLE

Navets are white turnips with a light mauve near the stems. They are always available in American markets.

This pickle is a dynamic concoction that adds immeasurably to dining. A slice or two chili-hot, with meat dishes, will activate the taste buds.

2 pounds navets, peeled and sliced into rounds 1/4 inch thick
2 tablespoons salt
6 cloves garlic, crushed in a garlic press

1 semi-hot fresh or dried red chili, crushed
1/2 cup cider or white wine vinegar
1 tablespoon olive oil

1. Combine the turnip slices and salt. Let stand in a bowl, covered, for 24 hours. Drain off the accumulated liquid.

2. Crush the garlic and chili together in a mortar. Mix the paste with the vinegar and oil. Pour it over the turnips. Let stand 1 day before serving.

Serve with any kind of Tunisian food. Makes about 2 cups.

SWEETS AND BEVERAGES

❈ SAMSA ❈

ALMOND-FILLED PASTRY TRIANGLES

The coffee shops in Tunis are filled with traditional pastries, juices and the inevitable Arab (Turkish) coffee. Samsa is especially appreciated for its almond crunch, perfumed with geranium or rose water and orange peel.

FOR THE ALMOND PASTE

1 cup blanched almonds
2/3 cup sugar
1 teaspoon grated orange peel

3 tablespoons geranium or rose
water (available at Middle
Eastern groceries)

FOR THE SYRUP

2 cups sugar
juice of 1 lemon

1 1/4 cups water

FOR THE TRIANGLES

10 brik leaves (fillo sheets), each
6 inches wide and 11 inches long

2 cups vegetable oil for deep-frying
2 tablespoons sesame seeds

1. *Prepare the Almond Paste:* Grind the almonds and sugar into a paste in a food processor, adding the orange peel and geranium or rose water during the process. Take heaping teaspoons of the paste and roll them into balls, each 1 inch in diameter. Set aside. Makes 10.

2. *For the Syrup:* Mix the sugar, lemon and water together in a pan and bring to a boil over moderate heat. Turn the heat to low and simmer for 15 to 20 minutes, until the syrup thickens somewhat. Keep warm.

3. *Prepare the Triangles:* Fold each fillo sheet over lengthwise so that it is 3 inches wide and 11 inches long. Put 1 almond ball at the lower right hand corner and fold it over to the left to shape a triangle. Fold the triangle over from side to side 4 more times, until you reach the end of the sheet. The last small bit of the fillo sheet should be tucked into the last triangle fold to seal the packet.

4. Heat the oil in a skillet and drop in the triangles. Fry over moderate heat on both sides for 2 minutes. Remove the triangles and plunge them into the warm syrup for 5 seconds. Remove them with a slotted spoon to a tray and sprinkle with the sesame seeds.

Eat at room temperature. Makes 10 triangles.

❈ GHRIABA ❈

CHICK-PEA FLOUR SWEET

This sweet, almost a fudge, is of Turkish origin, like so many of the sweets in Tunisia. Nevertheless, Ghriaba, or The Stranger, has come to be a traditional sweet in the Tunisian way of life. For me, the taste of chick-pea flour is known, having lived as I did for many years in India.

1 pound chick-pea flour *1/4 pound butter, melted*
1 pound white flour *1 cup olive oil*
1/2 pound powdered sugar

1. Mix the flours together. Mix in the sugar. Stir in the butter and oil. Knead the dough to a smooth consistency.

2. By hand, roll or push the dough out into a long cylinder, 1/2 inch in diameter. Cut the cylinder on the diagonal into 2-inch pieces. Put them on a cookie sheet and bake in a 250 degree oven for 15 minutes. The bottom of the pastry will become a light tan. Should you bake them 5 minutes longer, which some prefer, the bottom will

become a little darker. The sweet is ready. Remove from the oven and cool well. Store in an airtight tin.

Makes 24 sweets.

NOTE: In earlier times Ghriaba was made in the shape of a mountain peak, as drawn here actual size.

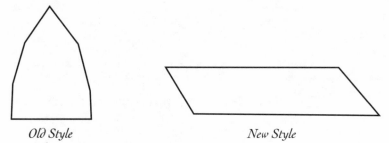

Old Style   *New Style*

❖ BOULETTES AUX AMANDES ❖

ALMOND BALLS

Here is another sweet that uses almond paste in a more complex and perhaps grander manner. These are a Tunisian delicacy.

1 cup sugar
1/2 cup water
1 teaspoon geranium or rose water (available at Middle Eastern groceries)
1/2 recipe Almond Paste (see Samsa, page 297)

1/4 cup coarsely crushed blanched almonds
several pistachio nuts or walnut pieces

1. Prepare a syrup by mixing the sugar, water and geranium or rose water together in a pan. Bring to a boil over moderate heat, turn the heat down to low and simmer for 10 minutes to lightly thicken. Set aside.

2. *Prepare Nut Balls:* Break off enough almond paste to roll balls, each 1 inch in diameter. Plunge the balls, one at a time, into the hot syrup, then roll them in the crushed almonds.

Should you wish, stuff each ball with a pistachio nut or a piece of walnut about the size of a pistachio.

Let the almond balls air-dry.

Makes 20 balls.

❋ YOYO ❋

TUNISIAN HONEY-DIPPED DONUTS

Walking along through the streets of metropolitan Tunis, one sees in the coffee shops the large, impressive donuts (*yoyo*) among the other *patisserie*. The donuts are wonderful with the Arab coffee.

Old-time cooks in the homes prepared the donuts by hand and they can still be made that way today. A piece of egg dough, about 1/4 cup, is rolled out into a cigar shape. The two ends are connected by twisting them together. The dough is then deep-fried. Nowadays, a donut cutter is effective and the taste is not altered.

FOR THE DONUTS

2 eggs, beaten
2 tablespoons sugar
2 tablespoons corn oil
1/2 teaspoon baking powder
1 cup flour

orange peel strip 3 inches long, 1/4 inch wide, chopped fine
1/2 teaspoon bottled orange flower water
oil for deep-frying

FOR THE HONEY DIP

2 cups sugar
1/4 teaspoon fresh lemon juice
1/4 teaspoon bottled orange flower water

1/8 teaspoon vanilla
1/4 teaspoon cornstarch dissolved in 2 tablespoons cold water
water to cover

1. *Prepare the Donuts:* Mix the egg, sugar, 2 tablespoons oil, baking powder, flour, orange peel and orange flower water together into a firm dough that can be handled. If too moist, dust with flour.

2. Roll out the dough into a 1/2-inch-thick flat round. Use a 3-inch donut cutter to cut out donuts. Set aside.

3. Heat the oil until hot over moderate heat. Then reduce the heat to low. Add a few donuts at a time and deep-fry them for 2 or 3 minutes, until brown on both sides. They will rise to the top of the oil when done. Remove and drain on paper towels for 1 minute.

4. *Make the Honey Dip:* Mix the sugar, lemon juice, orange flower water and vanilla in a pan. Just cover this with water. Simmer the mixture over low heat for about 1/2 hour to thicken slightly. Stir the dissolved cornstarch in rapidly; the mixture provides a glossy sheen to the donut. Keep the dip warm over very low heat.

5. Plunge the donuts, one at a time, into the hot honey dip. Use a fork or chopstick to remove them to a strainer to catch the excess syrup. Let the donuts air-dry for an hour or more. The excess syrup can be reserved for use at another time.

Makes 10 to 12 donuts

❀ HLALIM HLUWA ❀
CUSTARD WITH DATES AND NUTS

This soothing, comforting, smooth dessert is a concoction from the island of Jerba. I was served this several times without losing interest in it. *Eau de fleurs d'orange* (orange blossom water) perfumed the custard. Continental desserts, as we know, use vanilla extract.

1/4 cup cornstarch
1 quart milk
4 egg yolks
1 cup sugar
1/3 cup dates, chopped, plus 4 halves for garnish

1/4 cup walnuts, chopped, plus 4 halves for garnish
1 teaspoon orange blossom or geranium water (available at Middle Eastern groceries)

1. Dissolve the cornstarch in 1 cup of the milk, stirring briskly. Put the balance of the milk in a pan and simmer slowly over low heat.

2. Beat the egg yolks and sugar together until creamy. When the milk just begins to simmer, add the sugar mixture, stirring constantly, then the cornstarch. Add the dates, walnuts and orange or geranium water. Simmer over low heat for 5 minutes.

Remove the custard from the heat and pour into 4 cups.

Garnish each cup with a date and walnut halves. Refrigerate.

Serve chilled. Serves 4.

❂ DATTES FARCIES ❂

STUFFED DATES

Dates are ubiquitous in Tunisia and one sees them in several styles in the markets. There are bunches of ripe dates still attached to the stem, date paste that is smoothly ground and ready for the *pâtisserie* shops and these stuffed dates. Most of them have been lightly colored with a pale green paste, giving additional color to the natural brown.

1 pound blanched almonds (2 cups)
3/4 cup granulated sugar
2 teaspoons geranium or rose water (available in Middle Eastern groceries)

green food coloring (optional)
2 pounds dates, pits removed through a 1-inch lengthwise slit
powdered sugar (optional)

1. In a food processor grind the almonds and granulated sugar into a paste. Add the geranium or rose water; the liquid will moisten the mixture.

2. Should you wish to color the almond paste, add 1 or 2 drops of green food coloring. This is optional, and I personally do not care to use it.

3. Stuff each date with 1 heaping teaspoon nugget of the almond paste so that the stuffing is visible. Smooth over the surface but do not close the date opening. Roll in powdered sugar, if you wish, or leave them as is.

Serve at the tea or coffee hour. Makes about 40 stuffed dates.

❋ MARFOUSA ❋

DATE AND GOAT BUTTER

This recipe is offered for informational purposes as an example of the food of the nomads of Tunisia. It is simple, primitive and ingenuous.

The *kesra mille*, or bread in the sand, is prepared by mixing flour, salt and water. The dough is rolled out into rounds that are 1/2 inch thick and 10 inches in diameter. A hole is dug in the sand. A fire of charcoal or wood or both is made in it. When the sand has become very hot, the fire is allowed to die down and wheat stalks are placed over the coals. The bread rounds are placed on the wheat and covered with hot sand. The bread will bake in about 1/2 hour.

My Bedouin chef was enthusiastic about this simple desert dessert. Goats, not cows, provide the milk in the Sahara and it is logical that both the butter and buttermilk should be used. Dates are everywhere, a staff of life in the inhospitable surroundings of the desert.

1 pound pitted dates   *1/2 pound goat butter*
1 kesra mille *(bread in the sand)*

1. Cut the dates and *kesra* into 1/2-inch pieces. Add the butter and knead it all together.

2. Put the mixture in a skillet and stir-fry it over low heat for 5 minutes.

Serve warm, with glasses of the buttermilk that remains after the preparation of goat butter.

❋ ROB ❋

DATE JAM

The desert has its own agenda and the Bedouin who live there have their ancient system of utilizing what the desert presents to them for food. This jam—something sweet and nourishing—is not difficult to prepare.

5 pounds dates	*8 cups water*

1. Mix the dates and water together in a large pan and cook over low heat for 2 hours. The thick, viscous mixture must then be strained to produce the jam.

   Traditionally, the mixture is then put in the top (*kesskess*) of a *couscousier* and cup by cup strained through the holes. The seeds and other foreign material that did not dissolve are discarded. The strained mixture is now the jam in its soft form. The longer one cooks the dates, the firmer the jam.

2. My suggestion is to strain the mixture cup by cup through a metal sieve. Help it along by pushing the jam through with a wooden spoon.

3. The jam may be stored in glass jars and refrigerated for a month or more. It is a very fine sauce over ice cream.

Makes about 1 quart.

❈ SLATET FONDOUK GHALIA ❈

Assorted Fruit Salad

Flower of orange, rose and geranium are justifiably popular flavoring essences in *pâtisseries* and fruit dishes in Tunisia. (Vanilla would be the equivalent in our culture, but since it is a tropical plant of North America, vanilla has not been adopted by the Tunisians.) The flavor of flowers, aromatic and romantic, takes its place.

assorted fruits, such as ripe	*about 1 tablespoon flower of*
peaches, apricots, orange, pear,	*orange (a bottled essence,*
apple, melons	*available at Middle Eastern*
1/4 cup sugar, more or less to taste	*groceries)*

1. Cut 2 pounds of assorted seasonal fruits, peeled and pitted if need be, into bite-size pieces.

2. Sprinkle with sugar to taste and the flower of orange. Refrigerate.

Serve cold as a dessert. Serves 6.

✦ LEYMOUN ✦

LEMONADE REFRESHMENT

Leymoun, cool and delicious, is drunk at the breaking of the Fast at Ramadhan, just before dining, since the beverage is believed to prevent intense thirst.

2 cups sugar   *1 cup fresh lemon juice*
2 cups water

1. In a pan, mix the sugar and water together over low heat, stirring continuously, until dissolved.

2. Add the lemon juice and continue to stir until it just comes to a boil. Remove from the heat and cool. This is the lemon concentrate.

3. To serve, pour 1/4 cup of the concentrate into a glass and add water and ice cubes. Serve.
    Refrigerate the concentrate for future use.

Makes 4 cups concentrate.

✦ ROUZATA ✦

ALMOND REFRESHMENT

Rouzata is a popular drink at engagement parties and other romantic celebrations. When the temperature is high and energy is flagging in the desert air, the almond drink is refreshing and restorative.

1/2 pound sweet almonds, blanched   *3 cups sugar*
1/2 pound bitter almonds,   *4 cups water*
    blanched

1. Crush the almonds very fine in a processor. Add the water and process very well. Strain the liquid through a fine sieve into a bowl and discard the pulp.

2. Take 1 cup of the almond liquid and add it to the sugar in a pan. Dissolve the sugar over moderate heat, stirring continuously. Add the balance of the water, 3 cups, stir well and bring just to a boil.

3. Remove from the heat immediately and cool. This is the almond concentrate.

4. To serve, pour 1/4 cup of the concentrate into a glass and add water and ice cubes. Serve.
   Refrigerate the concentrate for future use.

Makes 4 cups concentrate.

❊ THÉ À LA MENTHE ❊
MINT TEA

This marvelous tea, reminiscent of the minted tea of Morocco, is habit forming, and I drank this pleasant addiction all over Tunisia whenever the mood directed me. Mint tea is considered to be a digestive after couscous or any other substantial food.

Note that there are many varieties of the herb mint. The one used in this tea is spearmint.

2 cups water	*1/2 cup fresh spearmint leaves*
3 tablespoons green tea (Chinese or Indian)	*2 tablespoons sugar, more or less to taste*

1. Boil the water in a pan, add the tea and remove the pan from the heat. Steep for 2 minutes.

2. Add the mint leaves to a teapot with the sugar. Pour the tea but not the leaves over the mint and sugar. Stir well.

Serve hot with 1 mint leaf in each glass. Serves about 6.

THE JEWISH CUISINE OF TUNISIA

COUSCOUS ROYALE
TUNISIAN JEWISH COUSCOUS

Tunisia is couscous country. It goes without saying that there are many variations on its preparation from one family to another. Nuances in the cooking become part of the nostalgia in later years, when one ruminates on lost cooking skills and the recipes themselves, which could be doomed to disappear in the 20th century.

The regional couscous of Jerba, Zarzis and Kairouan, of the Bedouin and the city of Tunis all contribute mightily to the national addiction, with its enduring hold on the palate of the country. In my opinion, the Jewish *Couscous Royale* is one of the great couscous combinations in Tunisia or the rest of the Maghreb.

The complete couscous presentation consists of stuffed vegetables cooked in a light tomato sauce; the couscous itself, which should be homemade but can be purchased; bouillon; and beef and vegetables (called *boulettes*), each of the four components served separately. In addition, a battery of salads and table condiments are *de rigueur* at the dining table. On one Sabbath evening couscous I participated in there were ten different salads covering the table in a colorful and generous display.

FOR THE STUFFING

*1 rib celery with leaves, strings
    removed and chopped
5 sprigs fresh dill, chopped
5 sprigs flat-leaf parsley, chopped
5 sprigs fresh coriander, chopped
1 teaspoon salt, or to taste
1 large onion, chopped (1 cup)
1 pound ground beef*

*3 inches day-old French or Italian
    bread, soaked in water, squeezed
    dry and chopped
1/2 teaspoon black pepper
1 clove garlic, crushed in a garlic
    press
1 tablespoon dried mint, crumbled
1 egg, beaten*

Prepare the Stuffing: Mix all the stuffing ingredients together rather well. Set aside.

FOR THE SAUCE

2 ripe tomatoes (1 pound), chopped, or equal amount canned
1/2 teaspoon salt

2 teaspoons sweet paprika
1/4 teaspoon black pepper
1 clove garlic, chopped
1 1/2 cups water

Prepare the Sauce: Mix the tomatoes, salt, paprika, pepper and garlic together in a pan. Simmer over low heat for 10 minutes. Add the water and simmer 5 minutes more. Set aside.

FOR THE VEGETABLES

All the vegetables, regardless of which ones you decide to use, are cut open just enough so that the incisions can be opened and filled with 2 or 3 generous tablespoons of the stuffing.

4 very small eggplant, halved lengthwise from the bottom to within 1 inch of the stem end
2 zucchini (1 pound), halved crosswise, each half cut lengthwise to about 1 inch of the end
4 small potatoes, peeled and halved lengthwise, each half cut lengthwise almost to the end

4 chunks cabbage, 3-inch pieces held together by the stem but with open leaves
salt
flour for dusting
1 whole egg plus 1 egg white
1 tablespoon tomato paste
2 tablespoons corn oil
oil for deep-frying (about 1 cup)

1. Sprinkle the cut vegetables with salt inside and out and let stand for 15 minutes. Rinse with cold water and dry.

2. Open the incisions and stuff each vegetable with 2 to 3 tablespoons of the prepared stuffing. Gently press the vegetables and stuffing together. Dust each stuffed vegetable with flour and set aside.

3. Mix vigorously together into a batter the egg and egg white, tomato paste and the 2 tablespoons oil. Dip each stuffed vegetable in the batter.

4. Heat the oil for deep-frying over moderate heat and brown the vegetables, several at a time, for about 5 minutes. As each is fried, trans-

fer it to one or two skillets, arranging the vegetables in a single layer. Pour the prepared tomato sauce over all and cook, uncovered, until nearly all the liquid has evaporated. This should take about 1/2 hour over low heat.

FOR THE BOUILLON, BEEF AND VEGETABLE SOUP

2 tablespoons corn oil
2 pounds boneless beef chuck, cut
  into 10 pieces
6 cups water
1 teaspoon salt
1/4 teaspoon black pepper
1 small ripe tomato, quartered
1 rib celery with leaves, quartered

3 whole carrots
3 medium whole zucchini
1/2 pound cabbage in 1 piece,
  blanched in boiling water 5
  minutes to remove its strong
  smell
4 whole sprigs flat-leaf parsley
4 whole sprigs dill

1. *Prepare the Soup:* Put the oil, beef, water, salt and pepper in a large pan or the bottom (*makfoul*) of a *couscousier.* Bring to a boil, reduce the heat to low, cover and simmer for 1 hour, or until the beef is almost tender.

2. Add all the remaining soup ingredients and simmer for 20 minutes more. Should the liquid evaporate too quickly during this period, add another 1/2 cup water. Set aside.

FOR THE COUSCOUS

2–3 pounds prepared couscous

Prepared couscous, a convenience, is available in Middle Eastern groceries and some supermarkets. There are several brands imported from France and Tunisia. Cooking instructions are written on the boxes.

For the traditional and superior method of cooking couscous, refer to the instructions at the beginning of this chapter.

TO SERVE

Each diner will be served or help himself or herself to the couscous, a cup of the bouillon, the beef and vegetables in one platter and the *boullettes* (vegetables) in another.

Serve warm. Serves 10.

SOUPE DE PESACH

PASSOVER SOUP

This idiosyncratic combination contains the unfamiliar cardoon, the turnip-like kohlrabi, carrots and herbs to season the soup for Passover. It is the thick celery-like stalks of the cardoon, smooth and melting when cooked, that are so attractive. This little-known member of the artichoke family is sometimes available in Italian neighborhoods in New York.

3 stalks cardoon, trimmed and cut into 1-inch cubes
3 kohlrabi (1 pound), peeled and cut into 1-inch cubes
5 carrots (1/2 pound), sliced diagonally
6 sprigs flat-leaf parsley, chopped
6 sprigs fresh coriander, chopped

1 pound boneless beef chuck, cut into thin slices 2 inches long
1/2 teaspoon white pepper
1 teaspoon salt, or to taste
1 teaspoon sweet paprika
5 cups water
3 sheets matzoh, broken into 1-inch square pieces

1. Put all the ingredients, except the water and matzoh, in a pan large enough to hold them. Cook over low heat for 10 minutes, shaking the pan vigorously every now and then. Add the water and bring to a boil. Simmer over low heat for 1 hour.

2. When the meat is tender, put the matzoh on top of the soup, cover the pan and simmer for 10 minutes more. Do not stir.

Serve warm, the meat and vegetables together. Serves 6 or more.

AKOUD

SWEETBREADS IN RED SAUCE

In olden times Akoud was traditionally prepared with the genitalia of beef. Nowadays, it is made with sweetbreads in an enormously effective way that involves cooking them over low heat. The sweetbreads take on a melting texture and the well-seasoned sauce is a masterpiece of flavors.

1 pound beef or veal sweetbreads
2 tablespoons corn or other
    vegetable oil
4 cloves garlic, crushed in a garlic
    press
1/2 teaspoon salt
3 tablespoons tomato paste

2 cups water
1 teaspoon sweet paprika
1 teaspoon ground caraway
2 teaspoons ground cumin
1 teaspoon Harissa (see page 89),
    more or less to taste

1. Soak the sweetbreads in cold water for 15 minutes. Pull off and discard the loose skin. Cut into 1-inch cubes.

2. Heat the oil in a pan, add the garlic and stir-fry over moderate heat for a few seconds. Add the salt, tomato paste, water, sweetbreads, paprika, caraway, cumin and *harissa* to taste. Bring to a boil.

3. Reduce the heat to low, cover the pan and cook for about 45 minutes, or until the sweetbreads are tender and the sauce has thickened.

Serve warm as an appetizer. Serves 6.

❈ BCHEELA ❈

SWISS CHARD WITH LAMB

The Jewish quarter on the island of Jerba is about 1 1/2 miles from the famous ancient synagogue of La Ghriba. In that district we were ushered into a home where we observed a corner filled with well-washed, fluffy wool that was to be used by the family. They were weavers.

There we were treated to a tasting of Bcheela in a black sauce that was fragrant and thick. Sweet dates were also served with a paste prepared from finely ground sorghum flour and honey. Each person pitted the date and stuffed it with the honey paste.

Coffee was served in demitasse cups and was a mixture—half standard coffee grounds and half chick-peas and coriander seeds toasted together until black. They were then ground, mixed with the real coffee and brewed. Had we not been told of the mixture—a tasty brew sweetened with cubes of sugar—no one would have been the wiser. I pre-

Amphora market day in Houmt Souk, Jerba

sumed that the adulterants were an inexpensive substitute for real coffee grounds, but they were entirely compatible with it.

We sat in the kitchen around a small wood table with the warm hospitality flowing around. Then the rains came with a vengeance and we dashed for the bus.

4 pounds fresh green Swiss chard	*3 large scallions, sliced thin*
1/4 cup olive oil	*3 tablespoons dried white haricot*
4 cloves garlic, crushed in a garlic	*beans, soaked overnight in*
press	*water and drained*
6 sprigs flat-leaf parsley, chopped	*1 pound lamb, cut into 6 pieces,*
fine	*with or without bone*
6 sprigs fennel leaves (or an equal	*1/4 teaspoon black pepper*
amount to parsley), chopped	*3 cups water*
fine	

1. Rinse the Swiss chard well in cold water and strip off the green leaves on both sides of the stems. Discard the stems. Chop the leaves rather well.

2. Heat the oil in a large pan and stir-fry the chard slowly over low heat for 15 minutes or more to reduce it to a dark green mixture. During

312   TUNISIA

this time mash the chard with the oil using the back of a wooden spoon.

3. Add the garlic, parsley, fennel leaves, scallion, beans, lamb, pepper and 1 cup of the water. Note that there is no salt in this dish. Bring to a boil and simmer everything together for 10 minutes. Add the balance of the water, 2 cups, and cook until the lamb is tender and everything else has reduced to a thick, dark mélange.

Serve warm. Serves 6 with bread.

GANAOUIA AVEC POULET

CHICKEN AND OKRA

Okra, that uncommon vegetable in Tunisia, must be handled with respect. If overcooked, it disintegrates into a viscous mass that is unpleasant. It should be crunchy, cooked just enough to integrate with the chicken and seasonings. This dish does just that. The Jews of Calcutta have a similar combination, with like seasonings, but that is culinary coincidence rather than an intentional connection.

3 tablespoons corn oil
3 large onions (2 pounds), sliced thin
2 ripe tomatoes (1 pound), fresh or canned, sliced
4 cloves garlic, sliced thin
1 teaspoon salt, or to taste
1/4 teaspoon black pepper
1/4 teaspoon ground turmeric
a 3-inch cinnamon stick, halved
3 pounds boneless chicken breast and thighs, cut into 3-inch pieces
2 cups water
1 pound fresh okra, stem ends trimmed

1. Heat 2 tablespoons of the oil in a pan, add the onions and stir-fry over moderate heat until golden, about 4 minutes. Add the tomatoes, garlic, salt, pepper, turmeric and cinnamon stick and stir-fry for 3 minutes.

2. Place the chicken pieces on top, add the water and bring to a boil. Cover the pan and cook over moderate heat for 1/2 hour.

3. Meanwhile, put the remaining 1 tablespoon oil in a skillet, add the okra and stir-fry over moderate heat for about 3 minutes, or until the color changes. Add the okra to the chicken, cover the pan and simmer over low heat for 15 minutes, shaking the pan vigorously now and then. The sauce will be thick and aromatic, the chicken tender and the okra cooked to perfection.

Serve warm with bread and several traditional salads. Serves 6.

❁ HARAIMI ❁

FISH IN SPICE SAUCE

This Jewish recipe is from one of the members of the ancient Jewish community on the island of Jerba. The seasonings are quintessentially Tunisian and include caraway, tomato paste, garlic, pepper and lemon.

*2 tablespoons olive oil
3 cloves garlic, finely chopped
2 teaspoons ground caraway
2 teaspoons hot red chili powder
1/2 teaspoon salt
1/4 teaspoon black pepper
1 tablespoon tomato paste*

*1/2 cup water
3 tablespoons fresh lemon juice, or
    more to taste
2 pounds ocean fish, such as red
    snapper or* mérou, *cut into
    1-inch-thick slices*

1. Heat the oil in a pan and add the garlic, caraway, chili powder, salt and pepper and stir-fry over moderate heat for 1 minute. Add the tomato paste, water and lemon juice. Simmer for 3 minutes.

2. Add the fish slices and cover the pan. Cook over low heat for 20 to 30 minutes. Shake the pan now and then to integrate the seasonings.

Serve hot. Serves 6.

❖ KEFTA DE LA GHRIBA ❖

GROUND MEAT PATTIES

El Ghriba on the island of Jerba is reputed to be the oldest known active synagogue in existence. The name means "the stranger" and implies that people who were different from the indigenous population came from another place in that early era and settled down. At one time Jerba was known as the Jewish island; the synagogue there is a splendid edifice that has an inscribed date of 641 A.D. Pilgrims from Europe and other places visit the synagogue during the Jewish holidays.

FOR THE PATTIES

2 pounds ground lamb, chicken, or fish

10 sprigs flat-leaf parsley, chopped

1 teaspoon salt

1 teaspoon black pepper

1 teaspoon hot red chili powder, or more to taste

2 cups French bread, soaked in water, squeezed dry and chopped

1 large onion, chopped (1 cup)

flour

4 eggs, beaten

1/4 cup olive oil for pan-frying

FOR THE SAUCE

2 tablespoons olive oil

6 cloves garlic, crushed in a garlic press

2 tablespoons tomato paste

1 teaspoon hot red chili powder, more or less to taste

2 cups water

1. *Prepare the Patties:* Mix the meat or fish, parsley, salt, pepper, chili powder, bread and onions together.

2. Form patties, each 3 inches in diameter and 1/2 inch thick. Makes 8 to 10 patties.

3. Dredge the patties in the flour, then dip them in the egg.

4. Heat the oil in a skillet and brown the patties over moderate heat for 2 or 3 minutes. Drain on paper towels.

5. *Prepare the Sauce:* Heat the oil in a large skillet and fry the garlic over moderate heat for 1 minute. Add the tomato paste, chili powder and

water. Bring to a boil and cook the sauce slowly over low heat for 15 minutes.

6. Add the prepared patties and simmer, basting them until all the sauce has evaporated, about 15 minutes.

Serve warm. Serves 6 with other dishes.

❈ AJLOOK (JEWISH) ❈
ZUCCHINI LEMON SALAD

Ajlook is not so much a salad as a condiment that is served with others at family gatherings. It makes a good appetizer when served with bread, crackers or matzoh on Passover.

*2 zucchini (1 pound), ends
    trimmed, cooked whole until
    tender and drained
1 teaspoon Harissa (see page 89)
1/2 teaspoon sweet paprika
1/2 teaspoon salt*

*1/2 teaspoon ground caraway
1/2 teaspoon lightly toasted
    caraway seed
2 tablespoons fresh lemon juice
1 teaspoon olive oil*

Mash the zucchini with a fork but not too smoothly, leaving some texture. Pour off excess liquid. Add all the remaining ingredients. Refrigerate.

Serve cool. Serves 6.

BIBLIOGRAPHY

Bahloul, Joelle, *Le culte de la table dressée: rites et traditions de la table juive algerienne*, Editions A.M. Metailie, Paris, 1983.

Encyclopaedia Judaica, Keter Publishing House Ltd., Jerusalem, Israel, 1972 (Macmillan).

Hacohen, Dvora and Menachem, *One People: The Story of the Eastern Jews*, Adama Books, New York, 1986.

Hourani, Albert, *A History of the Arab Peoples*, The Belknap Press of Harvard University Press, Cambridge, MA, 1991.

Kennedy, Richard, *The International Dictionary of Religion*, The Crossroad Publishing Co., New York, 1984.

The Oxford Book of Food Plants, Oxford University Press, London, 1969.

Ruedy, John, *Modern Algeria: The Origins and Development of a Nation*, Indiana University Press, 1992.

The Times Atlas of World History, Times Books Ltd., London, 1984.

Von Welanetz, Diana and Paul, *The Von Welanetz Guide to Ethnic Ingredients*, Warner Books, Inc., New York, 1982.

INDEX

319